THE WORLD GOVERNMENT

A Blueprint for a Universal World State

First published by O-Books, 2010
O Books is an imprint of John Hunt Publishing Ltd., The Bothy, Deershot Lodge, Park Lane, Ropley, Hants, SO24 0BE, UK
office1@o-books.net
www.o-books.com

For distributor details and how to order please visit the 'Ordering' section on our website.

ISBN: 978 1 84694 388 1

A CIP catalogue record for this book is available from the British Library.

Design: Stuart Davies

Printed in the UK by CPI Antony Rowe
Printed in the USA by Offset Paperback Mfrs, Inc

THE WORLD GOVERNMENT

A Blueprint for a Universal World State

Nicholas Hagger

BOOKS

Winchester, UK
Washington, USA

Books Published by Nicholas Hagger

The Fire and the Stones
Selected Poems
The Universe and the Light
A White Radiance
A Mystic Way
Awakening to the Light
A Spade Fresh with Mud
The Warlords
Overlord
A Smell of Leaves and Summer
The Tragedy of Prince Tudor
The One and the Many
Wheeling Bats and a Harvest Moon
The Warm Glow of the Monastery Courtyard
The Syndicate
The Secret History of the West
The Light of Civilization
Classical Odes
Overlord, one-volume edition
Collected Poems 1958 – 2005
Collected Verse Plays
Collected Stories
The Secret Founding of America
The Last Tourist in Iran
The Rise and Fall of Civilizations
The New Philosophy of Universalism
The Libyan Revolution
Armageddon

Acknowledgments

I acknowledge the memory of Churchill and Eisenhower, Einstein and Russell, who, tempered in the fire of the Second World War and atomic explosions, all called for a world government and world law that would enforce peace. I lived through the Second World War in the path of V-1 and V-2 rockets, and remember listening in bed at night for the cut-out and crash of flying bombs, and lying in a Morrison shelter in my school's grounds during an air raid. I wanted to know why Hitler had inflicted random war on my childhood and why my generation of children were subjected to a new nuclear threat. I visited the D-Day beaches while staying with a French family when I was fourteen and I visited Hiroshima's peace dome while living in Japan. I wrote my first poetic epic *Overlord* about Eisenhower's triumph over Hitler, and followed it up with another, *Armageddon*, on Bush's fortunes during the War on Terror. The more I researched into battles and generals, the more I longed for a world free from the scourge of war. I came to see that there needed to be a fundamental change to the world order, and the calls for a world government by these four men inspired the conception of this work.

I am grateful to the philosopher Kant for his thinking on perpetual peace, and to Francis Fukuyama for his thinking on universal liberal democracy, which I saw as a stage within the rise and fall of civilizations.

I am particularly grateful to John Hunt, who saw my *New Philosophy of Universalism* into print and asked me to expand on political Universalism in a book about world government. This work owes much to his penetrating assessment of the way forward. And I am grateful to my PA, Ingrid, for keeping up with my cracking pace and helping me to deliver the structure of the World State (and subordination of the Syndicate) on one page (p143), a seemingly impossible task.

"Human society can be saved only by Universalism."

Emery Reves, *The Anatomy of Peace*, 1945

"Mankind can be saved only if a supranational system, based on law, is created to eliminate the methods of brute force."

Albert Einstein, 1950

"History is now choosing the founders of the World Federation. Any person who can be among that number and fails to do so has lost the noblest opportunity of a lifetime."

Carl van Doren

*

To the memory of General Eisenhower, Supreme Commander of the Allied forces in Europe, who dreamt of world law that would abolish war and warned against the "military-industrial complex" of the Syndicate; and to President Obama, who has it within his power to lay this blueprint for a partial World State before the UN and a World Constitutional Convention. (See pp157 and 176.)

CONTENTS

PART THREE
THE STATECRAFT OF WORLD GOVERNMENT:
A BLUEPRINT FOR A WORLD STATE

Prologue

World Government and Peace

Plato wrote his *Politeia* (*Republic*) c.380BC, following his visit to Italy and Sicily when he was about forty in 388BC. In it he set out his ideal state and government for Dionysus I of Syracuse, who promised to implement his political ideas. Plato argued that a society is best ruled by a single individual. Later in his *Laws*, which he wrote towards the end of his life, he proposed replacing a single ruler with a set of laws, an executive, a group of oligarchs and all citizens.

Ever since Plato philosophy has been interested in proposals for the ideal state, and the thinking of Kant in *Perpetual Peace: A Philosophical Sketch* (1795), is particularly relevant. However, it is only relatively recently that a philosopher could realistically contemplate an ideal World State, for it is only relatively recently that 20th-century air travel, instant communications via the Internet and globalization have made world government a realistic possibility.

These days world government is often mentioned, and has been on the lips of some of the most famous people of our time as the following passages demonstrate:

> "Unless we establish some form of world government, it will not be possible for us to avert a World War III in the future."
>
> Winston Churchill, Prime Minister of Great Britain, 1945

> "The emergency committee of atomic scientists, having explored for two years all means other than world government for making responsible the control of atomic energy effective [meaning nuclear weapons, really, and by implication, all weapons of mass destruction], has become convinced that no other method than world government can be expected to prove effective, and that the attainment of world government is therefore the most urgent problem now facing mankind."
>
> 1948 UN Resolution

> "There is no salvation for civilization, or even the human race, other than the creation of a world government."
>
> Albert Einstein, 1945

> "The world no longer has a choice between force and law; if civilization is to survive, it must choose the rule of law."
>
> President Dwight D. Eisenhower

> "There is an increasing awareness of the need for some form of global government."
>
> Mikhail Gorbachev

> "The international community should support a system of laws to regularise international relations and maintain the peace in the same manner that law governs national order."
>
> Pope John Paul II

Yet despite such views at the highest level and despite a world federalist movement in the aftermath of the First and Second World Wars, there has surprisingly been no accessible study of the concept of world government. In fact, so far as I am aware this is the first book to be entitled *The World Government*.

World government is the concept of a political body that would make, interpret and enforce international law within a system that would allow it to have legally-binding authority over sovereign nation-states. Under a world government, all humankind would be united under one common political authority.

The actual starting-point of this book is a section on political Universalism in my challenge to modern philosophy, *The New Philosophy of Universalism*. Besides restoring the universe to philosophy after a hundred years of focusing on logic and language, Universalism returns to the view of the universe of the Presocratic Greeks, Plato, Aristotle and Kant. It identifies a universal principle of order and focuses on universality. It sees the universe as latently contained within an infinitesimal point that preceded the Big Bang. It sees all humankind as having emerged from an interconnected unity, from one cell and later one species. Universalism therefore treats all humankind as a whole in all disciplines.

In the course of covering the applications of Universalism, which include political Universalism, I wrote:

> "Political Universalism sees the whole world as being ordered as one political entity, an interconnected unity, a whole. In short, under a world government it would be a reflection of the unity of the cosmos (or ordered universe). As all humans are world citizens they have human rights, which include a human right to live under a world government that has abolished war, famine and disease. The world order's world government must be democratic so every member of humankind has a democratic vote. Political Universalism affirms a world government…that is not totalitarian but allows each human being the maximum freedom and attacks poverty…. Political Universalism minimises the conflicts that divide people and eliminates divisions by negotiation…. Political Universalism is Utopian in wanting to improve the lot of humankind and bringing universal freedom, democracy and relief from poverty, war, famine and disease."[1]

This book examines the concept of world government in more depth than space permitted in my challenge to philosophy.

Political philosophy is philosophical reflection on how best to arrange our political institutions and social practices, our economic system and family life. Political philosophers – such as Plato, Aristotle, Augustine, Aquinas, Hobbes, Locke, Hume, Hegel and J.S. Mill – establish principles that justify a particular form of state, and this involves analysing and interpreting the concepts of freedom, justice, authority and democracy with a view to portraying an ideal state. Social and political thinkers who have contributed to political philosophy include Cicero, Marsilius of Padua, Machiavelli, Grotius, Rousseau, Bentham, Fichte and Marx.

I have always been interested in universal states. I have a classical background – I had to translate several books of Plato's *Republic* at school – and in Ancient History I studied the Athenian Empire and its hold over the Aegean, and the Roman Empire and its hold over the known world, and was encouraged to draw parallels between them and the British Empire, which had been battered by two world wars. I had to translate a report of a Second-World-War battle into Latin. Montgomery had to be spelt "Montegomerius".

In Japan, where I was a Professor, I taught a course on Gibbon, Spengler and Toynbee to eight doctorate students. I steeped myself in Toynbee's view of civilizations' universal states and his conviction (expressed in Book 12) that all civilizations would eventually pass into a world-wide civilization. My poem 'Archangel' (1966) ends with a glimpse of a future world government under a "World-Lord". (See pp167-168.) However, although seeing nation-states as being within civilizations like Toynbee, I had criticisms of Toynbee's choice of civilizations and his uniform dating. Toynbee admitted at the end of his work that he had been unable to find the motive force of civilizations. I was convinced that I had the answer: civilizations rise after someone has had a vision of a metaphysical reality, round which followers gather and a new religion is formed that develops into a civilization. This insight enabled me to propose the Law of History.

I had seen a fourth way of accounting for the rise and fall of civilizations that differed from Gibbon's, Spengler's and Toynbee's. It enabled me to identify 61 stages through which 25 civilizations have passed or will pass. After 25 years of research I implemented the details of this view in *The Fire and the Stones*, a work of philosophy of history. This has recently been updated in two parts, the second of which is titled *The Rise and Fall of Civilizations*.

In the course of my research I came up against a group of contemporary oligarchs who were trying to effect a world government by secrecy and deception. (See ch. 6.) In the late 1980s I dismissed them as I was convinced history was, is and always will be the endless interplay of stages within civilizations. The attempt of these *élite*s to create a world government would, if successful, bring this interplay to an end as they wished to subsume all civilizations. I felt, and still feel, that any world government will be a tier above the rise and fall of civilizations, which will continue their rise-and-fall patterns. Nevertheless, in a chart in *The Fire and the Stones*, which also appeared in *The Light of Civilizations* and which I reproduce in this book (see pp178-179), I followed Toynbee in showing all civilizations as passing into one world-wide civilization for a while. It could be said that the world-wide civilization would occupy a tier above the lower tier of rising and falling civilizations, which would continue beneath this higher tier.

I kept track of this group and found that by 2003 its *élite*s were actually doing rather well. They seemed self-interested rather than philanthropic, and I distanced myself from what they were trying to achieve in *The Syndicate* (2004). It was not the institution of a World State that I was distancing myself from, but the would-be incumbents, as I made clear at the end of that work.[2]

In 1992 I had heard Francis Fukuyama, who was representative of their way of thinking, speak in London. In *The End of History* he claimed that in a

Hegelian sense history as an evolutionary process has a direction and will reach an end when it achieves a form of society that satisfies humankind's deepest longings. For Hegel this meant a liberal state, for Marx a communist society. Fukuyama suggested that history reached its "end" with the end of the Cold War as there would now be permanent liberal democracy. He seemed to be saying that the world was about to pass very soon into a permanent World State. In support of this view, it is worth noting that while there were no liberal democracies with universal suffrage in the world in 1900, in 2009 119 out of the 193 nation-states (including Taiwan) were deemed to have an electoral liberal democracy.[3] (See pp230-231.)

In 2009 a more precise survey found that 89 nation-states were deemed to be free, 62 were deemed to be partly free and 42 not free.[4] (See pp231-235 and 235-242.) 119 were deemed "electoral democracies" when only 89 were deemed free. Thus the 119 figure includes 30 partly free.

I hope that a World State – of the right kind, with the most appropriate incumbents, form and structure – is ahead for the world, but it has not happened yet and, though (as I shall explain in ch. 8) it could happen quite rapidly, there is no immediate prospect of its happening. In the meantime, civilizations continue in their rise-and-fall pattern, which will continue beneath a World State if one comes into being. The rise and fall of civilizations has been endless, for when a civilization ends it passes into another civilization. As a way of distancing myself from Fukuyama's belief that a universal state would replace civilizations, my most recent book on civilizations was originally entitled *The Endless Rise and Fall of Civilizations*, the word "endless" making it clear that the rise-and-fall pattern of civilizations will never end so long as there are historical events.

My encounter with Fukuyama made me think carefully as to whether world government can be superimposed on civilizations forever. I have concluded that it cannot, as world government is itself the expression of a stage within a civilization, and no stage can last for more than a limited period of time. I have concluded that I have lived during the development of a stage within the system of civilizations which will express itself for a while as a World State that will be above the continuing events of civilizations. Civilizations flow under a world-wide civilization and continue beneath it, as river currents continue under a majestic cloud.

The theme of this book is that eventually, through the evolutionary process of government and the state, there will be an ideal world government. I describe as a philosophical concept, but also as a practical and feasible course of action, what its model, structure and feel would be, and the process by which it would come into being. The book describes the human dream and longing for a world government; the reality that is already unfolding in our time; and the form it will ideally take. Just as Plato in an effort of statecraft wrote his *Republic*, for which a better translation might have been *Constitution*, so this work in an equivalent effort of statecraft offers a World State. It can be read at both philosophical and practical levels. In a similar vein Jean Monnet devised the EU in conjunction with the Council on Foreign Relations in the early 1920s, and lived to see it brought to birth via various intermediary stages in the 1957 Treaty of Rome and in the European Parliament, which opened in the year he died, 1979. (The European Parliamentary elections were held in July 1979, a few months after Monnet died in March.)

There are many practical difficulties to be overcome before there can be a world government, and bringing it into being will be even more of a process than was the EU. It may take until the 22nd century to realise and implement the idea fully to achieve a minimum standard of living for all humankind. This work is nevertheless timely in our age of globalization, and even though some parts of my thesis may not be fulfilled for another hundred years, Universalism requires that the concept of world government should receive a fuller treatment than the two pages in my work of philosophy.

Having written two epic poems of contemporary war I can see very clearly that contemporary wars are linked to the interests of nation-states or empires, to a clash of interests which cannot be resolved by current international law as the legal framework does not exist. World government would create this legal framework and prevent wars. Most epic poets who have lived through wars yearn for peace. As we shall see, the epic poet Virgil was aware of a new order of world rule in the 'Fourth Eclogue' and in the *Aeneid*; the epic poet Dante was extremely interested in world government; and the epic poet Milton who wrote *Paradise Lost* had been Latin Secretary to Cromwell who saw himself as founding a universal republic. Milton proposed an ideal republic in *The Ready and Easy Way to Establish a Free Commonwealth* (1660).[5] James Harrington wrote that the duty of a free Commonwealth was "the intent that the whole world may be governed with righteousness".[6] I ask myself if there is a special link between epic poetry and the conviction that there should be a World State that prevents war.

All my works are innovatory in some way. My innovatory philosophical and historical works have been thrown up by the need to address philosophical and historical issues I encountered in my innovatory literary, often poetic, work. It was my literary, poetic work that gave me my first glimpse of a World State: see pp167-168 for the end of my 1966 poem 'Archangel' and the glimpse that came to me in Moscow. Many of my philosophical and historical probings work out what has gone wrong in the past and in the present, and suggest a way forward, as does this present work.

This is a work that begins in philosophy and ends with an innovative proposal for a World State with a fair amount of precision as to how to realise it – and a safeguard for such a state against the wiles of self-interested *élite*s. As such it is a contribution both to political philosophy and to the philosophy of history, and may in the fullness of time, when attitudes have changed, be used as a blueprint to benefit the lot of humankind which has been living through a long time of trial and tribulation.

PART ONE

THE DREAM OF WORLD GOVERNMENT

1

History's Inexorable Flow towards World Government

A philosopher who seeks to propose a universal World State would do well to start with an overview of how the course of history has led to such a possibility.

The panorama it shows is surprising. For, like a river flowing towards the open sea, history drifts slowly and imperceptibly in one direction, from the parochial to the global. History's civilizations spring up in primitive conditions, pass into more complex city and national organization and widen towards world government. Humankind's groupings and attempts at government have evolved into control of ever-wider areas.

The Evolution of Government

Civilization began with recorded history, c.3000BC. However, Neolithic farmers roamed Europe long before then and left their historical traces. *Homo sapiens* appeared outside Africa c.70,000BC, and co-existed with Cro-Magnon man, who inhabited the Dordogne from c.30,000 to c.10,000BC. Near history's source in Neolithic times and from at least c.10,000BC, the first primitive government was within the tribe.

The tribe was a loose association of families, who in early times were nomadic. They wandered the steppes looking for new pastures for their animals and fought and conquered the territories of other tribes. A conquering tribe superimposed its leadership over the governments of the tribes they subjugated, but often allowed them to continue as they had been – so long as they acknowledged their new leadership. Tribes thus exercised a loose rather than a tight control over their subjects. In due course nomads settled in small villages. Priest-kings evolved, and primitive religion and government became enmeshed. Tribal leaders found that primitive religion – shamanism which began the painting of animals in dark caves as far back as c.50,000BC – was a good way to perpetuate their control over tribes.

Over the years tribes were brought together round religious buildings as in early Sumer. The Sumerians first appeared c.3500BC. By c.2500BC, stunning temples came to be built on high mounds, man-made mountains called *ziggurat*s, and these brought more tribes in from far and wide. The first cities were born. These were really only enlarged villages, and their heads gradually turned themselves into monarchs, ruling by one-man rule. Village councils gradually took on division of labour. Some tribal villagers specialised as priests who protected their city from attack and natural disasters and others specialised as warriors, farmers or tax collectors.

Settled agriculture and the cultivation of fields became prevalent and organization became more complex. The early Sumerian cities were soon in conflict as to which city owned a nearby river's water. The Tigris and Euphrates had to be subjected to central planning so both upstream and downstream fields could be watered. Nomads eyed cities' wealth and in their plunder brought war to their walls.

In the ancient Greek city-states monarchies under tribal kings developed into military aristocracies and later plutocracies which extended citizenship to more and more classes. There were conflicts between aristocratic, plutocratic and democratic factions within city-states, and different city-states had different emphases. While Athens developed as a democratic power, Sparta remained an aristocratic power and the democratic-aristocratic collision was behind the Peloponnesian Wars of 431-404BC which weakened the Athenian Empire and Greek power.

The organization of the Roman state was more complex. It was a blend of monarchy, aristocracy and democracy, which the Romans themselves referred to as a "public thing", *res publica* or republic. Headed by divine Caesar, who commanded the legions, it combined an executive power of two consuls with a legislative Senate which was at first drawn from the aristocratic classes and eventually from all classes of citizens. The unity of the state was captured in letters on Rome's buildings and on battle standards: "SPQR", *Senatus Populusque Romanus*, the Senate and the People of Rome. The third-century city-states were heavily taxed by the imperial administration and many were bankrupted.

Before the Roman Empire declined into tyranny, Roman law, faced with the problem of Christianity, separated Church and state, setting a precedent for the future. The Roman Empire eventually fell to the barbarian Visigoths from the steppes.

After the collapse of the Roman Empire, barons became crucial to government. There were uprisings by landless peasants and attacks by invaders from neighbouring lands, making day-to-day living dangerous. A feudal system evolved in which all sought and achieved protection. Landless freemen and small landowners went to the most powerful lord in the neighbourhood for protected shelter in peacetime. In return they offered their services in war. The feudal lord had financial, juridical and military sovereignty over his land and had power to tax, try and arm his subjects. A subject gave himself and his lands to a baron and received food, shelter and protection, and equipment in war. In return he tilled the baron's soil, paid taxes and fought his battles. Both vassal and lord were bound by their contractual relationship. In due course the lords became vassals of the king.

The medieval and Renaissance baronial states were run by kings and their military aristocrats, the barons or feudal armoured lords – warlords – who provided standing armies the kings, unable to tax like Roman emperors, could not afford. There were strong monarchies in England, France and Spain, and as trade brought wealth to cities that could be spent on fortifying walls the city-state revived in Italy, the Rhineland and Low Countries.

In the 16th-18th centuries the nation-state was born. The concepts of the nation and state were strengthened by the writings of Machiavelli, Bodin and Hobbes, who supported secular governmental authority against that of the Church. Monarchies were now territorial, and kings sought to impose uniformity on their peoples. The English kings fought the Welsh, Scots and Irish to bring them under their sovereign rule. The French kings drove into the Alps, Pyrenees and Rhine. The Spanish forced Christianity on their Jewish and Moorish subjects. Absolute monarchs made royal decrees that were administered by a class of bookkeepers, letter-writers and annalists, a new bureaucracy.

In the 17th-18th centuries absolutist monarchies fell, giving way in England to a constitutional monarchy that split legislation and enforcement into an executive, legislature and judiciary and eventually an electorate; and in France to a republic, whose monarch-free structure brought the nation-state to maturity. In America the Constitution opened the way to liberal democracy. In all three countries the idea of the sovereign nation-state was reinforced. The nation-states were originally set up and received their power from their peoples to protect their citizens, guarantee their security and maintain law and order.

Controlled from Europe, a new form of government rose with colonies, throwbacks to the early Phoenician and Greek colonies, and of course the Roman *colonas*. Starting in the 16th century in Latin America and continuing in the 17th century in America and in the 19th century, when India became an empire, the European imperial powers set up colonies in the Americas, Africa, Asia, Oceania and many other parts of the world. The colonial power pumped money to a colony's leadership and in return transferred its natural resources for use in its own country. The benefits colonies acquired from this arrangement varied, but in some colonies the people lived in poverty and derived little or no benefit from the colonial contact, which merely enriched the few who surrounded the leadership.

The colonialist and imperialist nation-state was nationalist. It asserted its nation-statehood against other nations in imperial competition, which led to the First World War. While these colonialist and imperialist constitutional monarchies and republics vied for empire, the 20th-century totalitarian dictatorships of Stalin and Hitler came into being, the government by constraint of largely unconsenting peoples. Such dictatorships were copied in smaller states, especially during the Cold War between the USSR and the West.

Hitler had aspirations to rule the world. He selected Nuremberg, the city of the Holy Roman Emperors, to be his seat after the Second World War, when he planned to be crowned Kaiser Adolf I, Emperor of Germany. After accepting the surrender of the Soviet Union, the US, the British Empire including India and in due course his ally Japan he would be Emperor of the whole world, whose representatives would meet in Nuremberg. In Nuremberg he began an impressive building program modelled on ancient Rome. He built the Colosseum, an open New Congress Hall modelled on Rome's Colosseum, which would seat 50,000 world representatives. Near this was the grandstand of the Zeppelinfeld from which Hitler addressed 1.6 million people one day in 1938. A nearby lake was gouged out and turned into a Stadium to accommodate a crowd of 350,000 to 450,000 people. A two-kilometre-long route was constructed to lead to the Castle where electors would meet to elect Hitler Emperor. Nuremberg would be the centre of the world, and Hitler's new buildings there, which can now be visited, would be the seat of his world government, which would be imposed by conquest, not voluntary association.

Incompatibility between nations which led to the Second World War is surfacing again in the incompatible claims of the US and Islam, of Israel and Iran. Incompatible claims of city-states ruined ancient Greece, and incompatible claims of nations threaten to ruin the modern world.

In our time the flow of government has widened into regions. The most obvious of these is the European Union or EU, which grew out of a European Economic Community of six members and is now a Union with its own legal personality of 27 member nation-states, and 48 European nation-states ultimately eligible for membership.[1] Other regional groups include the African

Union, and an American Union and Asia-Pacific Union are mooted. We shall be looking at these more closely in ch. 4.

A further widening of government has been a consequence of superpowerdom. Following the fall of the Berlin Wall in 1989 and the collapse of the USSR (one of the two world powers) in 1991, the US was left as the world's only remaining superpower in a globalized order whose consumers followed American films, bought American clothes and aspired to the American way of life, the American dream in which any immigrant had a chance to succeed. There are now not many parts of the world which do not look to America as a model for the way of life they admire, but there are parts of the world – notably within the more primitive tribal regions of Islam – which actively dissent from having anything to do with the American way of life.

In our time there have been splinter trends as emerging peoples hail their newly-fledged nation-states and resent being "regionalised" into large blocs. When Yugoslavia fragmented, nationalism swept through the Balkans and was behind wars involving Serbia, Bosnia and Kosovo. The Taliban are such a splinter group, fighting to regain control of Afghanistan, expel US puppets and restore Sharia law. Such nationalistic groups are swimming against the current of history and may find they do not succeed in resisting wider grouping. It can be expected that in due course there will be a Middle-Eastern Union, a region that will subsume Islamic nation-states.

The trend, the flow, is thus inexorably in the direction of global governance, and, further on, world government. We have reached a point where globalization is so strong a force that it would not be surprising if a world government were suddenly declared. Although, as we shall see, there are obstacles and things are not as simple as that.

The Pros and Cons of World Governance

In international relations theory there are four different schools, the first three of which incline towards global governance rather than a coercive world government.

Neo-realists hold that world government is not feasible and impractical. "International society" theorists hold that world government is unnecessary as sovereign states can relate to each other in a non-lawless way. Liberal internationalists combat global ills such as poverty, denial of human rights, threat of war, environmental degradation and lack of democratic accountability without calling for world government. Constructivists see the formation of a

World State as inevitable.

Constructivism holds that significant aspects of international relations are historically and socially contingent rather than consequences of human nature. In other words, international relations can be socially constructed and transformed by human practice; they are not given by nature. So it is possible to construct a World State even though human nature has promoted national interests that lead to war.

The German social constructivist Alexander Wendt, one of the most influential scholars of international relations in the world, has argued[2] that a World State with a global monopoly on the legitimate use of force is "inevitable". Using Aristotelian and Hegelian insights, Wendt traces the development of world order from a system of anarchic states to a World State – broadly the course we have been following in this chapter. He argues that the "logic of anarchy" contains within it the seeds of transformation towards a "global monopoly on the legitimate use of organized violence – a World State."[3] Following Kant (whose purposive view of history I consider at the beginning of ch. 3), Wendt sees the development as teleological, as being purposive. He argues that states struggle for recognition and are at the mercy of destructive technology (weapons of mass destruction).

Daniel Deudney[4] held in the 1990s that destructive technology makes states as vulnerable as individuals. The formation of a World State would serve as "a universal security community" whose members resolved conflicts peacefully rather than through the use of force. It would be a "universal collective security" system that would protect each member. A "universal supranational authority" could make binding authoritative decisions about the collective use of force.

Wendt holds that a World State could take various forms. While collectivising organized violence, it need not collectivise culture, economy or local politics on a global scale. While requiring a structure that "can command and enforce a collective response to threats", it need not abolish national armies, or require a single UN army. And while requiring a procedure for making binding choices, "it would not even require a world 'government', if by this we mean a unitary body with one leader whose decisions are final".[5]

Enough has been said to establish my main point, that government evolves and develops through various forms into a global model which may become a world government, which to some is inevitable.

This raises the question, is world government a good thing? We have seen that neo-realists, "international society" theorists and liberal internationalists have their doubts. The neo-realist Kenneth Waltz has argued that a world government would be driven to pursue its own exclusive organizational interests at the expense of the interests and freedom of states, and that an atomistic order of sovereign states is better. "International society" theorists such as Martin Wight and Chris Brown have seen a world government as unnecessary. Liberal internationalists such as Richard Falk have seen global governance as more desirable than world government. Liberal theorists such as Charles Beitz and Thomas Pogge have seen humanity as a common, cosmopolitan moral community of free and equal persons and have not seen a World State as being part of a liberal ideal for world order. Communitarian liberals such as Michael Walzer have seen centralised world government as a threat to social pluralism. Many liberals have seen a world government as politically tyrannical and inefficient, homogeneous (in obliterating distinct cultures and communities) and soulless, and have called for a global politics of non-domination. These are arguments that supporters of world government can counter. Indeed, some of these liberal arguments are at the level of ideological opinion.

This having been said, constructivists like Alexander Wendt do think world government may be a good thing. I would say that it all depends on who is doing the governing. If a World State is being organized by oligarchs for their own financial benefit, dictatorially, so they can hijack and profit from selling the Earth's natural resources, then world government is a bad thing. On the other hand, if a World State is being organized altruistically and philanthropically for humankind's benefit, it may be a good thing. The process in itself is neutral, and whether it is bad or good depends on who is running the world government, the motivation and integrity of the incumbents. To prevent a World State from falling into wrong hands, into the hands of bad, autocratic and dictatorial incumbents, the structure of the World State should strengthen the regions at the expense of the rulers. In other words, a World State must be democratic with built-in safety measures to prevent abuse of power.

History has taken humankind from primitive tribal groups to complex regional organization, and a World State is inevitably and inexorably ahead – just as the open sea is ahead of the widening river. However, not too much should be made of this parallel, for a World State only resembles the open sea if it is to last forever, and I am convinced it will only last for a while. It would be more accurate to see the river of history as flowing into a great lake, from which it will emerge the other side.

Philosophical Summary

So what can a philosopher proposing a World State take from an overview of the evolution of government? The development of complexity in government. Doubters about world government. Hitler's world-government organization in Nuremberg. Wendt's constructivism. The incumbents in a world government.

To sum up, a philosopher proposing a World State can distil from the course of history:

government progresses from tribe to complex organization;
government progresses from small locality to more global extent;
splinter groups resist global government;
progression towards a World State is inevitable (Wendt);
Hitler's world-government organization in Nuremberg;
the quality of a world government depends on its incumbents.

The evolution of government into more complex forms of organization and wider, more global localities has taken place because behind it and driving it there is profound yearning for a united world.

2

The Long Yearning for a World State

A philosopher who seeks to propose a World State would do well to form an overview of the development of this yearning for a united world. It was not until relatively recently that humans have been able to think of the governance of the *whole* world. America was not settled until the 16th century and Australia was not discovered by Europeans until the 17th century. For much of human history before then great powers thought in terms of the *known* world, which often did not extend far beyond their own borders.

However, this did not stop empires and dictatorships conquering substantial portions of the known world. The Macedonian Empire of Alexander the Great controlled from the Balkans to India, which at that time was considered to be the end of the world. The Roman Empire ruled the world it knew. The Ch'in (now written Qin), Han and Tang dynasties of the Chinese Empire conquered the known world of Chinese civilization. The Mongol Empire at its greatest extent in 1279 stretched from the Danube to the Sea of Japan and from the Arctic to Cambodia. It covered 22 million square kilometres, a fifth of the Earth's total land area, and ruled a population of over 100 million. The Inca Empire encompassed virtually all of the world known to the Incans. The British Empire conquered a quarter of the world's land surface and a third of the world's population, and was the nearest the world has come to total political unification.

All these empires ruled massive parts of the world in their different times. No complete world government has ever existed, and until the present era of US superpowerdom, the British have come nearest to the ideal of world government.

Even in the limited knowledge and horizons of the ancient world men yearned for perpetual peace and pondered a world government and world citizenship.

The Ancient World

The idea is present in ancient Egyptian thought. From at least c.2600BC the Pharaoh embodied the sun and ruled where the sun shone as Ra, the sun-god. Hence the two sons of Khufu, builder of the Great Pyramid, were called after

Ra: Djedefra (also written Djedefre) and Khafra (also written Khafre or Chephren). Rule of the known world was implicit in the Pharaonic sun-cult.

The idea is also present in ancient Indian thought. In *Rig Veda*, the oldest of the four *Vedas*, the earliest sacred literature in India, c.1500-1200BC, *rta*, unity and cosmic order, is universal.[1] The unitary vision of Vedic man enabled him to conceive a oneness within all levels of the universe, including the social level. There should be universal harmony as a reflection of the cosmic order, and this oneness extended to the people on Earth, who could all open to the cosmic order's "universal Light". This notion of the One illumining all humankind passed into later Brahmanism (c.600BC), the *Upanisad*s (5th century BC) and the *Bhagavadgita* (5th or 3rd centuries BC, or 1st and 2nd centuries AD), in which Arjuna tells Krishna that he is reluctant to fight in the battle of Kurukshetra as he does not want to kill his kinsmen who may be absorbed in Brahman and thus be illumined. Krishna explains that he must fight and can still be illumined, but the feeling is that universal peace better reflects the oneness of the cosmic order. The *Bhagavadgita* was the greatest single influence on Mahatma Gandhi's espousal of non-violence.

The idea can be found in ancient Chinese thought. The theme in many Chinese texts is that the Emperor was mediator between Heaven, *T'ien*, the Earth and Man, all of which are within cosmic unity. Texts such as the *I Ching* reach back to the origins of Chinese civilization, and reflect the oneness of Heaven, Earth and Man in the Chou dynasty (from 112 to 481BC), which towards its end included Confucius and Lao-Tze. In both Confucian and Taoist philosophy, Heaven and Earth denote the Great Whole of the universe, and the world of Man denotes the Great Whole of man's society.[2] The Great Whole is the One, and as the universe within the cosmic order of Heaven, Earth and Man is one, so all known mankind is one. Later, the illumined man was mediator between Heaven and Earth. To Confucius "without knowing the Mandate of Heaven, one cannot become a superior man".[3] Mo-tzu (5th century BC) taught "universal love" and denounced war, arguing that it is the will of Heaven that men should love universally. This philosophical shift strengthened the idea that the cosmic order involved Heaven, Earth and all Man, not just Chinese man.

The idea can be found in Graeco-Roman thought. According to Plutarch, Socrates said in the 5th century BC, "I am a citizen, not of Athens, or Greece, but of the world."[4] Plato's *Republic* focused on an ideal luxurious city in a time of city-states, and though the city is also an image that reflects the state of one's soul (the will, reason and desires combined in the human body) and by implication has universal applications, it is not in itself a blueprint for a World State.

In Stoic thought, the world is a unity, the one great city, and man as a world citizen must live according to the unity and orderly arrangement of Nature and the world design, and with a sense of the universal brotherhood of mankind. (This thinking rubbed off on St Augustine, whose *De Civitate Dei* or *City of God*, 415-420, saw the world as filled with Christian souls who all had equality before God.) The Graeco-Roman Stoics were close to supporting the idea of a world government.

Such thinking was a reflection of the concept of unity. It was felt that as the universe was regarded as a unity in Eastern thought, this unity should be expressed in a political form – a view that has also shaped the thinking of Universalism. In Western thought, Stoic ideas about the oneness of the universe inspired medieval Christian proposals for a global political authority.

Dante's Universal Monarch

The Italian poet and philosopher Dante articulated the Christian ideal of human unity and its expression in a world governed by a universal monarch or Emperor. In *Convivio* (*The Banquet*, 1304), Dante argued that wars and their causes would be eliminated if "the whole Earth and all that humans can possess be a monarchy, that is one government under one ruler. Because he possesses everything, the ruler would not desire to possess anything further, and thus, he would hold kings contentedly within the borders of their kingdoms, and keep peace among them."[5]

Dante had been offered hospitality in his exile by the ruler of Verona, Can Grande della Scala, and he became his guest in 1315-1316. The new Holy Roman Emperor, Henry VII, had conferred the title Imperial Vicar on Can Grande. This title Pope John XXII challenged. Dante was asked to write in defence of Can Grande and prove to the clergy of Verona that the Pope's decree was without authority. As a persecuted White Guelf seeking aid from the Ghibelline Can Grande, Dante supported the Emperor whereas their opponents, the Black Guelfs, supported the Papacy, which meant that the Popes reciprocally supported the Black Guelfs.

It is likely that Dante wrote *De Monarchia* (*On Monarchy*, sometimes translated as *On World Government*) in 1317-1318, when he was starting *Paradiso*. We know this because a reference to *Paradiso*, recently confirmed as being authentic,[6] spoke of monarchy as "the greatest gift conferred by God on human nature: *sicut in Paradiso Comedie iam dixi* ('as I have already said in the *Commedia Paradiso*')". Dante argued for a universal Emperor whose temporal power was distinct from the Pope's religious power, and he envisaged that Pope and Emperor would forge a co-operative rather than a competitive relationship. At one level he was undoubtedly thinking of the Holy Roman Emperor and the Pope, but he probably hoped that Can Grande della Scala, ruler of Verona, would act as universal Emperor. He sent him batches of cantos from his *Paradiso* after moving to Ravenna in 1319 until his death in 1321, in the hope that he would take on the role of universal Emperor.

De Monarchia was a political treatise affirming universal monarchy. Drawing on Aristotle, Dante argued that human unity stems from a shared effort to develop humankind's intellectual potential. Peace is vital to realise this end, and cannot be maintained if humanity is divided. Just as "every kingdom divided against itself shall be laid waste", since humankind shares one goal, "there must therefore be one person who directs and rules mankind, and he is properly called 'Monarch' or 'Emperor'. And thus it is apparent that the well-being of the world requires that there be monarchy or empire." When conflicts arise between two rulers who are equals, "there must be a third party of wider jurisdiction who rules over both of them by right" (i.e. Can Grande). A universal monarch is necessary as "a first and supreme judge, whose judgment resolves all disputes either directly or indirectly". In the absence of a universal monarch, humankind is "transformed into a many-headed beast", striving after "conflicting things". Humankind ordered under a universal monarch "will most closely resemble God, by mirroring the principle of oneness or unity of which he is the supreme example". The Roman Empire was "a part of God's providential plan for humanity".[7]

By "monarchy", Dante does not merely mean the rule of a single individual, the Holy Roman Emperor, although he did believe that legitimate monarchy, as opposed to tyranny, is the most perfect form of government. He is referring to the structure of the international system with an argument that is almost Hegelian. Universal government is necessary because it is the way to universal peace, the only way humankind can attain its end or purpose – which is the realisation of "possible intellect". Dante insists that the ideal political order is a universal polity. The universality of a universal monarch requires that he should bring in universal law, which would guarantee freedom as the perfect condition of humankind.

As we shall see, Dante's reasoning is similar to Kant's and to Francis Fukuyama's view that liberal democracy satisfies all aspects of human nature and is therefore the Hegelian end of history. The Holy Roman Empire thus guarantees the highest level of human freedom that is possible. Dante argues from first principles, but his conclusions have much in common with Kant's Enlightenment thinking.[8]

Dante urges that the Holy Roman Emperor should be universally accepted as the temporal sovereign authority who could unite the world in peace under one rule of law. Several passages in *De Monarchia* reinforce the message that humankind needs unity and peace:

> "Since individual men find that they grow in prudence and wisdom when they can sit quietly, it is evident that mankind, too, is most free and easy to carry on its work when it enjoys the quiet and tranquillity of peace." (1:4.)
>
> "Justice has greatest power under a unitary government; therefore the best order of the world demands world government." (1:11.)
>
> "The human race is at its best when most free." (1:12.)
>
> "All concord depends on a unity of wills; the best state of mankind is a kind of concord, for as a man is in excellent health when he enjoys concord in soul and body, and similarly a family, city or state, so is mankind as a whole. Therefore, the well-being of mankind depends on the unity of its wills." (1:15.)
>
> "Behold how good and pleasant it is for brethren to dwell together in unity." (1:16.)[9]

These sentiments are reflected by Dante's contemporaries Marsilius of Padua, who completed *Defensor Pacis* (*The Defender of Peace*) in 1324, three years after Dante died, and Petrarch, who met Dante in 1310:

> "The fruits of peace or tranquillity, then, are the greatest goods, as we have said, while those of its opposite, strife, are unbearable evils. Hence we ought to wish for peace, to seek it if we do not already have it, to conserve it once it is attained, and to repel with all our strength the strife which is

opposed to it. To this end individual brethren, and in even greater degree groups and communities, are obliged to help one another, both from the feeling of heavenly love and from the bond or law of human society."

Marsilius of Padua *The Defender of Peace* (1:1:4)

"The authority to make or establish the laws, and to give a command with the guard to their observance, belongs only to the whole body of the citizens or to the weightier part thereof as efficient cause, or else to the person or persons to whom the aforesaid whole has granted this authority."

Marsilius of Padua *The Defender of Peace* (1:13:8)[10]

"Just as the love of the people is gained more easily by mercy and generosity than by any other quality, so, conversely, nothing is more guaranteed to provoke a people's hatred than cruelty and greed."

Petrarch, 'How a Ruler ought to Govern His State'

"My song, be humble, for you are addressed to haughty folk, ever hostile to the truth. Speak then to those few high hearts that love virtue. Say to them: 'Who gives me strength to speak, as I go crying: "Peace! Peace! Peace!"'"

Petrarch, 'My Italy'[11]

It is clear that in the early 14th century there was a great longing for unity and peace within the known world, and that there were clear views as to how this could be achieved.

Utopias, Federations and Morally-Perfect States

Sir Thomas More modelled his *Utopia* on the island of Atlantis (its topography, its plain, harbours, mountains, baths, temples, army, government, population, products and bull-sacrifice) which Plato described in *Critias*. More took the idea of an ideal state from Plato's *Republic*, and was also indebted to the *Timaeus* and *Laws*. He followed Plato in borrowing his communism, contempt for gold and equality in training and pursuits between men and women.

However, More's purpose was not to portray an ideal commonwealth, as Plato had done, but to expose the social and political evils of England satirically. In this aim he was close to Erasmus's *In Praise of Folly* (also translated as *Praise of Folly* or *The Praise of Folly*), and he borrowed techniques from Plutarch's *Instituta Laconica* and from Tacitus' *Germania.* Tacitus described the manners and customs of uncivilized Germans and while doing so by implication satirised the evils of Roman life in his own time.

Utopia was probably suggested by a narrative of the voyages of Vespucci, which was printed in 1507. Its subject is the search for the best possible form of government. In Antwerp More meets a traveller, Raphael Hythloday, who has discovered the "island of Utopia", "Nowhere land". Its best possible form of government is one that a world government would be proud of. Its communism offers equality to all, there is a universal system of education for men and women, and there is toleration of religion. More anticipates Sir Francis Bacon's *New Atlantis*, Defoe's *Robinson Crusoe* and Swift's *Gulliver's Travels* in using a remote island – Swift used Lilliput – to present a society that by implication satirises English society.

Utopian works held up a representation of a perfect society by which the author's own imperfect society could be judged. They were by definition about specific places with good government, and did not encompass the world. No hint of world government can therefore be found in More's *Utopia*, or in Bacon's *New Atlantis*, which was set in the New World. However, it may be implied that the principles of the ideal states were to be followed by states throughout the world

We shall see (on pp71-72) that the Dutch Hugo Grotius, living in the turmoil of warfare during the Eighty and Thirty Years' Wars, was concerned to resolve international conflicts. After the Peace of Westphalia (1648), which concluded the exhausting Thirty Years' War, the system of sovereign states was strengthened as states pledged not to interfere in each others' affairs. Uniting humankind under one monarch or Emperor became a remoter possibility.

Soon afterwards, the English philosopher Thomas Hobbes anticipated the development of international law and collective security organizations such as the League of Nations and the UN: "Leagues between Common-wealths, over whom there is no humane Power established, to keep them all in awe, are not onely lawfull [because they are allowed by the commonwealth], but also profitable for the time they last."[12] Hobbes argued that a world government or World State is unnecessary, but held that a lawful interstate order is both possible and desirable.

Charles-Irénée Castel, Abbé de Saint-Pierre, an inspirer of Rousseau and Kant, held *Project for Making Peace Perpetual in Europe* (*Extrait du projet de paix perpétuelle*, 1713) that Europe's princes should form a federation of states by social contract. The contracting sovereigns would form a perpetual alliance and establish a permanent Diet or Congress. This would adjudicate all conflicts between the contracting princes. The decisions of the federation would be enforced by armed action.[13] In other words, the European princes would surrender their sovereign rights to make war or peace to a superior, federal body that would guarantee their protection.

This was a serious attempt to prevent war by international law. Jean-Jacques Rousseau, in *A Lasting Peace through the Federation of Europe and The State of War* (1756), supported the idea in principle: "Realise this Commonwealth of Europe for a single day, and you may be sure it will last forever; so fully would experience convince men that their own gain is to be found in the good of all." However, Rousseau held that societies had corrupted humans' natural innocence. He thought that the Abbé's proposals would not be followed "because men are crazy". Furthermore, the European sovereigns would be unlikely to volunteer to liquidate their power: "No Federation could ever be established except by a revolution."[14] To Rousseau, the best way of abolishing war was to establish well-governed societies as he outlined in *The Social Contract* (1762). Thus to achieve perpetual peace states should be made morally perfect. According to Rousseau, the moral perfection of states would establish perpetual peace, not a world government. A world of ideal states or societies would have no cause for war, and therefore would not need a world government.

In the late 18th century the idea of a federation gained momentum after the American Declaration of Independence of 1776 and the first modern democratic federation, the US, was established (i.e. finally ratified) in 1788. The US's multi-state federation of 1788 looked back to Rousseau's ideal, morally perfect states.

Nevertheless, it must be said that Rousseau's view was excessively idealistic as there will never be a world of ideal, morally perfect states. Therefore there *is* a need for a world government.

Kant's Federation of Free States

The philosopher Immanuel Kant thought deeply about a world government. In his *Idea for a Universal History with a Cosmopolitan Purpose* (1784)[15] – "cosmopolitan" suggests "relating to world citizens" – he linked the development of the domestic state to the "slow development of man's original [rational] capacities". He argued that war logically leads to an international state. War moves states "to take the step which reason could have suggested to them even without so many sad experiences – that of abandoning a lawless state of savagery and entering a federation of peoples in which every state, even the smallest, could expect to derive its security and rights not from its own power or its own legal judgment, but solely from this great federation (*Foedus Amphictyonum)*, from a united power and the law-governed decisions of a united will." Kant was referring to a federation like the Amphictyonic League of Greek tribes.

The federation Kant envisaged would be the "inevitable outcome" of human history. Soon afterwards, in a treatise, *Perpetual Peace: A Philosophical Sketch* (1795), a title that owes much to Abbé de Saint-Pierre, he reinforced the idea of the inevitability of such a federation. He argued that rationality dictated the formation of "an international state (*civitas gentium*), which would necessarily continue to grow until it embraced all the peoples of the Earth."[16] This international state would be a world government. However, Kant conceded that "the positive idea of a world republic cannot be realised" in the conditions of his day, the 1790s when Europe was still reeling from the French Revolution.

In *Perpetual Peace* Kant argued that in a world of distinct but interacting states the threat of a future war could be abolished by following a three-step plan. First, the civil constitution of each state should be republican and guarantee the freedom and equality of citizens through the rule of law and representative political institutions. Secondly, the law of nations should be founded on a federation of free states, a "federation of peoples" which is distinct from an "international state". A "pacific federation (*foedus pacificum*)...does not aim to acquire any power like that of a state, but merely to preserve and secure the freedom of each state in itself, along with that of the other confederated states". He argued that a federal Union of free and independent states "is still to be preferred to an amalgamation of the separate nations under a single power which has overruled the rest and created a universal monarchy". Kant believed that a universal monarchy would be a world government that seemed to be all-powerful but would in fact be powerless: "For the laws progressively lose their impact as the government increases its range, and a soulless despotism, after crushing the germs of goodness, will finally lapse into anarchy." A "universal despotism" would end "in the graveyard of freedom".

The third step for permanently abolishing war is the observance of cosmopolitan right, which Kant limits to universal hospitality. The rights of people as citizens of the world should be limited to the conditions of universal hospitality. In other words people should be allowed to visit other countries, but not to stay unless invited. For although humans share a right to the Earth's surface, strangers require the inhabitants' agreement to settle on their territory. There is thus no right to conquer foreign lands as, Kant states, happened in "America, the negro countries, the Spice Islands, the Cape" and East India.[17]

Kant, then, writing in the mid 1790s when Europe was in turmoil, saw the need for an "international state (*civitas gentium*)", and he saw it as a process, for it would "necessarily continue to grow until it embraced all the peoples of the Earth". But realistically this world republic was not going to happen overnight, and so he focused on a second-best, a "pacific federation" (*foedus pacificum*) between states, an intermediate means of abolishing war immediately, and his principle of "universal hospitality" was undoubtedly conceived with French revolutionary troops in mind. (In early 1795 the republican armies conquered Belgium and then the left bank of the Rhine and the United Provinces, which would have alarmed Kant in Köningsberg, East Prussia.) They should withdraw back to France for humans had the right to visit other countries but not conquer them and occupy them. Kant thus had world government as an aim but was clear that it should not be a "universal despotism" under a despot like Napoleon. (Napoleon declared to Benjamin Constant before the Battle of Waterloo, "I wanted to rule the world, and in order to do this I needed ultimate power....I wanted to rule the world – who wouldn't have in my place? The world begged me to govern it."[18])

Kant thus endorsed the ideal of human unity and saw a world republic of free and equal individuals as an ideal end of the progress of human history. He was opposed to a universal monarchy as he felt that monarchy, as distinct from a republic, does not guarantee the freedom and equality of individual citizens: "Under a constitution where the subject is not a citizen, and which is therefore not republican, it is the simplest thing in the world to go to war."[19] A world republic remained his political ideal, but his short-term "realistic utopia"[20] would comprise a federation of free republican states short of a World State, the nearest achievable approximation, he felt, to the ideal of a world republic.

A contemporary of Kant's, the radical political cosmopolitan Anarcharsis Cloots (Jean-Baptiste du Val-de-Grâce, Baron de Cloots), who died in 1794, basing his thinking on the social-contract theory outlined in Rousseau's *The*

Social Contract (1762), went further than Kant. He argued that the sovereign-state system should be abolished in favour of a universal republic that embraced all humankind.[21]

19th- and 20th-Century Federations

The idea of a world republic was taken up by a German philosopher, Karl Krause, in an essay, 'The Archetype of Humanity' (1811). He proposed the formation of five regional federations: Europe, Asia, Africa, America and Australia. These would be aggregated under a world republic.[22]

The idea of a world federation and universal law that would bring perpetual peace was in the thoughts of Englishmen when the British army were fighting in Afghanistan from 1838 to 1842. In 1842 the English poet Tennyson published 'Locksley Hall' (written in 1837-8), which included the lines:

> "For I dipt into the future, far as human eye could see;
> Saw the Vision of the world, and all the wonder that would be...
>
> Till the war-drum throbb'd no longer, and the battle-flags were furled
> In the Parliament of man, the Federation of the world.
>
> There the common sense of most shall hold a fretful realm in awe
> And the kindly earth shall slumber, lapt in universal law."

Federations in Switzerland in 1848 and Canada in 1867 reflected the US multi-state federation of 1788. Their federations united distinct ethnic, cultural and lingual regions under a common government. However, although there had been International Peace Congresses in Europe every two years from 1843 to 1853 the momentum for further federalism was temporarily lost after the outbreak of first the Crimean War and then the American Civil War. Ulysses S. Grant, the Northern US Civil-War general, with the carnage of the American Civil War of the 1860s fresh in his mind, said: "I believe at some future day, the nations of the Earth will agree on some sort of congress which will take cognizance of international questions of difficulty and whose decisions will be as binding as the decisions of the Supreme Court are upon us."[23]

Bahá'u'lláh founded the Bahá'i Faith between 1852 and 1892. He saw a global commonwealth of nations as being fundamental to the new religion. It would have a world legislature, an international court and an international executive. The Bahá'i religion advocated universal weights and measures, currency unification and a global language.

There was now a surge of internationalism in Europe. Many international organizations were formed, starting with the International Red Cross in 1863, the Telegraphic Union in 1865, the Institute of International Law in 1873 and the Universal Postal Union in 1874. There was growing interest in world government. James Lorimer explored the idea of a world government establishing a global rule of law in *The Institutes of the Law of Nations* (1883). An embryonic world parliament, the Inter-Parliamentary Union, was founded in 1886 by Cremer and Passy. There were around 450 international organizations by 1914.

The author H.G. Wells was a champion of world government. He had been the first to foresee the dangers of an "atomic bomb" in his novel *The World Set Free* (1914), which in 1932 inspired the scientist Leo Szilard to work out how to start the nuclear chain reaction needed to build an atomic bomb. Wells foresaw the consequences of nation-states' developing atomic weapons and using them against each other. *The Outline of History* (1920, revised 1931) presented the world's history in one volume. At the end of his *Outline*, in a section headed 'Some Possibilities of a Federal World State', Wells called directly for world federation: "A federation of all humanity, together with a sufficient measure of social justice to ensure health, education and a rough equality of opportunity, would mean such a release and increase of human energy as to open up a new phase in human history."[24] In *The Shape of Things to Come* (1933, the year Hitler came to power) Wells saw a dictatorship to enforce world government as beneficial to humankind. This is not a view that democratic world federalists would share.

Aldous Huxley in *Brave New World* (1932) wrote of a World State, a unified government, ruled by a World Controller, that administers the entire planet except for a few isolated areas. Set in 2059 following a Nine-Years' War that broke out in 2049, the novel shows a world economy regulated by the State. Humans live in racial, social and economic harmony. The vision is dystopian and there is no place for individualism in regimented living conditions.

There had been various attempts to establish global institutions to resolve international disputes and to regulate the conduct of wars by laws. The Hague Conferences of 1899 and 1907 failed to prevent the First World War, and the League of Nations failed to prevent the Second World War.

The Second World War was responsible for over 60 million dead, 90 million according to some estimates. The atomic bombings of Hiroshima and Nagasaki were deeply shocking, and atomic scientists lobbied for the international control of atomic energy as the main function of a world federalist government. The United Nations was established by charter in 1945, when it had 51 members, and adopted the Universal Declaration of Human Rights in 1948. Many felt that it presided over discussions and co-ordination between sovereign governments, and such prominent thinkers as Albert Einstein, Winston Churchill, Mahatma Gandhi and Bertrand Russell called for the forming of a federal world government:

> "It will be just as easy for nations to get along in a republic of the world as it is for you to get along in the republic of the United States. When Kansas and Colorado have a quarrel over the water in the Arkansas River, they don't call out the National Guard in each state and declare war over it. They bring a suit in the Supreme Court of the United States and abide by the decision. There isn't a reason in the world why we can't do that internationally."
>
> Harry S. Truman

> "A world government with powers adequate to guarantee security is not a remote ideal for the distant future. It is an urgent necessity if our civilization is to survive."
>
> Albert Einstein

> "There is no salvation for civilisation, or even the human race, other than the creation of a world government."
>
> Albert Einstein

> "As long as there are sovereign nations possessing great power, war is inevitable."
>
> Albert Einstein

> "A world government must be created which is able to solve conflicts between nations by judicial decision. This government must be based on a clear-cut constitution which is approved by the governments and nations and which gives it the sole disposition of offensive weapons."[25]
>
> Albert Einstein

"With all my heart I believe that the world's present system of sovereign nations can only lead to barbarism, war and inhumanity, and that only World law can assure progress towards a civilized peaceful community."

Albert Einstein

"Unless some effective world supergovernment for the purpose of preventing war can be set up...the prospects for peace and human progress are dark....If...it is found possible to build a world organization of irresistible force and inviolable authority for the purpose of securing peace, there are no limits to the blessings which all men enjoy and share."

Winston Churchill

"Unless we establish some form of world government, it will not be possible for us to avert a World War III in the future."

Winston Churchill

"I would not like to live in this world if it is not to be one world."

Mahatma Gandhi[26]

"It is entirely clear that there is only one way in which great wars can be permanently prevented, and that is the establishment of an international government with a monopoly of serious armed force."

Bertrand Russell, 1945[27]

"A scientific world society cannot be stable unless there is a world government."

Bertrand Russell[28]

"We invite this Congress, and through it the scientists of the world and the general public, to subscribe to the following resolution: 'In view of the fact that in any future world war nuclear weapons will certainly be employed, and that such weapons threaten the continued existence of mankind, we urge the governments of the world to realise, and to acknowledge publicly, that their purpose cannot be furthered by a world war, and we urge them, consequently, to find peaceful means for the settlement of all matters of dispute between them.'"

The Russell-Einstein Manifesto, 1955[29]

World Federalists

Towards the end of the Second World War two federalist books appeared.

Wendell Willkie's *One World* (1943) sold over 2 million copies. Most of the book is Willkie's description of his wartime tour of the Middle East, the Soviet Union and China as Roosevelt's personal representative in 1942. Willkie, a Democrat, had lost to Roosevelt in the 1940 presidential campaign, and then worked with Roosevelt, rousing the US from isolationism. It is only at the very end of his book that he touches on the federal theme: "America must choose one of three courses after this war: narrow nationalism, which inevitably means the ultimate loss of our own liberty; international imperialism, which means the sacrifice of some other nation's liberty; or the creation of a world in which there shall be an equality of opportunity for every race and every nation. I am convinced the American people will choose, by overwhelming majority, the last of these courses." [30]

Emery Reves' *The Anatomy of Peace* (1945) argued that the United Nations should be replaced by a federal world government as an association of nation-states can never prevent a new war: "What chance have we to create a world government before the next war? Not much." [31] This book became the "bible" of world federalists and was commended by Einstein in 1947.[32]

The first world federalist organization had been launched in 1937: the Campaign for World Government. A Federal Union was set up in the UK in 1938, and another Federal Union (now the Association to Unite the Democracies) followed in the US in 1939. This called for a Federation of Atlantic Democracies. In 1940 a *Mouvement populaire Suisse en faveur d'une federation des peoples* was established in Geneva. Altiero Spinelli's plan for a European federation was circulated among the anti-Fascist resistance movements during the Second World War. In 1945, the Committee to Frame a World Constitution convened at the University of Chicago and drafted a Constitution for the World.[33]

In 1947 grassroots federalists formed the United World Federalists (UWF), later renamed World Federalist Association, and then Citizens for Global Solutions. They called for the transformation of the United Nations into a universal federation of states with powers to control armaments. States should surrender their sovereign rights to stockpile weapons and wage war, and they should submit their disputes to authoritative international institutions of adjudication and enforcement. World peace would only be achieved by establishing world law.

At the same time similar movements formed in many countries. In 1947 a global coalition, now known as the World Federalist Movement – Institute for Global Policy (WFM-IGP) was formed in Montreux, Switzerland. This body was created when five small world federalist organizations agreed to merge in Asheville, North Carolina. In August 1947 more than 51 organizations from 24 countries attended the Conference for the World Movement for World Federal Government, which made the Montreux Declaration. The World Movement met again in Luxembourg in 1948 and founded an association of parliamentarians for world government, which came into existence in 1951.

In 1948 Garry Davis renounced his US citizenship, declared himself a "citizen of the world" and called for world government from the balcony of the UN General Assembly in Paris,[34] until he was dragged away by guards. Davis founded a Registry of World Citizens. Opinion polls carried out by UNESCO in 1948-49 found world government was preferred in six European countries, and rejected in the US. On 4 September 1953 Davis, speaking from the City Hall of Ellsworth, Maine, announced the formation of the "World Government of World Citizens". He based this on three "World Laws": One God (or Absolute Value); One World; and One Humanity. Claiming that his mandate was article 21(3) of the Universal Declaration of Human Rights, he founded the United World Service Authority in New York City as the administrative agency of the new world government. It then designed and issued a "World Passport" based on article 13(2) of the Universal Declaration of Human Rights Some 800,000 passports have been issued and these have been recognised by over 151 countries.[35]

Some federalists did not reject the nation-state, only authoritarian, non-democratic states. In 1949 Clarence Streit founded the Atlantic Union Committee (AUC), which called for a federal Union of democratic states that would be the genesis of a "free-world government, as nations are encouraged by example to practise the principles which would make them eligible for membership, namely the principles of representative government and protection of individual liberty by law".[36]

In 1954 E. Adamson Hoebel, a legal anthropologist, broadened the legal realist tradition to include non-Western nations: "Whatever the idealist may desire, force and the threat of force are the ultimate power in the determination of international behaviour, as in the law within the nation or tribe. But until force and the threat of force in international relations are brought under social control by the world community, by and for the world society, they remain the instruments of social anarchy and not the sanctions of world law. The creation in clear-cut terms of the corpus of world law cries for the doing. If world law, however, is to be realised at all, there will have to be minimum of general agreement as to the nature of the physical and ideational world and the relation of men in society to it. An important and valuable next step will be found in deep-cutting analysis of the major law systems of the contemporary world in order to lay bare their basic postulates – postulates that are too generally hidden; postulates felt, perhaps, by those who live by them, but so much taken for granted that they are rarely expressed or exposed for examination. When this is done – and it will take the efforts of many keen intellects steeped in the law of at least a dozen lands and also aware of the social nexus of the law – then mankind will be able to see clearly for the first time and clearly where the common consensus of the great living social and law systems lies. Here will be found the common postulates and values upon which the world community can build. At the same time the truly basic points of conflict that will have to be worked upon for resolution will be revealed. Law is inherently purposive."[37] This call for all nations to pool their laws and create from them a system of international law is just as relevant today as it was in 1954.

In 1962 the Secretary-General of the United Nations, U Thant, called for world government in a speech at Uppsala, Sweden.

The world movement for World Federal Government had hoped that a UN review conference in 1955, planned under article 109 of the UN Charter, would turn the UN into a world federal system. Due to the Cold War, there was no political will for such a conference. In 1965 the movement established offices near the UN, and appointed a UN observer and advocate. The focus was on amendments to the UN Charter with a view to making the Security Council more representative, creating a World Court with compulsory jurisdiction and authority to conduct judicial reviews, and to turn the General Assembly into a democratically elected world parliament. Federalists proposed a commission on sustainable development, an international development authority, a standing peacekeeping corps and an international criminal court.

In 1969 the American landing on the moon brought a new perspective to the Earth. The first astronauts on the moon's surface saw the Earth as a blue ball against a black sky, and it seemed a unity, one. Film they took was relayed to

Earth and humankind saw the Earth as seen from the moon. Suddenly millions of people thought it inconceivable that there could not be a World State with a world government.

Support for multinational federalism led to the formation of the European Union. However, the intensification of the Cold War (1945-1989) had divided the world into two ideologically opposed camps, led by the US and the USSR, and world government came to be seen as one of the two opponents ruling the world by conquering the other. Progress towards global federation was halted and, indeed, went into reverse. The US was accused of attempting to impose "American monopolistic capitalism" on the world, and universal federation faced the same accusation. Public discussion of world government ceased.

Now the Soviet Union became the historical conveyer of socialist or communist thinking. Socialist ideas were linked to the French Revolution, and the State was held up to be coercive on behalf of the proletarian class. It was to coerce and oppress the bourgeoisie. Such notions of the State crowded out the concept of a philanthropic World State. There was talk of a world socialist economy governed by a "Bolshevik World State".[38] Soviet apologists argued that the real cause of war was capitalism. In practice, Soviet Communism was based on repression and had little to do with socialist ideals.

In spite of the Cold War recent world leaders have continued to urge world government:

> "We have been warned by the power of modern weapons that peace may be the only climate possible for human life itself....There must be law, steadily invoked and respected, for without law, the world promises only such meagre justice as the pity of the strong upon the weak."
>
> Dwight D. Eisenhower

> "We must create world-wide law and law enforcement as we outlaw world-wide war and weapons."
>
> John F. Kennedy

> "There is an increasing awareness of the need for some form of global government."
>
> Mikhail Gorbachev

> "Our goals are the same as those of the UN's founders, who sought to replace a world at war with one where the rule of law would prevail, where human rights were honoured, where development would blossom, where conflict would give way to freedom from violence."
>
> Ronald Reagan, in his address to the UN General Assembly, September 26, 1983

Following the dissolution of the USSR in 1991, there was a revival of interest in federal world government and in the global protection of human rights. In 1992 the Maastricht Treaty paved the way for the European Union (EU), which was enlarged to include half a billion people in 27 member nation-states. In 1998 the Rome Statute led to the establishment in 2002 of the International Criminal Court. The African Union was founded in 2002 and the Union of South American Nations in 2008 (replacing the 2004 South American Community of Nations).

The concept of world government has seeped throughout Western culture. Robert A Heinlein's *Starship Troopers*, a literary work adapted into a series of films, presents a world government with a socialist ideology. Orson Scott Card's *Shadow of the Giant* shows a "Hegemon" over the Earth. The TV series *Star Trek* presents the Earth as united under one government in the 22nd century. It is called United Earth following the unification of Earth in the 22nd century. United Earth is a political subdivision of the United Federation of Planets, which was founded in 2161. The concept of world government also appears in comics, animation and video games.

Today a number of international organizations promote world government. The World Federalist Movement (WFM) is a movement of global citizens with 23 member organizations and 16 associated organizations around the globe. It seeks to establish a federated world government. The US member organization is Citizens for Global Solutions. The Centre for International Governance Innovation (CIGI) is a research and education centre in Canada. It is creating a global online research community to strengthen governance around the world. One World Trust (OWT) is a UK-based charity and member of the World Federalist Movement. It seeks to make existing global organizations more accountable. Civitatis International is a UK-based non-governmental organization. It does legal research and promotes increased systems of global governance to policymakers. The Committee for a Democratic UN is a network of parliamentarians and non-governmental organizations from Germany,

Switzerland and Austria. It has a world federalist philosophy. Democratic World Federalists is a San-Francisco-based civil-society organization. It promotes a democratic federal system of world government. Vote World Government (VWG) is a Canadian non-governmental organization which has embarked on a global referendum that asks, "Do you support the creation of a directly-elected, representative and democratic world government?"

The Japanese-based World Party campaigns for a world parliament with seats allocated in proportion to the populations of nation-states. It co-operates with the World Government Institute, which is the theoretical wing of the world-government movement, and with the World Citizen Network.

Once again there is a consensus for global governance, and a renewed yearning for a World State. In every part of the world people yearn for a world government that stops short of being coercive, authoritarian and dictatorial, but which can put an end to war. In a time when images of wars in Iraq and Afghanistan fill television screens, there has never been a greater need for a supranational World Authority.

Philosophical Summary

What can the Universalist deviser of a World State take from the long yearning for one world? Eastern unity reflected in humankind's oneness. Dante's universal monarchy to bring peace. Grotius' international law. Abbé de Saint-Pierre's federation by social contract. Rousseau's morally perfect states. Kant's federation of free states. Cloot's universal republic to replace sovereign states. Federations like the US are a step towards world government. Krause's five federations to become a world republic. H.G. Wells' world federation and a federation of all humanity. Groups of world federalists. The European Union.

To sum up, the philosopher devising a universal World State can distil from humankind's yearning:

cosmic unity should be reflected in a oneness of humankind;
a universal monarch can bring peace;
international law to make peace;
forming a federation of states by social contract;
morally perfect states will not happen;
a universal republic gives more security than a monarchy;
there should be a federation of free states;
a universal republic should replace sovereign states;

a federation of all humanity;
the atomic bomb has increased the urgency for permanent peace;
movements of world federalists want a world government;
federal regions like the EU are a step towards world government;
many world leaders have called for a world government.

This focus on a World State has raised questions about history's progress to an end-point following the collapse of the certainties we have known, the collapse of the old world and with it of the old order.

3

History's Progress to an End-Point: The Collapse of the Old Order

A philosopher who proposes a World State should consider Kant's Enlightenment view of the progress of history to its goal – an end-point that I would say will last for a while and not forever – in the light of the disarray we have all been witnessing in the system that ran Europe until the 20th century.

Universal History

Kant's Enlightenment view of history as progress can be found in his 1784 essay of 16 pages, *An Idea for a Universal History from a Cosmopolitan Purpose*, to which I have already referred. The title, *Idee zu einer allgemeinen Geschichte in weltbürgerlicher Absicht* is variously translated as ending "with a Cosmopolitan Purpose" and "from a Cosmopolitan Point of View", Fukuyama's preference, and "purpose" is arguably the better translation. That is the translation I have adopted, and it is supported by a short notice in the twelfth number of the *Gothaische gelehrte Zeitung* for 1784, which said: "A favourite idea of Professor Kant's is that the ultimate *purpose* of the human race is to achieve the most perfect civic constitution and he wishes that a philosophical historian might undertake to give us a history of humanity from this *point of view*, and to show to what extent humanity in various ages has approached or drawn away from this final *purpose* and what remains to be done in order to reach it." (My italics.)

Kant is saying that the purpose of the human race is to achieve a perfect civic constitution – for a World State. This constitution would enshrine the "freedom of the human will". History has "a regular movement" in it that carries the human race to this end-point. History, and Nature, are therefore teleological, for their purpose is to bring about this "natural end": the "goal" of a "society with the greatest freedom". Kant believed that history was a progressive evolution with an end-point, a final purpose that made the whole of history intelligible, in which "the human race finally achieves the condition in which all the seeds planted in it by Nature can fully develop and in which the destiny of the race can be fulfilled here on Earth".

An Idea for a Universal History with a Cosmopolitan Purpose is really a list of nine theses and exegeses. The fifth thesis asserts, "The greatest problem for the human race, to the solution of which Nature drives man, is the achievement of a universal civic society which administers law among men." The sixth thesis asserts, "This problem is the most difficult and the last to be solved by mankind." The seventh thesis asserts, "The problem of establishing a perfect civic constitution is dependent upon the problem of a lawful external relation among states."

The eighth thesis asserts, "The history of mankind can be seen, in the large, as the realisation of Nature's secret plan to bring forth a perfectly constituted state as the only condition in which the capacities of mankind can be fully developed, and also bring forth that external relation among states which is perfectly adequate to this end." The ninth thesis speaks of the "union of the human race": "A philosophical attempt to work out a universal history according to a natural plan directed to achieving the civic union of the human race must be regarded as possible, and, indeed, as contributing to this end of Nature."

The accompanying exegesis asserts that it can be assumed "that Nature, even in the play of human freedom, works not without plan or purpose". The idea that history has a plan and purpose that challenges the work of "empirical historians" is "only a suggestion of what a philosophical mind...could essay from another point of view". "A philosophical history" can see Nature and history as having a plan and purpose.[1]

Writing after the American Declaration of Independence and in the run-up to the French Revolution, then, Kant saw the end-point of history as the realisation of human freedom. A Universal History would determine whether history is a general human progress in the direction of republican government, which today we think of as liberal democracy.[2] Kant believed that Universal History is both philosophical and empirical. He called for a Kepler or Newton who could explain the universal laws of the evolution of human history. "We leave it to Nature to produce the man capable of composing it."

Kant was looking for a Universal History that showed the progressive evolution of humankind within the societies the civilizations have thrown up. He was looking for the idea of progress, an Enlightenment idea rather discredited by two world wars and the wars of our time: "If one follows the influence of Greek history on the construction and misconstruction of the Roman state which swallowed up the Greek, then the Roman influence on the barbarians who in turn destroyed it, and so on down to our times; if one adds episodes from the national histories of other peoples in so far as they are known from the history of the enlightened nations, one will discover a regular progress in the constitution of states on our continent (which will probably give law, eventually, to all the others)."

H.G. Wells' *Outline of History* came close to charting the progress of humankind and answering Kant's call. But Wells stopped at the end of the First World War when, despite the League of Nations, progress seemed to be going into reverse: the regress of the Second World War and the Holocaust. Kant would also have been looking for periods of freedom, democracy and egalitarianism, cultural periods like the late 5th- and early 4th-century-BC Greek culture, aspects of the Renaissance (discounting the tyrannies), and the Enlightenment culture that created the Declaration of Independence in America and (shortly after 1784) the French Revolution, and he would have undoubtedly included the culture within the British Empire.

Kant's project of writing a Universal History that is philosophically serious and also empirical – history with progress and purpose that also refers to precise periods and dates – was initially taken up by Hegel. Hegel, seeing liberty, equality and fraternity as the ideals of the French Revolution and believing that they offered "the society with the greatest freedom" and that they would shape the society that followed the French Revolution, believed that the end-point of world history came in 1806 when revolutionary France under Napoleon beat the Prussians at Jena and ensured that the rights of man would triumph. Alexandre Kojève, the Russian-French philosopher, Hegel's interpreter, thought the same, as Francis Fukuyama points out in *The End of History*.[3]

The lesson of Hegel is that one should beware of believing that one's own time is the end-point of world history, a warning that applies to Fukuyama. Jacques Derrida complained that we have not reached the perfection of the ideal of liberal democracy as "never have violence, inequality, exclusion, famine and thus economic repression affected as many human beings in the history of the earth and of humanity".[4]

I find that the baton has passed to me, and that I am now grappling with Kant's idea of pinpointing the end-point of world history. In my Universalist history[5] I have traced the progress of each of 25 civilizations, covering the whole of the recorded history of the last 5,000 years, from their birth in response to a metaphysical idea, their growth and empires, and then their decline into secularisation when the idea is lost – but also into outer equality and democracy, Unions and federations.

Each of my 25 civilizations goes through 61 similar stages. When a civilization reaches its end, stage 61, it passes into another civilization, just as the Mesopotamian and Egyptian civilizations passed into the Arab civilization in 642, when they adopted Islam and Allah. Most of my living civilizations are in stage 43 or 46, union or federalist stages. I see all my living civilizations as ultimately flowing into, or more accurately beneath, a supranational world-wide civilization for a while (see p4). It is a law in my Universalist history that in any conflict between civilizations, the younger is victorious over the older, and the youngest living civilization dominates all the rest.

Thus this world-wide civilization must necessarily be influenced by the youngest extant civilization, the North-American, which is in stage 15 of its 61 stages, the same stage that the Roman civilization was in 341-218BC during the rise of the Roman Empire. The world-wide civilization that my living civilizations will all pass into, or rather beneath, will not be a formal American Empire as the Declaration of Independence supports the freedom and equality of all peoples and therefore opposes turning them into colonial dependents; but it will be strengthened by American encouragement and leadership.

It can therefore be said that although civilizations rise and fall, grow and decay, they will all reach a time when many are in Union or federalist stages and one is in a dominant, stage-15, "pre-Roman-Empire" stage, a time when all growing-decaying civilizations progress to an end-point which will be a world-wide civilization that espouses liberal democracy. The entry into this world-wide civilization and "civic constitution" will coincide with the requirements of the rise-and-fall patterns of all the living civilizations, most of which are looking for Unions and federations under a dominant younger civilization. The entry into a world-wide civilization will thus happen naturally – in the sense that the rise-and-fall patterns demand it at that particular period of time.[6]

However, it is important to recognise that until the beginning of the world-wide civilization actually happens, the rise-and-fall pattern of civilizations will continue. It is the norm, and the world-wide civilization will be superimposed on the norm, which will continue beneath it.

In Kant's Universal History, civilizations flow towards the open sea of universal freedom and liberal democracy forever. My scheme shows a similar flow. Many of my civilizations have just passed through stage 42, a period of egalitarianism, and I show several stage-43 and stage-46 civilizations passing under the influence of the stage-15 US. At some point all living civilizations will flow into, or under, the influence of a world-wide civilization for a while as if flowing into, and through, an intermediary great lake. I would say that they will resume as themselves with their original identities as civilizations, the other side of the lake.

For both of us, history is therefore a progressive and unitary history of mankind, even though I hold that the individual civilizations which carry forward this progressive evolutionary thrust rise and fall, decline and disintegrate on their way to historical unity. Kant would have recognised my Universalist history as Universal History.

The progress of history to an end-point therefore resembles the flow in the chart on pp178-179, in which all civilizations ultimately flow into, or under, a world-wide civilization for a while and remain there in Hegel's sense for a while. Events continue, individual civilizations continue to go through their stages and die into other civilizations just as the currents from rivers continue when they have merged in a great lake, but history will have reached its end-point for a while in widespread liberal democracy. This end-point will be the goal of history, but it will not terminate the progress of history and last forever – no historical arrangement has ever lasted forever, not the Roman Empire, not the British Empire. That is the view as to what will happen of Universal History, which includes my Universalist history.

Despite this *caveat* the chart on pp178-179, 'From One to One', reveals history to have a very satisfying symmetry – one that is in history's civilizations rather than in the eye and mind of the beholder.

The Collapse of the Old World

A world-wide civilization with liberal democracy has been made more likely by the convulsive death-throes of the old order that have taken place towards the end of the first decade of the 21st century.

Capitalism

The existing world order has been underpinned by the capitalist system, the system of free enterprise, free trade and free competition under which the means of production are privately owned and production is guided, and income distributed, through the operation of markets.

The system began with the break-up of feudalism and gathered strength in the 16th century in the course of the growth of the English cloth industry. The excess of production over consumption, when ploughed back into the means of production, enlarged productive capacity and was not invested in unproductive projects such as cathedrals. Hard work and frugality were encouraged by the 16th-century Protestant Reformation. Prices rose faster than wages, and the capitalists benefited from the ensuing inflation. From c.1500 to c.1750 the early capitalists of the mercantilist era were supported by strong national states, nation-states which achieved uniform monetary systems and legal codes that aided economic development.

In 18th-century England during the Industrial Revolution, capitalism shifted from being based on commerce to being based on industry. Capitalists invested their profits in advancing technical knowledge that promoted industrial growth. Adam Smith, in *Inquiry into the Nature and Causes of the Wealth of Nations* (1776), advocated leaving economic decisions to market forces and not the state bureaucracy, which, he felt, should be disbanded. This was a theory of *laissez-faire*: the abstention of government from interfering in the workings of the market.

In the 19th century after the French Revolution and the Napoleonic Wars, capitalism became dominant. Political liberalism stood for free trade, sound money linked to the gold standard, balanced budgets and minimum poor relief. There was a good measure of economic freedom, although the free economy was in fact a system of warring national economies guided by political rather than economic considerations.

This form of capitalism collapsed with the First World War, when trade was disrupted by air attacks on ships. In the 1920s international markets shrank, the gold standard was abandoned during the Great Depression of the 1930s in favour of managed national currencies and banking supremacy passed from Europe to the United States. There were revolts against European colonialism in Africa and Asia, and trade barriers multiplied. Protectionism replaced economic freedom. The Great Depression of the 1930s discouraged the State from interfering in economic decisions, but warring national economies undermined free trade.

The Second World War intensified protectionism. Air attacks on ships again disrupted sea trade. By the end of the war economies had become even more national and protected, currencies were not convertible and international trade continued to suffer. The Bretton Woods Conference of July 1944 had set up the International Bank for Reconstruction and Development to make capital available to states needing foreign aid, and the International Monetary Fund to finance short-term imbalances in international payments and to stabilise exchange rates. In Britain socialist measures attacked monopolies and inheritance and introduced social welfare, weakening capitalism. However, after the war US firms moved into Europe and the rest of the world, and US multinational corporations dominated the car, chemicals and computer industries. Capitalism revived. This was the beginning of global capitalism.

Global capitalism was a consequence of developed global financial markets and the growth of transnational corporations and their domination over national economies. It was strengthened through the offshore market in Eurodollars (deposits in US-dollar denominations held at banks outside the US) in the 1970s. It was reinforced around 1980, when Margaret Thatcher and Ronald Reagan removed the State from the economy and allowed market forces to thrive, including privatisation. Private enterprise proved better at creating wealth than the State. To attract and retain capital other countries had to follow their lead. There was strict monetary discipline, and as a result there was a recession and the international debt crisis of 1982 followed.

In 1989 the Berlin Wall fell, the Soviet Empire began to disintegrate and capitalism swept through the ex-Soviet Union, becoming truly global. The spread of communications, including television and the Internet, reinforced it. Information and culture slowly became globalized through the widening use of telephones, faxes and computers. Air travel reached all parts of the globe more quickly. The technology for this information revolution was developed from the early, relatively unsophisticated computers that had directed NASA's landing on the moon in 1969. It was US technology.

New York and London were the world's financial centres. The global economy expanded until 1997. Then the removal of the currency peg in Thailand led to the Thai *baht*'s being floated and halved in value, and to financial markets ruining economies in the developing countries.

Globalization offered individual freedom – free competition on a global scale – that could not be matched by national states. It probably accelerated global growth. However, globalization hindered national states' taxation, which had traditionally raised revenues to fund their expenditure. For every nation-state's consumers bought goods from many different countries throughout the globe, which meant that they bought fewer domestic goods. Welfare states suffered from the reduction in taxation. Multinational corporations and international financial markets were in conflict with national politics, whose politicians endeavour to please their electorates in order to retain power.

Then came the financial crisis. The housing bubble in the subprime mortgage market burst following widespread 100-per-cent borrowing on inflated house prices without any need for the borrowers to place a deposit. This led to the collapse of the financial system. The theory that financial markets tend towards equilibrium was proved wrong. In August 2007 the crisis spread to other markets. Hedge funds collapsed, and some lightly regulated financial institutions such as Lehman Brothers, whose creditworthiness proved untrustworthy, crumbled. The financial system went into meltdown. A large money-market fund that had invested in commercial paper issued by Lehman Brothers found that its asset value was below the amount it had deposited. There was a run on money-market funds, which stopped buying commercial paper. The issuers of commercial paper drew down their credit lines, ending interbank lending. The Federal Reserve System injected $1,800 billion into the system. Soon outlays by the Federal Reserve and US government agencies staggeringly came to over $13.5 trillion.

The stock market slumped. Everywhere, consumers were late in settling their bills. Businesses had to pay their staff out of reduced cash flow, and the banks were not lending. Small and medium-sized businesses went into administration.

In the US, Britain, Europe and in many other countries the State bailed out banks and became a majority shareholder. The Thatcher-Reagan revolution went into reverse. A form of nationalisation replaced privatisation as taxpayers' money was injected into the financial system which it would take a generation for taxpayers to repay. Western governments adopted the policy of printing money – quantitative easing – advocated by Keynes in 1932. Expansionist monetary policies replaced tight monetary control to head off a new Great Depression. Levels of government debt rose. Countries looked as if they might go bankrupt: Iceland; Greece; Britain; China. In such countries the State, burdened with a massive bureaucracy and Welfare State, and in America's case trying to expand the State's provision of healthcare, was unable to create the wealth that private enterprise had created in the mid-1990s. Bankers were reviled for having created financial chaos and for being rewarded with inflated bonuses they did not deserve.

The future for global capitalism looked dismal. The old financial order seemed to have run its course, and to be waiting for a new model.

Socialism

If capitalism has played a large part in bringing history to an end-point in permanent liberal democracy by its collapse, socialism has also undermined the old order. It has promoted equality and fraternity – and has similarly underpinned the old order, modifying and weakening unbridled capitalism and in the process losing its own inspirational utopian drive and collapsing under etiolating compromises.

Socialism's roots can be traced back to Plato's *Republic* and More's *Utopia*, but as a movement it really began as a reaction to the harsh social and economic conditions created by the Industrial Revolution. In the early days of the Industrial Revolution, the injustice, inequalities and suffering were appalling. Employers exploited their workers, who produced the goods from which both made a living. Extreme socialists dreamed that the masses would wrest control of the means of production and of the government from capitalists. Some urged the complete nationalisation of all the means of production. Others advocated selective nationalisation with controlled private ownership permitted in some industries. Market socialists sought to control the market economy by socialist planning.

Socialism began in the early 19th century with utopian thinkers: in France, where François-Marie-Charles Fourier and Comte Henri de Saint-Simon dreamt of a new society in which all would have an equal opportunity to rise in relation to their talents regardless of capitalist competition; and in England, where Robert Owen, a capitalist employer in textile works, supported growing trade unionism. Pierre-Joseph Proudhon was more anarchistic and attacked private property. Karl Marx produced the Communist Manifesto in 1848, a year of European revolutions. This saw society in terms of class struggle and antithetical, antagonistic forces: out of the clash between the capitalists and labour would come a new synthesis, a socialist, communist society.

The Marxist movement came to dominate socialist thinking during the last third of the 19th century. Influenced by Marx, moderate German social democracy was born in 1869. It urged government to provide capital to emancipate labour from capitalist domination. There were Social-Democratic parties in France, Scandinavia and Central Europe, and there was a rise in anarchism. The Second International of 1889 provided a kind of international parliament of socialist movements, and under German leadership conveyed Marxist revolutionary ideas. British Fabianism, on the other hand, pursued a socialist, non-Marxist course: a "gradual", non-revolutionary reform of society to improve the conditions of the masses.

The rise of Russian socialism in the 1860s and 1870s incorporated Marxism, and under the Leninists led to the October Revolution of 1917 and a city-based communism. The Third International of 1919 strengthened communist parties and advocated world revolution. The masses did not in fact now own the means of production, and the communist state did not wither away, as promised, but became repressive. It soon became clear that the masses had not been liberated as a result of class struggle, but were being oppressed under a dictatorship, and that the revolution seemed more of a national Russian revolution than a socialist one. The Soviet Union turned violent under Stalin's Great Purge of the 1930s, and European socialists split from communists. Socialists achieved power in Germany, the United Kingdom, Italy, France and Sweden. Nazi Fascism was opposed by the Free World, including the Soviet Union, and this confrontation between left-of-centre and far-right gave socialism a temporary ideological boost that owed much to opposing Fascism.

After the Second World War, a new agrarian socialism spread among peasants in the backward, developing countries, notably China, and fueled liberation struggles against colonialism. In Europe, socialism evolved from class struggle to concern for social welfare within free markets, and post-war socialist parties came to power in Germany, Britain, France and Italy. Meanwhile socialism swept Africa, the Arab world and South-East Asia. The British-Commonwealth countries Australia, New Zealand and Canada also saw a growth of socialism, as did Latin America, notably Chile. During these years, socialism seemed to be undergoing something of a revival.

The spread of socialism created egalitarian, democratic and fraternal societies of a moderate socialist nature. They were more concerned with social security and aspects of the welfare state than with class struggle and revolution. Their middle-of-the-road egalitarianism perfectly reflected stage 42 of my 61 rise-and-fall stages. Extreme Marxist socialism, which espoused revolutions to overthrow states in the name of the masses, who were then oppressed, largely collapsed when the Berlin Wall fell in 1989 and the Soviet Empire broke up in 1991. Communism lingered on in China, where it was mixed with capitalism and moderate socialism, and in extreme dictatorial states such as North Korea. But Communism looked finished. With the demise of extreme Marxism, socialism as a strong modifying force that would advance the masses could be deemed to have run its course and to have failed. It looked a pallid form of its previous self.

Most of the world's liberal democracies had a uniform, left-of-centre, watered-down socialism that paid lip-service to liberty, equality and fraternity. They governed from near the centre. Fairness and equality of opportunity were combined with some private ownership. In general, liberal democracies steered clear of class struggle and anti-capitalist measures. The EU encouraged this process and political posture: as Western Europe joined together with Eastern Europe, both could meet in the centre, and so Western-European liberal democracies tended to shift leftwards and East-European liberal democracies tended to shift rightwards. A similar process moved most parties onto common centre ground. There was soon little to choose between governments and opposition parties on this uniform, central ground.

The pervading uniformity of states' outlooks had the effect of watering down socialism. British New Labour had been created as a deliberate watering-down of socialism, mixing it with private enterprise and investment and abolishing the extreme-socialist Clause 4. Socialism seemed a pale imitation of the socialism that was known in earlier times.

The financial crisis seemed to reinstate socialism as in a number of countries the State poured huge amounts of funds into banks, taking stakes in them on behalf of taxpayers and using "quantitative easing" to print money, a measure that in the past has always resulted in inflation. Socialism seemed to revive when across the world, in the US, Europe and Far East, politicians acting on behalf of taxpayers handed $3 trillion in bail-outs to banks, whose leaders then carried on as if there had never been a crisis.

The revival of socialism was an illusion. For there was now less money available for public spending and welfare, and there would have to be cutbacks in most areas of government. In many ways the financial crisis had brought about the collapse of socialism just as it had brought about the collapse of capitalism. Only an uninspiring, watered-down socialism survived within the uniform, left-of-centre governments of many liberal democracies.

In truth, the socialism of the old order had passed, not with the dramatic suddenness of Soviet Marxism, but it had nevertheless unobtrusively fallen sick and quietly died.

Totalitarianism

Totalitarianism, another feature of the old order, has also run its course: a form of government that permits no individual freedom and subordinates individuals' lives, and all social life, to the totalitarian government's authority.

Benito Mussolini coined the word *totalitario* (the Italian for "totalitarian") in the early 1920s and reflected its sense in his 1932 entry in the *Enciclopedia Italiana* which described the Italian Fascist state: "All within the State, none outside the State, none against the State." Totalitarianism soon came to mean single-party government.

By the Second World War, Germany's Hitler and the Soviet Union's Stalin had shown themselves to be totalitarians as did Spain's Franco and Japan's Tojo. They used central rule to coerce and repress after the manner of the Indian Maurya dynasty and the Chinese Ch'in (now written Qin) dynasty of the 3rd and 2nd centuries BC. Under their totalitarianism all legal, social and political traditions were swept away. Their totalitarian nation-states pursued a special goal linked to conquest, and any dissent was branded evil and punished. Whole classes of people were liquidated: Jews in Germany, *kulak*s or wealthy peasant farmers in the Soviet Union. Their police operated without any regulation or constraint by law, and laws were made by one man, who behaved deliberately unpredictably to rule by terror and repress dissent. Conformity was enforced by propaganda, censorship, regulation and force.

Hannah Arendt, in *The Origins of Totalitarianism* (1951) tracked the origins of totalitarianism back to 19th-century anti-Semitism and imperialism, and saw its rise as a consequence of the disintegration of the nation-state. Thus, in Germany, the Weimar republic collapsed amid hyper-inflation and high unemployment, and Hitler rose out of its ruins.

Since the Second World War there have been numerous totalitarian regimes. Mao's China is an obvious example. Individuals were herded into communes and every aspect of their lives was controlled by the State. Any dissent or failure to conform was punished, often by execution. The 1966 Cultural Revolution imposed conformity in the form of the *Little Red Book* of Mao's sayings, which citizens had to wave. It identified unreliable citizens and locked them up or did away with them after a brief hearing in a local court. China is still totalitarian, but the harshness of the regime has eased.

Many other nation-states are totalitarian. As we saw on p5, out of 192 nation-states within the UN and Taiwan, in 2009 89 were assessed as free and 62 as partly free, making a total of 151 free/partly free liberal democracies (of which 119 were considered to be "electoral democracies") and leaving 42 assessed as not free, that are considered not to be democracies.[7] These include: the Russian Federation and many ex-USSR states; Arab and African totalitarian states like Iran, Iraq, Libya and Zimbabwe; Asian totalitarian states like North

Korea and Myanmar (Burma); and the Latin-American Cuba. (See pp231-234 and 235-242.) I lived in Libya under Col. Gaddafi during the first year of the Libyan Revolution, and witnessed the dismantling of the monarchy and its parliamentary institutions and their replacement by a totalitarian government in which the threat of execution (one night dramatically exercised against me) asserted terror and repression and controlled dissent.[8]

By the outbreak of the financial crisis it was apparent that totalitarianism had reached a dead end. China faced bankruptcy and under Deng took a capitalist direction while the totalitarian Mao's portrait remained in Tiananmen Square. North Korea, unable to feed its own people, claimed to have renounced weapons of mass destruction and in return received American cash and tons of food aid. It then became apparent that it had built a couple of nuclear bombs. After 40 years of totalitarianism, during which billions of dollars were squandered on terrorism and supporting anti-American and anti-British causes, Gaddafi renounced weapons of mass destruction and returned oil-rich Libya to the policies in operation under the monarchy.

All round the world in our global time, repressive rule by autocrats is opposed. Strong rulers such as Saddam Hussein, Iran's Supreme Leader Khameini and Ahmadinejad (the heirs of Ayatollah Khomeini), and Mugabe may all have believed they could control and repress public opinion in a globalized world, but their local peoples used the Internet and Twitter to send messages to the outside world and their totalitarian regimes could not stop them.

Totalitarianism is now completely discredited, and the last totalitarian regimes are ready to throw off the tyrants who have ruled them just as Romania threw off the Ceausescu regime. Totalitarianism belongs to the old order of the old world. It is among the flotsam and jetsam of history, and in our time the totalitarian tyrants (see p243) inspire loathing and contempt for their colossal mistreatments of their peoples.

The Nation-State

Capitalism, socialism and in some countries totalitarianism have all operated through the nation-state, another feature of the old order which now looks to be in decline.

A nation is a body of people who share a real (or imagined) common history, culture, language, religion, ethnic origin and common descent and who typically inhabit a particular country or territory.[9] Historically, the concept developed slowly. Cicero, in *Philippics Against Mark Antony* (44BC), contrasts external, inferior races of "people" (*nationes*) with the Roman "community" (*civitas*). St Jerome uses the term of non-Christians. Liutprand, Bishop of Cremona, uses it in conjunction with language and territory (in 968). Medieval universities used the term "nation" (*natio*) to refer to a subdivision of students who spoke the same language. This was the case in the University of Paris; also in the University of Prague, where subdivisions included Bohemian, Bavarian, Saxon and Polish "nations" (*nationes*).

The nation as primary focus of political allegiance, grew out of the Westphalian system that was created by the 1648 Treaty of Westphalia, which established the notion of territorial sovereignty as a doctrine of non-interference in the affairs of other nations. Until the 18th century the focus was on a smaller political unit: a feudal fiefdom, a religious group, a city or the immediate neighbourhood. The religious unit had revealed itself during the Crusades, when Crusaders had allegiance to the supranational Christian community as a whole, known as Christendom. Until the 18th century the state was therefore one of a number of focal points for political activity.

At the beginning of the 18th century Europe was dominated by multi-ethnic empires: the Austro-Hungarian Empire, the Russian Empire, the Ottoman Empire, the French Empire and the British Empire. They were all monarchies ruled by a king, emperor or sultan. Each empire was dominated by one ethnic group and its language was the language used in public administration. Some smaller European states were dynastic, ruled by a royal house (such as Savoy).

The rise of large centralised states ended the feudal structures and local city allegiances, and the national ruler came to be viewed as the state's head. The new nation-states were sovereign, territorial units. Nations as sociological, cultural units had a long historical narrative in their early phases but became nation-states when they developed modern industrial states and nationalist movements. This happened towards the end of the 18th century when formulations of political demands occurred after the American and French Revolutions, during the writing of the American Constitution of 1788 and of the French Constitutions of 1791 (in which sovereignty was held by parliament) and 1793 (when sovereignty was transferred to the people).

The state was a political and geopolitical entity. The nation was a cultural and often an ethnic entity. A nation-state was born when the social concept of a "nation" coincided with the political concept of a "state". The nation-state was thus a combination of the political, geopolitical, cultural and ethnic. Often its boundaries did not coincide with its ethnic and cultural boundaries, but it claimed sovereignty within its own territory.

The early nation-state, such as England and France, guarded its borders and considered itself an economic unity, as did Germany when its customs union, the Zollverein, was created in 1818. The United Kingdom was formed by the merger of two independent kingdoms (the Kingdom of England and the Kingdom of Scotland). Each state continued with its own distinct features, and the UK is now variously regarded as a nation-state and as a multinational state (including Wales and Northern Ireland), "countries within a country". Portugal and the Dutch Republic were early nation-states, and Italy was created during its 19th-century unification. More nation-states were created as the empires broke up: Austria, Hungary and Bosnia and Herzegovina grew out of the break-up of the Austria-Hungarian Empire. The Russian Empire broke up into the states of the Soviet Union. The ethnically-diverse Ottoman Empire broke up into the many nation-states extending from the Balkans through Turkey to Morocco.

Independent regions had their identities subordinated to national identity: Alsace-Lorraine to both France and Germany at different times; Catalonia to Spain; Brittany and Corsica to France; and Sicily and Sardinia to Italy. Some smaller states survived and became nation-states: Lichtenstein, Andorra, Monaco and San Marino. Switzerland is a confederation of cantons with four official languages, but it also has a Swiss national identity.

Some nation-states had political boundaries that did not correspond to their ethnic and cultural boundaries, and disputes led to late transfers of peoples into nation-states: for example the Hatay Province was transferred from Syria to Turkey. The Kurds are a people without territory between northern Iraq, eastern Turkey and western Iran. Denmark has sovereignty of the Faroe Islands and Greenland. China includes the Han ethnic group and 55 ethnic minorities.

An anomaly of the nation-state system is that some members of nations live outside their nation-states' borders. These are thus ethnic minorities in another nation-state. The nation-states that have absentee members want to annex areas to include these populations. Irredentist claims (claims like those made in 19th-century Italy that any territory formerly belonging to a nation should be restored to it) have led to nations asserting that they have a "Greater" nation, one that restores their own ethnic absentees living in other territories. For example, Belgium seceded from the United Kingdom of the Netherlands in 1830 and its Flemish population in the north speaks Dutch and is often claimed by Dutch supporters of a Greater Netherlands ideal.

It is worth listing the many similar instances to underline the muddle that exists within the nation-state system: Greater Albania; Greater Balochistan; Greater China; Greater Croatia; Greater Finland; Greater Germany; Greater Hungary; Greater India; Greater Indonesia; Greater Israel; Greater Iran; United Macedonia; Greater Mongolia; Greater Morocco; Greater Netherlands; Greater Portugal; Greater Romania; Greater Serbia; Greater Somalia; Greater Syria; Greater Greece (*Megali Idea*); Pan-Turkism. All these claims may lead to attempts to recover areas and could lead to local wars.

It is clear that there is an arbitrariness about the borders of existing nation-states. Their boundaries often do not include all the ethnic, cultural and linguistic groups that properly belong with them. In the feudal time there were feudal fiefdoms that divided humankind into warring groups, each under different laws of medieval dukes, counts and barons. It is now being grasped that the new nation-states returned the multi-ethnic empires to the equivalent of feudal states, each with its own laws and with institutions replacing the king, emperor or sultan as instruments of government. Nation-states subdivide humankind into segregated groups and rule on their behalf while ignoring the rest of humankind.

There has been a growing realisation that conflicting nation-states led to the First and Second World Wars and have produced many wars during the 19th and 20th centuries. Nation-states have now become more interdependent, taking part in rounds of meetings like the G20, and in Europe the federalism of the European Union has placed a new tier over the nation-states and removed over 80 per cent of their right to make laws. A German source puts the figure at 84 per cent. The President of the European Union Parliament, Hans Gert Pöttering, said that once the Lisbon Treaty was fully implemented, the EU would be responsible for "nearly 100 per cent" of all laws made in Europe.[10]

In the Lisbon Treaty the EU state was given a legal entity which was above that of its component nation-states and signalled the subordination of the nation-state to a new federal structure. Devolution has weakened the nation-state, or multinational state, in the UK.

If nation-states did indeed have a social contract with their peoples under which they provided security and harmonious living in return for taxation and other duties, including military service in harm's way when demanded, some nation-states have forfeited adherence to this contract by breaking their side of the bargain. In the case of the UK, after Churchill cashed in the British Empire to fight for freedom and protect the British people from Nazi rule, the spivs of New Labour borrowed and pretended their brilliance had created a boom by letting 3 million immigrants in to share it, and when it went bust, carried on borrowing and saddled the British people with a deficit of over £800 billion which would take decades for taxpayers to repay. A British taxpayer, called on to pay for nation-state recklessness in the face of war and financial crisis, could be forgiven for concluding that a deceptive Government had broken its side of the contract, and that there must be a better way of running everyday life to provide harmonious living. The nation-state has to earn its respect. It cannot take respect for granted.

There is a widespread feeling that the haphazard nation-state system no longer merits support as a receptacle for combining those who share a culture, history, common language, religion, ethnic origin, and common descent, and that in a regional time the concept of the nation-state has become discredited and has passed, although it still wields power structures over its peoples. The nation-state has run is course and is a remnant of the old order that has undergone a protracted collapse.

Colonialism

Colonialism was the building and maintaining of colonies in one territory by people from another territory, after the manner of the ancient Phoenicians, Greeks and Romans.

The era of European colonialism was from the 15th to the 20th centuries. It began with the emerging European nation-states – England, France, Portugal, Spain and the Low Countries – shortly before c.1500 and with the early voyages of discovery. Nine European nation-states had empires: the British (who had two, one in America and then one in the rest of the world), the French, the Portuguese, the Spanish, the Italians, the Dutch, the Germans and the Belgians (in the Congo). At the same time the United States had an empire in the Philippines.

The colonial pattern was the same under all the empires. The mother country settled a colony, installed a garrison to hold it and sent out more settlers. The mother country then imported its natural resources, and as the colony became established exported its own goods. In due course it acted as a civilizing force, educating and training the locals. The amount of training *colon*s received varied between empires.

Colonialism had run its course by the middle of the 20th century. Decolonization accelerated from 1945. Great Britain granted India and Pakistan their independence, and the greater part of the British Mediterranean, African, Asian, Pacific and West-Indian colonies received their independence in the ensuing decades. France, Belgium, Portugal and the Netherlands decolonized in most of their territories from the 1950s to the 1970s. Liberation movements sprang up in many colonies to press for independence.

The era of colonialism has now passed. It belonged to the old order. Although a few small colonies still remain, history has swept the colonial system away.

Nationalism

Nationalism, the creed of those who believe that fidelity to one's state is more important than fidelity to international principles or individual interests, is inextricably linked to the nation-state. Nationalism grew out of the creation of the early nation-states, and loyalty to these nation-states was strengthened during wars. Since the Second World War, as we have seen, the European nation-states weakened as a result of interdependence and the growth of the EU. Nationalism in Europe similarly weakened.

In some cases nationalism led to the creation of nation-states, particularly in post-war Asia and Africa where liberation movements, anti-colonialist movements, sprang up to press for independence. But as colonies were given independence, and became enmeshed in interdependent regional structures, nationalism weakened.

During the Second World War nationalism was associated with partisans and resistance-movement guerillas, who sought to liberate their countries from Nazi rule. In the mid-1980s I played a part in calling for the liberation of the East-European states from the Soviet Union. I wrote a paper entitled *FREE* ("Freedom for the Republics of Eastern Europe") and broadcast into Eastern Europe – not to stoke up their nationalism but to swell the regional Union, the European Community (which has since passed into the European Union).[11] In a world of regions and Unions, and very few remaining colonies, nationalism of this kind was to be found in the Middle East and Afghanistan, among guerillas fighting Western dominance.

The main expression of nationalism today can be found at international sporting fixtures. Just as the nation-state and colonialism had passed as remnants of the old order, so nationalism, which was inextricably linked with them, increasingly looked outmoded.

Sovereignty

Sovereignty is the ultimate law-making authority over a territory or a state's decision-making process and maintenance of order. In the Middle Ages medieval monarchs shared power, and therefore sovereignty, with the feudal aristocracy.

In 16th-century France Jean Bodin, the French jurist and political philosopher, reacting to the chaos caused by the French wars of religion, used the new concept of sovereignty to strengthen the French king's power of rebellious feudal lords and effect the replacement of feudalism by nationalism. Influenced by the Roman jurist Ulpian (2nd-3rd century AD), who held that the Roman *imperium* of the people was transferred to the Emperor, who was not bound by the law and whose word was law, Bodin wrote in *Six Books of the Republic* (*Six livres de la république*, 1576) that "the sovereign who makes the laws cannot be bound by the laws he makes" ("*majestas est summa in cives ac subditos legibusque soluta potestas*"). However, to Bodin the sovereign was restricted by the constitutional law of the state, though possessing absolute and perpetual sovereignty. According to Bodin sovereignty was conferred by divine law as the divine right of kings.

The English philosopher Thomas Hobbes identified the sovereign with might rather than law. He held that the sovereign could not be limited by the law he commands, and that sovereign power was therefore absolute. This led to sovereigns imposing their will on other sovereigns and therefore to a perpetual state of war. Like Bodin, Hobbes called for a strong central authority.

In *Leviathan* (1651) he defined sovereignty as supreme legal coercive authority over a particular population and territory. In this work Hobbes argues for a social contract and rule by an absolute sovereign. He analyses the twelve principal rights of a sovereign and three types of commonwealth. He writes that chaos or civil war, situations of a state of nature, could only be averted by strong central government.

The book was written during the English Civil War, and published after its end, and it is clear that Hobbes was a supporter of the Royalist cause. The frontispiece of *Leviathan* by Abraham Bosse, who discussed it with Hobbes, shows a giant Charles I rising over hills, beneath a quotation from the *Book of Job*, "*Non est potestas super terram quae comparetur ei*" ("There is no power on Earth to be compared to him"). This links the figure of Charles I to the monster leviathan in the *Book of Job*. However, Hobbes irritated both sides: the Royalists by his social contract theory, the Parliamentarians by his support for absolute monarchy. He fled to Paris where he taught the future Charles II mathematics. His thoughts on commonwealths were primarily linked to the situation in England.

Hobbes argued that although individuals surrender their liberties for protection, a plurality of sovereign states is not burdensome: "Because states uphold the Industry of their Subjects; there does not follow from the international state of nature, that misery, which accompanies the Liberty of particular men."[12]

In the 17th and 18th centuries, John Locke and Rousseau developed a theory of popular sovereignty: that a state is based on a compact of its citizens who entrust their powers to a government for common protection.

Rousseau, in the second book of *Du contrat social, ou Principes du droit politique* (1762), argues that sovereignty, or the general will, is inalienable and acts through laws. The legislator has no authority of his own; he is only a guide who drafts and proposes laws which the people alone (the sovereign or general will) has authority to pass and impose. In his *Of the Social Contract* (1763) Rousseau argues that "the more the Government has to use force to contain the people, the more force the Sovereign should have in order to contain the Government".

Rousseau's theory of popular sovereignty found expression in the American Declaration of Independence of 1776. Reflecting Rousseau's popular sovereignty, the French Constitution of 1791 stated: "Sovereignty is one, indivisible, unalienable and imprescriptible; it belongs to the Nation; no group can attribute sovereignty to itself nor can an individual arrogate it to himself."

In the ensuing years different views of sovereignty evolved. The 19th-century English jurist John Austin held that sovereignty was vested in a nation's parliament. The US Constitution was the fundamental law of the federal Union, not the legislature, a view that was reinforced by the Supreme Court's right to declare laws unconstitutional. Political scientists such as Léon Duguit, Hugo Krabbe and Harold J. Laski championed pluralistic sovereignty, locating sovereignty in various political, economic, social and religious groups.

For 200 years sovereign states had claimed the right to judge disputes with, and enforce war on, other sovereign states. In the 20th century the sovereignty of nation-states was restricted. The 1899 and 1907 Hague Conferences established rules about the conduct of war on land and at sea. The Covenant of the League of Nations restricted the right to go to war. The Briand-Kellogg Pact of 1928 condemned going to war to solve disputes. The Charter of the United Nations (Article 2) required member states to settle disputes "by peaceful means in such a manner that international peace and security, and justice, are not endangered" and to "refrain in their international relations from the threat or use of force". Somehow this injunction had to be reconciled with the UN's "principle of sovereign equality of all its Members".

States have now accepted a body of law limiting their sovereign right, by consent or autolimitation. States are sometimes considered bound even if acceptance has not been expressed or implied. There is thus a balance between states' sovereignty and the needs of international society. The principle of federalism established divided sovereignty (sovereignty divided between the federal Union and states). The growing interdependence of states has resulted in the pooling of sovereignty to establish Unions such as the European Union. States' national governments and organs of the world community are now exercising authority on behalf of peoples. Nation-states are often now considered the instruments of their sovereign peoples.

The spreading of divided sovereignty has undermined the investing of sovereignty in institutions, and to the extent that sovereignty has been invested in nation-states and nationalism, it has been further undermined by the decline of the nation-state as a result of the rise of regional Unions and interdependence. Austin held that British sovereignty was invested in parliaments. But as we saw on p54, in 2009 over 80 per cent of European laws were jointly decided between the European Parliament and the Council of Ministers. The British parliament, which used to make all Britain's laws, then enacted less than 20 per cent of laws as 80 per cent were enacted in Brussels by the European Union, which could therefore be regarded as having taken over 80 per cent of British sovereignty on a pooling basis.[13] As we have seen, after the ratification of the Lisbon Treaty the European Union was set to pass nearly 100 per cent of Europe's laws, leaving just over 0 per cent to national parliaments.

The sovereignty of nation-states' institutions is not as strong as it used to be. The people are sovereign according to many constitutional experts, which means all the people in the world, and splitting them up and dividing them into nation-states' territories has failed to remove sovereignty from the people of the world. The sovereignties of the last 200 years that were located in monarchs or nation-states belong to the old order and have passed. Only a World State with a world government can reflect, in the areas over which it has authority, the sovereignty of the peoples of the world.

Self-Determination

During the First and Second World Wars many peoples living under empires in occupied nations, and during the decolonizing time many *colon*s, dreamed of self-determination: of founding an independent nation-state with the right to determine its own government and allegiance. The occupied and downtrodden *colon*s longed to do as they wished within their own frontiers, no matter how harmful it was to the rest of the world. The longing for a new nation-state led to interdependent aggregates of peoples within an empire splitting themselves into smaller, newly-sovereign units in the name of "ending the occupation", "ending imperialism", "abolishing colonialism" and "national independence from empire".

Those who fought for self-determination then found themselves living in newly-sovereign nation-states – and facing the problems sovereign nation-states have suffered: disputes with other sovereign nation-states and new local wars, then a time of interdependent regions when nation-states were scorned. Within two decades many of the new nation-states created after 1919, after the Second World War and during decolonization were conquered and enslaved by other nation-states. Thus, the self-determination of Lithuania ended in its occupation by Poland, and Polish self-determination ended when Germany and later the USSR conquered Poland. Many East-European nation-states were swallowed by the Soviet Empire. Nationalism devoured its children.

Like the nation-state and sovereignty, in our regional world self-determination's time seems to have passed and increasingly appears to belong to the old order.

Internationalism

Internationalism is a political movement that advocates greater economic and political co-operation among nation-states for the prevention of wars. It means "inter-nationalism", a co-operation between nation-states.

Such co-operation failed during the first half of the 20th century. The Covenant of the League of Nations was based on the principles of national sovereignty, national self-determination and the right of every nation-state to do as it wished within its own boundaries. If Stalin wished to execute one million in his purge of 1934 and kill a further 10 million in the next few years, other nation-states should not interfere – the Westphalian approach to nation-states.

The League of Nations' replacement, the United Nations, was in 2009 an aggregate of 192 sovereign nation-states. We have seen that nation-states are competitive units whose disputes can slide into wars. The UN deals with a world in which until the Second World War nationalism, though weakening, still dominates democracy, capitalism, socialism, liberalism, Christianity, politics, religion, economics, monarchies and republics. Internationalism suggests that conflicting nationalisms can be bridged; that the UN can reconcile disputes between sovereign nation-states, conflicting nationalisms.

As the UN's powerlessness to prevent the 2003 war in Iraq demonstrates, powerful nation-states can ride roughshod over the UN, which has had no power to prevent any of the wars since 1945. Internationalism, being between conflicting nationalisms, looks outmoded and also belongs to the old order. There is a case for its being replaced by a better system.

Collective Security

Collective Security is a security arrangement in which nation-states co-operate collectively to provide security for all by taking action against any nation-states within groups (such as the Warsaw Pact) which have challenged the existing order by using force. It marshals nation-states into achieving a balance of power, as NATO did during the Cold War when it counterbalanced the power of the Soviet bloc within Eastern Europe.

Collective security, then, amounts to some nation-states banding together to act against other nation-states which have also banded together. Both bands see their cause as the more just. There is as much potentiality for conflict in the opposition of two conflicting systems of collective security as there is among conflicting nation-states. The collective security just takes place on a group level now.

The collective security of the League of Nations failed when Japan occupied Manchuria, part of China, in 1932. The League called for Japan to withdraw. As a member of the League of Nations, Japan vetoed the resolution. After two years the League passed a resolution condemning the invasion without committing the League's members to act. The Japanese left the League of Nations, and the problem was not solved.

The League's collective security also failed when it allowed Mussolini to get away with invading Abyssinia in 1935 because Britain and France, seeing Mussolini as an ally who might block the rise of Hitler's Germany, did not condemn the Italian invasion.

During the inter-war years the League fell down because some major states such as the US did not join or give support, and because every state had a veto which some were quick to use to their own advantage.

The successor to the League of Nations, the United Nations, suffered from similar weaknesses. Dealing with sovereign nation-states, the United Nations was positioned between them all. It was originally stymied because the General Assembly was composed of all UN member states, each of which had one vote, no matter how large or small. This meant that it was cumbersome for the great powers to secure agreement. The Security Council was developed to circumvent a paralysed General Assembly. However, the five most powerful nation-states within the Security Council, including the Soviet Union, had the veto and used it whenever it suited them, paralysing the UN's ability to resolve disputes.

Consequently, member states of the United Nations frequently failed to condemn aggressors. When Argentina invaded the Falkland Islands, overseas territories of the UK, many UN members stayed out of the dispute and the arguments within the UN Security Council as it did not affect them. The US sat on the fence as it was a member of the Inter-American Treaty of Reciprocal Assistance (the Rio Pact). It adopted an even-handed, balancing posture which did nothing to head off war.

NATO is the best-known collective-defence organization. Its Article 5 (see pp187-188) calls on, but does not commit, member states to assist other members under attack. This article was invoked after the September-11 attacks in the US, after which NATO members provided assistance to the US War on Terror in Afghanistan. In more recent times, NATO has supported Coalition troops in both Afghanistan and Iraq, defending the old order of sovereign nation-states against latter-day "barbarians": the Taliban and al-Qaeda, who would like to possess – and in al-Qaeda's case probably do possess – weapons of mass destruction and who have to be held in check by the West's military equivalent of the Roman legions.

During the Cold War the roles of the UN and NATO as a mediator between, and defender of, nation-states has not been without success. Since the Second World War, by 2009 there have been 111 military conflicts world-wide, according to one count.[14] Only nine have involved two or more states going to war with one another. The remainder have been civil wars, some internal, some in which other nations have intervened. The UN's and NATO's collective security has often not been effective in dealing with such situations as peace-keeping forces have been too small.

However, since the end of the Cold War in 1991, collective defence, which has to be against an enemy, has been turned against Islamic fundamentalism in Afghanistan, and specifically bin Laden's purchase of at least 20 nuclear-suitcase bombs from the Chechen Mafia from 1999 onwards (confirmed by Hans Blix of the IAEA in 2004). I have detailed the evidence for this in the Appendix[15] of my epic poem on the nightmare Armageddon threatening our generation: al-Qaeda's plan to detonate ten simultaneous nuclear explosions in ten American cities and bin Laden's attempt to revive the Caliphate – which was discontinued with the formal end of the Ottoman Empire in 1924 – in Baghdad, the seat of the Abbasid Caliphate. During my research for this work, I was able to confirm that this threat to the West is real and is reflected in the degree of the presence of Western troops in Afghanistan.

The fact remains, collective security amounts to one lot of nation-states banding against another lot, and just as the nation-state itself is outmoded, so too is the system of collective defence. Collective security's time is passing, and it, too, belongs to the old order.

Superpowerdom

There is a strong feeling that the Bush Administration deliberately exploited the September-11 attacks to pursue a policy of American supremacy, a supremacist ideology based on the 1997 Statement of Principles and mission statement of the Project for the New American Century (see pp190-192), a neo-conservative policy-advocacy group with a strong pro-Israeli outlook. It can be argued that, on the contrary, the Bush Administration saved America from the nuclear Armageddon of bin Laden's nuclear purchases, and that any exploitation of September 11 was perpetrated by the *élite*s pursuing an industrial agenda.

Whatever the truth, American superpowerdom following the collapse of the Berlin Wall in 1989 and the fall of Communism in 1991 is tantamount to one nation-state lording it over all the others, either to promote US industrial oil-and-gas-pipeline interests, or to harry the al-Qaeda leadership so they could not carry out a nuclear plot against the US. Superpowerdom comes across to the rest of the world as one nation-state bossing all the other nation-states either to its own advantage or for the "collective security" of all nation-states against the threat of modern Armageddon.

The American Administration has three choices. Either America can be isolationist; or it can pursue an American Empire; or it can build a World State, either out of industrial self-interest, or on the basis of philanthropy.

Studies have suggested that although at present only the US fulfils the criteria to be considered a superpower, other nation-states are rising and may reach superpowerdom at some point in the 20th century, notably: China; India; the European Union; and the Russian Federation. If just one of these four succeeds in becoming a rival superpower to the United States, then once again a great power's nation-state will be in competitive conflict with another.

Just as warring nation-states are of the old order, so conflicts between superpowers, which are inflated nation-states, also belong to the old order.

Religion

The organized religions command followings throughout the world. Christianity has the biggest following (about 2 billion), followed by Islam (1.1 billion), Hinduism (800 million) and Buddhism (350 million). There are many more faiths. In descending order of support they are: Sikhism, Judaism, the Bahá'i Faith, Confucianism, Jainism and Shinto.

Each organized religion has sects, which are subdivisions. Christianity includes: the Roman Catholic Church (1.05 billion); the Eastern Orthodox Church (240 million); the African Initiated Church; Pentecostalism; the Reformed/Presbyterian/Congregational/United Churches; Anglicanism/the Episcopal Church; the Baptist Church; Methodism; Lutheranism; the Jehovah's Witnesses; the Latter-day Saints; the Adventist Church; the Apostolic/New Apostolic Church; the Restoration Movement; New Thought/Unity/Christian Science; the Brethren (including Plymouth Brethren); the Mennonites; and the Friends/Quakers. Islam includes: Sunnis (940 million); Shias (120 million); Ahmadis; and Druzes. Hinduism includes: Vaisnavism; Saivism; Neo-Hindus and Reform Hindus; and Veerasaivas/Lingayats. Buddhism includes Mahayana, Theravada, and Vajrayana/Tibetan Buddhism.

Organized religions think of themselves as conveying universal truths. However, they segregate groups of people. Each organized religion cuts up and subdivides the whole of humanity into a part, and sects within an organized religion subdivide even more. Consequently universal truth is cut up, subdivided and replicated for a part of humankind, and its universality is thus compromised.

In the past, Christianity saw universal truth as Christianity-dominated, and Christian religion has evolved into national organizations. Thus the Catholic Church is based in Vatican City, which is a national institution although it is not listed by the UN as one of its 192 member states. The Church of England is a national organization and its head is the sovereign, the Queen. Its universal truth is compromised by its being enmeshed in the nation-state since the time of Henry VIII. Thus, today there are prayers for the Queen and the Government. The same is true of sects of Islam, which have become enmeshed with nation-states.

Originally Christianity taught a monotheism that was universalist. It taught that all men were created equal in the sight of God and are ruled by one God. The history of Christianity has been one of its evolution into a totalitarian hierarchy under an infallible Pope; and the reaction to it that led to schism and later to sectarianism. The universal has degenerated into centralised absolutism and separated, segregated sects and denominations.

The Christian churches have abandoned their initial universalism and their moral principles apply within their segregated groups of people within a nation-state. "Thou shalt not kill", originally a universal truth, now means "Thou shalt not kill a human being of one's own nation-state, but in times of war it is permissible to kill a human being of the same faith from another nation-state", which is what happened between English and German soldiers during the Second World War. In Islam, the universal teaching of Mohammed, the unity maintained by the *Koran* from Morocco to Pakistan, has been split up and subdivided into nationalist groups and became Pan-Turkism, Pan-Arabism or the creed of the Pakistani Muslims (whose first allegiance was not to Islam but to Pakistan).

Tom Paine, the American Founding Father, grasped that nation-states had corrupted the universality of religion and had had a segregating effect on the world when he wrote in *The Age of Reason* (1794): "I do not believe in the creed professed by the Jewish church, by the Roman church, by the Turkish church, by the Protestant church, nor by any church that I know of. My own mind is my own church. All national institutions of churches, whether Jewish, Christian or Turkish, appear to me no other than human inventions, set up to terrify and enslave mankind, and monopolise power and profits."[16]

A return to Universalist religion can be expected: to one world-wide religion of the Light which is common to all organized religions, the Divine Light called God by religious mystics in all cultures and civilizations which can be known as the inner Light. A federal world religion would have this Universalist tier, and beneath it the many regional, segregated organized religions, all of which espouse the Light amid the nation-state-ised focus of their worship. I set out the common ground for such a Universalist religion in Part One of *The Fire and the Stones*.[17]

It is now widely grasped that nation-state-ised organized religions have failed to convey universalism. Nation-state-ised religions belong to the old order.

Ptolemaic Old Order, Copernican World State

The old order that seems to be passing is a bit like the Ptolemaic view of the universe, the geocentric theory laid down by Ptolemy in 2nd-century-AD Alexandria which lasted 1,400 years. In *Almagest*, the climax of Greek astronomy, Ptolemy explained that the Earth was the centre of the universe, and that the sun, moon and stars revolved around it. The coming order of a World State is a bit like the Copernican theory of the 16th century, the heliocentric theory. Copernicus proposed that the Earth itself rotated and was no longer a stable point, and that it and the planets revolved round the sun. (In fact, the Copernican hypothesis was anticipated by Pythagoras in the 6th century BC and by Aristarchus of Samos in the 3rd century BC.)

Copernicus set out his view in a work titled *Hypothesis*. He did not claim it was based on scientific fact for he knew the Church would oppose his thesis as heresy, just as it would later oppose Galileo.

Our world is already Copernican in shifting to structures that reflect the unity of humankind – regions and Unions – and towards a Universalist World State. But our political and social conceptions are still Ptolemaic and tied to the notions of nation-state, sovereignty and the concepts behind the other headings in this chapter. We are in a time of transition between the institutions of a collapsing old order and a coming World State.

Philosophical Summary

What can the Universalist proposing a World State take from history's progress to an end-point and the collapse of the old order?

History is teleological and approaches its goal, an end-point which will last for a while and not forever. A philosophical history challenges empirical history by showing that history has a plan and purpose. The purpose of history is to achieve a civic constitution that enshrines freedom. History progresses towards a republican liberal democracy, the institutionalization of freedom. Human progress shows humankind evolving from barbarism to egalitarian unity in a World State while living in civilizations that rise and fall. All civilizations ultimately flow into a world-wide civilization within a World State for a while.

The system under which humankind has lived since c.1500 is outmoded and collapsing. Capitalism has weakened following the financial crisis. Socialism has weakened following the fall of Communism. What remains is a pale, watered-down mixture of capitalism and socialism. Totalitarianism is outmoded. The nation-state subdivides and segregates part of humankind from the whole of humankind, and has been weakened by interdependence and regional administration, as has nationalism (which is based on fidelity to the nation-state). Colonialism is defunct following the fall of empires and decolonization. Self-determination (the birth of a new nation-state) has weakened with the weakening of the nation-state before interdependence and regional administration.

Internationalism is outmoded as it urges co-operation between weakened but defiant nation-states to preserve peace, and should be replaced by a better system. Collective security (which is based on the collective defence of nation-states) has weakened. Superpowerdom (the dominance of one nation-state) is discredited as belonging to the old order. Organized religions segregate parts of humankind from the whole. A Universalist religion which is universal to humankind is needed. The World State involves a new Copernican perspective that will replace the Ptolemaic nation-state.

To sum up, the philosopher devising a universal World State can distil from the progress of history to freedom and the collapse of the old order:

history is teleological and approaches its goal, an end-point which will last for a while and not forever;

the purpose of history is to achieve a World State that enshrines freedom for a while;

history progresses towards liberal democracy, the institutionalization of freedom;

humankind evolves to egalitarian unity in a World State;

during their evolution to unity, human beings live within rising and falling civilizations;

all civilizations flow into, or beneath the influence of, a world-wide civilization for a while;

the system under which humankind has been living is outmoded and collapsing;

capitalism has been weakened by the financial crisis;

socialism has been weakened by the fall of Communism;

we live under a mixture of watered-down capitalism and socialism;

totalitarianism is finished;

the nation-state subdivides and segregates humankind and has been weakened by interdependence and regional administration;

nationalism (fidelity to the nation-state) has been weakened;

colonialism (running territories in empires) is defunct;

self-determination has weakened;

internationalism (co-operation between nation-states for the prevention of war) has weakened before the defiance of outmoded states and needs to be replaced;

collective security has weakened as it is based on weakened nation-states;

superpowerdom (the dominance of one nation-state) belongs to the old order;

organized religions segregate parts of humankind;

there should be a Universalist religion;

a Copernican perspective of a World State is ahead, and will replace the Ptolemaic conception of the nation-state.

The collapse of the old order has left a heap of problems for the world which the nation-state system has been unable to solve: war, poverty, pandemics, climate change, famine and financial crash. As we survey the *débris* of the old order in which we now conduct our lives in our time of transition to an interdependent, regional world that is not yet complete, we cannot help wondering what the best model is for the new supranational authority into which we are passing, and how it would work as a reality in our time.

PART TWO

THE WORLD GOVERNMENT AS A REALITY IN OUR TIME

4

Models of a Supranational Authority: the *Status Quo*

A philosopher who considers what kind of supranational authority could be set up to run a world government and prevent war should recall all the constructive ideas that have been put forward in the past within the field of international law. If I do this I will be in a position to list all the possible models for such an authority in our time, assess each option and eliminate those that would not work until I am left with one, which will be the way forward.

We have already taken a look in ch. 2 at the dreams of securing peace in past ages. We now need to revisit the past briefly from the perspective of international law.

International Law in the Past

The idea that international law can create a supranational authority which can compel sovereign political units to avoid war through binding arbitration goes back to the Middle Ages.

It can be found in the work of Pierre Dubois, whose *De Recuperatione Terrae Sanctae* (*On the Recovery of the Holy Land*, 1306) asserted that peace in France depended on extending the royal authority of Philip IV in his struggle with Pope Boniface VIII, and that peace in Europe depended on Philip IV's assuming the power of the position of Holy Roman Emperor, an office then vacant. Universal and perpetual peace would then be established by the international arbitration of a council, a confederation of equal Christian states, based in a headquarters at Toulouse. The council would be directed by Christian princes, one for each existing monarchy, who would be supported by a court. This would be composed of three lay prudent men and three wise ecclesiastics, who would be mediators in conflicts. This council would have the power to impose sanctions on a disobedient kingdom, which would include the power to place an embargo on food imports.

Dubois' idea for international arbitration seems to have been transmitted to George of Podebrady, who was chosen King of Bohemia in 1458. A French adventurer, Antonio Marini, probably conveyed Dubois' ideas to him. Podebrady's supranational project, *Congregatio Concordiae*, was very similar to that of Dubois.

We have seen (on pp20-21) that Dante wrote *De Monarchia* in 1317-1318, ten years after Dubois' work. Did Dante know of Dubois? Books on Dante make no connection between the two, but Dante also sees his "Monarch" or "Emperor" who would rule humankind as arbitrating conflicts. He invested the power of arbitration in a council: he proposed that disputes between sovereign princes be settled by means of arbitration by a council of appointed clerics and laymen from each nation. So it is possible that Dante did know of Dubois' work, and that he did not arrive at international arbitration independently.

Desiderius Erasmus served the future Emperor Charles V as councillor in 1516, and the next year he composed *Querela pacis* (*The Complaint of Peace*), condemning war as an instrument of tyranny. He warned temporal rulers to preserve Christian harmony. Erasmus kept the idea of international peace alive at a time when Europe was fragmenting as a result of Luther's Protestant Reformation, but he did not add anything to Dubois' international arbitration.

The Duc de Sully appeared to revive arbitration in 1595. In his *Economies royales* he credits Henry IV, whose minister he was, as organizing a coalition of all the states of his empire against the Habsburgs of Vienna and Madrid, and with planning their downfall. Europe would be redivided into 15 states. Perpetual peace between the 15 would be guaranteed by congresses of perpetual peace. In fact, it has been proved that this idea was the product of Sully's imagination. Henry IV did not plan to keep international peace by congresses.[1]

The pioneer of international arbitration was Émeric Crucé, who in *Le nouveau Cynée* (*The New Cyneas*, 1623) imagined he was the peacemaker Cineas at the court of the 3rd-century-AD Pyrrhus, King of the Molossians of Epirus. He called for a permanent assembly of princes or their delegates to arbitrate international disputes. Crucé saw this assembly as exercising moral pressure rather than sanctions to enforce settlements. His scope was global for his day, and arbitration would take place between the nations of Europe, Asia and Africa.

The Dutch jurist Hugo Grotius was thinking about international law's ability to keep peace when he wrote *De jure belli ac pacis* (*On the Laws of War and Peace*, 1625). This is generally taken to be the starting-point of modern international law, based on natural law.

Living during the Eighty Years' War between Spain and the Netherlands (1568-1648) and the Thirty Years' War between Catholic and Protestant

European nations (1618-1648), Grotius was preoccupied with the conflicts between nations and religions. He dedicated *De jure belli ac pacis* to his patron, Louis XIII of France and set out a system of principles of natural law which should bind all people and nations, regardless of local custom. In this work he writes:

> "Throughout the Christian world I observed a lack of restraint in relation to war, such as even barbarous races should be ashamed of; I observed that men rush to arms for slight causes, or no cause at all, and that when arms have once been taken up there is no longer respect for law."[2]

Grotius saw international law as a means of maintaining peace.

Grotius, a many-sided man who published works of poetry, philology, history and theology and became Swedish ambassador in Paris, helped form a concept of an international society as a community sharing the idea that states and rulers have rules that apply to all. All in this international community (today called a "world" or "global" community) should be subject to international law.

The Quaker William Penn, founder of Pennsylvania, put forward a plan for peace in his essay *Towards the Present and Future Peace of Europe* (1693). It included settling disputes between nations by arbitration rather than war, and his plan is today considered to be a prototype of the United Nations. Significantly, United Nations Day is celebrated on Penn's birthday (October 24). I attended Penn's school, Chigwell School in Essex, England, and it is appropriate that I should be writing this book, having trodden in his footsteps.

We have seen on (pp24-25) that Abbé de Saint-Pierre, in *Project for Making Peace Perpetual in Europe* (1713), envisaged that European sovereigns would contract to form a perpetual alliance and establish a permanent Diet or Congress that would arbitrate all disputes between the federation of princes. Arbitrating decisions would be enforced by armed action. This proposal gave teeth to the idea of arbitrating under international law.

We have also seen (on p25) that Rousseau was inspired by Abbé de Saint-Pierre but proposed a federation of morally-perfect states. In *The Social Contract* (1762) Rousseau does not advance the idea of arbitration in international law.

Jeremy Bentham, the English philosopher, took the idea up in *Plan for Universal and Perpetual Peace* (1789). His reconstructed skeleton, with a wax head that replaced his skull (which was mummified), dressed in his own clothes, can be seen sitting upright in a glass-fronted case in University College, London.

We have seen (on pp25-28) that Kant, in *Perpetual Peace: A Philosophical Sketch* (1795), a title that echoes Bentham's as well as Abbé de Saint-Pierre's, called for a federation of free states as an interim stage to an "international state" (*civitas gentium*) or world government. The idea of arbitrating disputes lies behind Kant's proposal, but he adds little detail to his forerunners in thinking about international law.

To these proposals must be added the more practical attempts to create a supranational authority that can use international law to bring permanent peace: the Hague Conference conventions of 1899 and 1907, the League of Nations and the United Nations coupled with the International Court of Justice. Their relative lack of overall success in abolishing wars in the 20th and 21st centuries has led some to believe that establishing world peace through international law is an enduring illusion. Others point out that the UN has failed to resolve conflicts between superpowers because it has never been given the power to do so.

To sum up, there is a tradition of proposals that disputes should be solved by arbitration. The arbitrator should be a council (Dubois) or a Monarch/Emperor (Dante). In Crucé the council has become a permanent assembly of princes or their delegates, and in Penn the assembly has become a prototype of the United Nations.

However, all these attempts to bring universal peace by international law assume arbitration between nation-states. Only Kant envisages a World State, and then concedes that in the prevailing conditions of his time a World State had no immediate prospects of being established.

The Goals of a Supranational Authority

The old order is collapsing, as we have just seen, and in consequence the world is faced with urgent problems that have to be solved. The goals of the kind of supranational authority that emerges are to solve these problems. They are:

(1) bringing peace between nation-states, and disarmament;
(2) sharing natural resources and energy so that all humankind can have a raised standard of living;
(3) solving environmental problems such as global warming, which seem

to be beyond self-interested nation-states;
(4) where possible, ending disease;
(5) where possible, ending famine;
(6) solving the world's financial crisis; and
(7) where possible, redistributing wealth to eliminate poverty.

The most desirable kind of supranational authority is the one that can best achieve all these goals.

I have to ask whether a loose, tightly federal or radically different model is best suited to achieving these goals. Are the world's problems best solved by continuing with a form of the existing system of nation-states and old order? By proceeding to a more federal arrangement with arbitration? Or by radically replacing the existing system with a new system?

Eight Models for a Supranational Authority

Proposals for abolishing war by international law envisage different kinds of supranational authority. Eight kinds of supranational arrangement can be identified:

(1) developing a sense of world community through regional and functional international organizations that operate in assistance of world law;
(2) sticking with the United Nations and the *status quo* and strengthening great-power agreement by using policy and non-constitutional sources of law such as international treaties, to resolve disputes;
(3) a World Constitutional Convention to draft a world constitution that nation-states would accept;
(4) revising the UN Charter to strengthen international law to give the UN the power to resolve disputes between superpowers and outlaw war;
(5) creating under treaty a new UN-related organization that would exist alongside the UN and strengthen it in observing international law in areas not covered by the UN Charter;
(6) advancing towards world government through *élite*s' exclusive groups and deceptive New World Order;
(7) democratizing the UN and making global governance accountable; and
(8) creating a tier of government of international law above the UN that would bring in a world government and abolish war.

I have not included the option of abolishing the United Nations and returning the world to the potentially warring and disputatious nation-states: the world that existed at the end of the 19th century. This would invite new empires and a host of wars and would not advance international peace at all. In fact, it would be completely retrogressive and counter-productive. It would be like abolishing the referee in a football match. The United Nations is imperfect, but its resolutions do blow the whistle on the activities of nation-states which contravene the spirit of international law. Abolition of the UN is an intellectual option but in practical terms it is merely an academic option as it carries the world away from rather than towards peace.

Nor have I included the two models of a fully federal United States of the World, and the model of a New World Order's federal Union, detailed on pp128-129, as these models involve a world government with total control of all global governance and not just the areas of the seven goals.

I now want to look at each of the eight models one by one. In each case I need to ask if a particular model is able to solve the world's problems and thus achieve the goals of a supranational authority.

Model 1: World Community through Organizations

The spreading of a world community has been happening since the Second World War. Leaving aside the 1945-established UN Charter (see Model 2), progress towards a world community has been through the planting and growth of international organizations that have given a sense of partial world community and interrelatedness.

In 1985, at the height of the Cold War when both the two conflicting superpowers and nation-states, the US and the USSR, were armed with 69,401 nuclear weapons,[3] the consensus was that the only way of keeping the peace was through a "balance of terror". Neither side dared fire nuclear weapons at the other as if it did it would bring about its own destruction. Peace was kept through "mutually assured destruction". In the US this strategy was linked to the US diplomat and political adviser George Kennan's policy of containing the Soviet Union, which meant preventing it from expanding. Two superpower nation-states pointing nuclear weapons at each other in a balance of terror was not a confidence-inspiring way of guaranteeing perpetual peace. Rather, it was a holding operation in an exceptionally difficult time.

It was against this background that seeds were planted to grow into a world community. The regional organizations referred to in (1) (on p74) have grown out of relatively small beginnings. The European Coal and Steel Community grew into the European Economic Community (EEC), which in turn grew into the European Community (EC), which has now grown into the European Union (EU). The 34-state Organization of American States (OAS) has been joined since 1994 by the 34-state Free Trade Area of the Americas (FTAA). This is an extension of the North American Free Trade Agreement (NAFTA); the Central American Free Trade Agreement (CAFTA); and the Latin American Free Trade Association (LAFTA), which was created in 1960 and replaced in 1980 by the Latin American Integration Association (LAIA). In 2008 the Union of South American Nations was established, and replaced the South American Community of Nations which had been created in 2004. Eventually there may be an American Union or Union of the Americas. The Caribbean Free Trade Association (CARIFTA) grew into the Caribbean Community (CARICOM). The Organization of African Unity (OAU) has grown into the African Union. The Asia-Pacific Economic Co-operation forum (APEC) and the South Asian Free Trade Area (SAFTA) are growing into an Asian Economic Community (AEC) and may eventually pass into an Asia-Pacific Union. All these developing Free Trade Associations and Unions have regional links based on geographical proximity and therefore common history and culture.

Of these, the European Union is an intergovernmental organization of European countries with at the time of writing 27 member states. It is the most powerful regional organization in existence, having been based on the German federal system while appearing to be a loose association of nations. Germany is a federal republic of 16 states that were countries until the Weimar constitution of 1919, and whose western states were federated in 1949. With massive Marshall-Plan US funding it has provided the impetus for what amounts to a Franco-German empire in which parts of other European nation-states will be provinces. Members have transferred a considerable degree of sovereignty to it, and following ratification of the Lisbon Treaty on the European Constitution the EU acquired a legal personality of its own and became a state over the member nation-states. It was now responsible for nearly 100 per cent of European legislation, as we have seen (see p59). The European Union was now a political rather than an economic union and had become a superstate.

Its legal base is a succession of international treaties: the Treaty of Rome (1957), the Treaty of Maastricht (1992), the Treaty of Amsterdam (1999), the Treaty of Nice (which was signed in 2001 and came into operation in 2003) and then the Treaty of Lisbon. Its structure is the interconnection of social institutions: the European Commission; the Council of the European Union (or "Council of Ministers"), the central decision-making authority in the EU; and the European Parliament. This institutional triangle forms the decision-making centre of the EU system and is supported by the European Court of Justice, the European Court of Auditors and the European Council, which was established as a result of summit meetings involving heads of state and governments in 1969. The buildings housing these institutions are all within walking distance of each other in Brussels, though the Parliament also meets in Strasbourg. Related to these institutions are the European Central Bank and the European Investment Bank.

To some the European Union would be a United States of Europe with redrawn European regions that would mix bits of nation-states to break down national Europe. For example:[4]

- The TransManche region would comprise the UK's Kent and East Sussex, and Northern France;
- The North Sea region would be north of the TransManche region and would include Eastern England, Eastern Scotland and chunks of Sweden, Denmark, Germany, Holland and the Flemish part of Belgium (with headquarters in Denmark);
- The Atlantic region would include Western Britain and Ireland, and parts of France, Spain and Portugal (with headquarters in Portugal);
- The Northern Periphery region would include North-West Scotland and parts of Norway, Sweden, Finland, Greenland and Iceland.

To others the EU would be too undemocratic to be a United States of Europe and would border on the totalitarian.

There is tension between intergovernmentalism and supranationalism within the EU. Intergovernmentalism is a method of decision-making in international organizations: member states have the power and decisions have to be unanimous. Government appointees speak for their member states. In a supranational body, on the other hand, appointed officials or representatives selected by legislatures, or the member states' peoples, have the power. Member state governments share their power, and a member state may be forced by other member states to implement a decision it opposed.

Supporters of intergovernmentalism, which is strong in the UK, Denmark and Sweden, argue that supranationalism is a threat to national sovereignty and democracy, and that only nation-states' national governments are democratically legitimate. Supporters of supranationalism, which is strong in France, Germany, Italy and the Benelux countries, argue that integration proceeds at a faster pace than when governments act unanimously. Intergovernmental decisions can take years. Intergovernmentalists argue that EU integration is the result of tough bargaining between member states.

The European Union has tried to balance both approaches. Model 1 is anchored on the intergovernmental approach. Supranationalists (and neofunctionalists) argue that supranational institutions have been the driving force behind integration.

There are 48 states in Europe (see pp256-257), and there is room for considerable expansion. As to future enlargement, Croatia was expected to join the EU around 2010, Macedonia around 2012, followed by Albania, Bosnia and Herzegovina, Kosovo, Montenegro, Serbia and Turkey. Chancellor Merkel of Germany stated in June 2008 that such enlargement would not take place without the Lisbon reform to the Nice rules. Eastern-partnership states, including Russia and the ex-Soviet states, are behind the Western-Balkan states, Turkey and Iceland in the queue.

The functional organizations referred to in (1) above include the World Bank and the International Monetary Fund (IMF), which were created at the Bretton Woods Conference in 1944. The World Bank is an international financial institution that provides loans to poor countries for capital programs that can reduce poverty. The International Monetary Fund (IMF) is an organization of 190 countries (see pp263-267) that work to foster global monetary co-operation, secure financial stability, facilitate international trade, promote high employment and sustainable economic growth, and reduce poverty around the world.

The original seeds that were planted were: the Food and Agriculture Organization of the UN; the World Health Organization; the International Bank for Reconstruction and Development, which passed into the World Bank; the International Labour Organization; the World Meteorological Organization; the UN's Governing Council for Environmental Programs; and the United Nations Development Programme. Other functional organizations co-ordinate air transportation, prevent airline hijacking and control the international traffic in drugs.

All these functional organizations had supranational authority in as much as their remit was to cross the borders and boundaries of nation-states, which have had to comply with their requirements. The scope of all these organizations is transnational.

Some supporters of Model 1 say that these organizations are meeting the world's practical needs in a gradualist manner while establishing a sense of community that makes conflict across national and ideological borders less likely and peaceful resolution more likely. Nationalist opponents of Model 1 say that these organizations should operate in ways that do not conflict with national self-interest as the fundamental psychological loyalty of each people should be to their nation-state. I have claimed in ch. 3 that the nation-state is withering away, and in our time of transition to a World State there is tension between nationalist and globalist approaches. Thus in Europe Universalist opponents of Model 1 argue that gradualism is too slow, that Model 1 would take too long to reach world government.

These days souls are divided between old loyalties to the nation-state and openness to the new structure of regions, Unions and a coming World State. Like Janus, we look both ways, back towards the certainties of the past, including the inviolability of the nation-state, and forward to the uncertainties of the future. All transitional times are bewildering to live in, and the soul is torn. Frequently there is schism in the soul.

I have to ask: can Model 1 guarantee perpetual peace? Model 1 represents the gradualist approach of the *status quo*, with nation-states grouping themselves, or being grouped, into membership of regions and membership of transnational organizations. The *status quo* has not prevented wars in our own time: wars in the Balkans, Iraq and Afghanistan. It has not prevented nuclear weapons from falling into the wrong hands, as seems to have happened when some of the ex-Soviet nuclear-suitcase bombs fell into the hands of the Chechen Mafia, who sold them on to bin Laden for use by al-Qaeda. Spreading world community through organizations has taken place under the umbrella of the US, which has acted as the world's policeman (Britain's role in the days of the British Empire).

The loose arrangement of Model 1 cannot solve any of the world's problems which have so far proved insoluble under the *status quo*. Something more fundamental than the *status quo* is needed to solve the world's problems. Model 1 is not the kind of supranational authority that can achieve my stated goals.

Model 2: Sticking with the UN and Strengthening Great-Power Agreement

The most significant apparently supranational authority embodying international law in our time has been the actually inter-national United Nations, which was established in June 1945 for 49 original member states to stop wars and provide a platform for dialogue.

Its stated aims are facilitating co-operation in international law, international security, economic development, social progress, human rights and the achieving of world peace. Its aims can be found at the beginning of its Charter:

"We the peoples of the United Nations determined

to save succeeding generations from the scourge of war, which twice in our lifetime has brought untold sorrow to mankind, and

to re reaffirm faith in fundamental human rights, in the dignity and worth of the human person, in the equal rights of men and women and of nations large and small, and

to establish conditions under which justice and respect for the obligations arising from treaties and other sources of international law can be maintained, and

to promote social progress and better standards of life in larger freedom,

and for these ends

to practise tolerance and live together in peace with one another as good neighbours, and

to unite our strength to maintain international peace and security, and

to ensure, by the acceptance of principles and the institution of methods, that armed force shall not be used, save in the common interest, and

to employ international machinery for the promotion of the economic and social advancement of all peoples,

have resolved to combine our efforts to accomplish these aims."

The UN's purposes are stated in Article 1:

"The Purposes of the United Nations are:

1. To maintain international peace and security, and to that end: to take effective collective measures for the prevention and removal of threats to the peace, and for the suppression of acts of aggression or breaches of the peace, and to bring about by peaceful means, and in conformity

with the principles of justice and international law, adjustment or settlement of international disputes or situations which might lead to a breach of the peace;

2. To develop friendly relations among nations based on respect for the principle of equal rights and self-determination of peoples, and to take other appropriate measures to strengthen universal peace;
3. To achieve international co-operation in solving international problems of an economic, social, cultural, or humanitarian character, and in promoting and encouraging respect for human rights and for fundamental freedoms for all without distinction as to race, sex, language, or religion; and
4. To be a centre for harmonizing the actions of nations in the attainment of these common ends."

The principles of the United Nations are:

"The Organization and its Members, in pursuit of the Purposes stated in Article 1, shall act in accordance with the following Principles.

1. The Organization is based on the principle of the sovereign equality of all its Members.
2. All Members, in order to ensure to all of them the rights and benefits resulting from membership, shall fulfil in good faith the obligations assumed by them in accordance with the present Charter.
3. All Members shall settle their international disputes by peaceful means in such a manner that international peace and security, and justice, are not endangered.
4. All Members shall refrain in their international relations from the threat or use of force against the territorial integrity or political independence of any state, or in any other manner inconsistent with the Purposes of the United Nations.
5. Members shall give the United Nations every assistance in any action it takes in accordance with the present Charter, and shall refrain from giving assistance to any state against which the United Nations is taking preventive or enforcement action.
6. The Organization shall ensure that states which are not Members of the United Nations act in accordance with these Principles so far as may be necessary for the maintenance of international peace and

security.

7. Nothing contained in the present Charter shall authorize the United Nations to intervene in matters which are essentially within the domestic jurisdiction of any state or shall require the Members to submit such matters to settlement under the present Charter; but this principle shall not prejudice the application of enforcement measures under Chapter VII."

I have already said that in 2009 there were 192 member states of the UN (see pp200-203), which include most sovereign states in existence. Its administrative organs are: the General Assembly; the Security Council; the Economic and Social Council; the Trusteeship Council (already virtually abolished); the Secretariat; and the International Court of Justice. Additional bodies deal with the governance of other UN system agencies, such as the World Health Organization (WHO) and the United National Children's Fund (UNICEF). It functions in six languages: Arabic, Chinese, English, French, Russian and Spanish. It is financed from assessed and voluntary contributions from member states.

The General Assembly is the main deliberative assembly of the UN. It is composed of all UN member states and meets yearly. Each state has a vote, and votes require a two-thirds majority. It was originally intended that the General Assembly would be the main UN chamber, but because every state, no matter how large or small, has one vote, getting business done became unwieldy, and in the early days ever more use was made of the Security Council. Over the years the focus shifted to the Security Council, which had fewer members and was less cumbersome.

The Security Council is charged with maintaining peace and security between nation-states. It consists of 15 members of the UN, 5 Permanent Members (China, France, the Russian Federation, the UK and the US) and 10 Non-Permanent Members (currently Austria, Burkina Faso – formerly the Republic of Upper Volta, Costa Rica, Croatia, Japan, Libya, Mexico, Turkey, Uganda and Vietnam. The 5 Permanent Members have the power to veto substantive but not procedural resolutions. The Soviet Union overused the veto in the early days, paralysing the Security Council. The Security Council has the power to make binding decisions that member governments have agreed to carry out, under the terms of Article 25: "The Members of the United Nations agree to accept and carry out the decisions of the Security Council in accordance with the present Charter." Its decisions are the UN resolutions that maintain peace and security.

The Security Council arbitrates between nation-states as the jurists and philosophers of the past dreamt an assembly or council would. However, the members of the Security Council have little power to coerce, and their resolutions are subject to agreement by the member governments. Each member has one vote, and decisions on substantive matters require an affirmative vote of nine members, including the concurring votes of the Permanent Members (under Article 27).

The UN has well-known weaknesses. In Article 2(4) and elsewhere by implication the Charter allows sovereign nations to use force that they claim is for defence. Many of the local wars since 1945 have been conducted on the basis that they were in self-defence: the invasion of Afghanistan in 2001 was for the self-defence of the US following 9/11; Russia invaded Georgia in August 2008 for reasons of self-defence; and Israel invaded Gaza in early 2009 for reasons of self-defence.

Another example of the UN Charter's weakness concerns sanctions. The Charter itself does not mention the word "sanctions". They are justified by Article 41, which states: "The Security Council may decide what measures not involving the use of armed force are to be employed to give effect to its decisions, and it may call upon the Members of the United Nations to apply such measures. These may include complete or partial interruption of economic relations and of rail, sea, air, postal, telegraphic, radio and other means of communication, and the severance of diplomatic relations." However, it can be argued that sanctions violate Article 2(3) and (4): that Members "shall settle their international disputes by peaceful means in such a manner that international peace and security, and justice, are not endangered", and that Members "shall refrain in their international relations from the threat or use of force against territorial integrity or political independence of any state, or in any other manner inconsistent with the Purposes of the United Nations". Any violation hinges on the interpretation of "peaceful means" and "political independence".

Sanctions were only used twice during the Cold War, between 1945 and 1990: against Southern Rhodesia (1968) and South Africa (1977). Between 1990 and 2000 the Security Council adopted 15 sanctions regimes: against Iraq (1990), former Yugoslavia (1991), the Federal Republic of Yugoslavia (1992), Libya (1992), Somalia (1992), Haiti (1993, lifted in 1994), UNITA

(1993), Rwanda (1994), Liberia (1994), the Bosnian Serbs (1994), Sudan (1996), Sierra Leone (1997), the Federal Republic of Yugoslavia again (1998), the Taliban (1999), Eritrea and Ethiopia (2000).

In 2009 the following countries were still enduring sanctions: Afghanistan, Côte d'Ivoire, the Democratic Republic of the Congo, the Democratic People's Republic of Korea (North Korea), Iran, Iraq, Lebanon, Liberia, Sierra Leone, Somalia and Sudan. In 2003-2004 the sanctions regime against Iraq was hit by scandal as UN officials, including Kofi Annan's son, were found to have taken bribes in administering the food-for-oil program.

In April 2000 the Security Council set up a working group on sanctions to consider whether the Security Council should change its practice when imposing new sanctions, and make them more humanitarian. The working group considered enlargement, questions of regional representation, criteria for membership, the relationship between the General Assembly and Security Council, accountability and the use of the veto. It took stock of these areas rather than made any fundamental changes

Article 42 provides for the use of armed force by the UN if other measures are considered to be unworkable: "Should the Security Council consider that measures provided for in Article 41 would be inadequate or have proved to be inadequate, it may take such action by air, sea or land forces as may be necessary to maintain or restore international peace and security. Such action may include demonstrations, blockade, and other operations by air, sea, or land forces of Members of the United Nations."

An example of non-constitutional sources of law that might strengthen great-power agreement have been international treaties, conventions, covenants and precedents, all of which can be found in the growth of regions and Unions. We have seen that the growth of the EU went through the treaties of Rome, Maastricht, Amsterdam, Nice and Lisbon. There was a constitutional convention to draft the European Constitution. Other regions have used such European measures as precedents.

Supporters of Model 2 argue that when the great powers – notably the permanent five on the Security Council – agree (and therefore do not use their veto), international law is expressed in the form of UN resolutions and sanctions. They claim that the Charter threatens enough force to make the UN work as an international power that can as a last resort use armed force to restrain a warring nation-state. They claim that it is thus not the UN structure that needs changing, for which public support would have to be won before changes could be pushed through, but great powers' agreements.

Does Model 2 guarantee perpetual peace? Although the UN has promoted agreement between the great powers it has fallen short of preventing wars between nation-states such as the 2003 war in Iraq. Because it is between nation-states and is only above them when the member states agree, the UN is part of the *status quo* and of the old Cold-War order which is outmoded. There is a case to be made that Model 2 does not go far enough in creating supranational authority, for the UN is only supranational when its member states agree. It is relatively powerless when they disagree.

Model 3: World Constitutional Convention

A supranational authority or world government can be formed by a World Constitutional Convention. A constitutional convention is a gathering for the purpose of writing a new constitution or revising an existing constitution.

Supporters of a World Constitutional Convention argue that nation-states and their national governments hinder the expression of a world community. Nation-states will not voluntarily give up a part of their sovereignty or accept international decisions that conflict with their national self-interest. They claim that as the UN is composed of representatives of nation-states and their national governments, there is no point in working through the UN.

For example, until recently the UN had not implemented the UN's provisions for reorganization. In 1997 Kofi Annan began a reform program: an attempt to change the Permanent Membership of the Security Council, which reflects the power relations of 1945; making the bureaucracy more transparent, accountable and efficient; making the UN more democratic; and imposing an international tariff on arms manufacturers. In 2005 the UN convened a World Summit "to take bold decisions in the areas of development, security, human rights and reform of the United Nations". But it has to be said that the reforms proposed were procedural and cosmetic rather than fundamental and substantive. And the issue of the Permanent Membership of the Security Council was not resolved.

The UN has failed to reform itself in other ways as well. The US adopted the Connally Reservation, which limits the jurisdiction of the International Court of Justice to those cases the US agrees it should hear. The USSR and other powers refused to grant any degree of compulsory jurisdiction to the International Court of Justice.

A call to reform the United Nations came from an unexpected source when, on 23 September 2009, the Libyan dictator and despot, Col. Gaddafi, addressed the UN General Assembly, an invitation that symbolised his international rehabilitation after renouncing nuclear weapons in 2003 and becoming President of the African Union. In a 96-minute speech that exceeded his slot of 15 minutes (an overrunning allowed by the Assembly's president, a former Libyan foreign minister), wearing a bronze tribal robe and black *fez* and a large lapel pin of Africa, Gaddafi confrontationally attempted a one-man revolution against the UN and attempted to terrorise the UN into reforming itself.

Gaddafi beginning by congratulating, "in the name of 1,000 African kingdoms", Barack Obama, "our son" (implying that he was an African born in Kenya), and remarking that swine flu "may be one of those viruses that was created in the laboratory and got out of control because it was meant to be a military weapon", said that the UN had failed as it had not achieved very much. It had allowed too many wars to take place since its inception in 1945 and that it should be reformed. Gaddafi maintained there have been 65 wars, but in fact there have been wars – sometimes multiple wars – involving 123 countries which the UN has failed to prevent since 1945. (See pp210-225 and 225-229.) This compares with the tally of 111 military conflicts since the Second World War that we encountered on p62.

He tackled the dominance of the five Permanent Members of the UN Security Council. He read out passages from an Arabic paperback copy of the UN Charter and said it was the work of a small clique of states: "The preamble says all nations are equal whether they are small or big. But the five Permanent Members of the Security Council have undermined other states. The veto [held by the five Permanent Members] is against the Charter. We do not accept it, we do not acknowledge it. Veto power should be annulled."

He tackled excessive US influence. He said it was difficult for the UN to act without the US taking the lead. Gaddafi's Libya had been bombed by President Reagan's planes acting on behalf of the UN in 1986, and, taking his revenge on the UN, he said that the UN was undemocratic and dictatorial and that the Charter did not refer to the Roman Senate's practice of allowing a dictator (such as Sulla and Julius Caesar) to hold office in a time of emergency. The implication was that Gaddafi's own dictatorship of 40 years had coped with a "time of emergency". He tossed the UN Charter dismissively onto the podium in front of him.

Gaddafi tackled the General Assembly's powerlessness to act. He told the General Assembly it was no more important than London's Speakers' Corner.

"You are like a Hyde Park. You just make a speech and disappear." He said he wanted the General Assembly to be the "Parliament of the World, the Congress of the World, the Master of the World", and said that UN Secretary-General Ban Ki-moon should see to it. He called on the General Assembly, which controls all member states, to take control of the Security Council: "The Security Council did not provide us with security but with terror and sanctions." He compared the current UN system to al-Qaeda terrorism, and said "The Security Council should be named 'the Terror Council'."

He demanded that the Permanent Seats should be redistributed. He said that the African Union should have a Permanent Seat on the UN Security Council. He said that the Security Council had allowed some Permanent Members – he meant the UK and France – to practise colonialism, and he called for $7.77 trillion to be paid in compensation to Africa. Speaking as President of the African Union, he said that if the Africans did not receive their $7.77 trillion they would "go and take it back". He said, "We are content and happy if Obama stays for ever as President", suggesting that Africa was more likely to receive its compensation if Obama (like Gaddafi himself) could be President-for-life.

He demanded that the location of the UN should be moved from the United States. He told the delegates he had woken at 4 a.m. New-York time "because it was morning in Libya", and complained of suffering from jet lag. He told the delegates who had not walked out that they were all suffering from jet lag and that the UN should be moved to the Eastern hemisphere. "It's been in the West for over 50 years, and now it should be moved to the East. You will thank me for the proposal of [reducing] the suffering of flying for hours to come to this place."

There was no applause when he finished. But he had powerfully and despotically towered over the UN and terrorised many of the delegates with his dictatorial finger-jabbing and menacing anger. He, a dictator, had accused the UN of dictatorship. He, who had closed Parliament and ended Libyan democracy 40 years previously, had accused the UN of being undemocratic. His attitudes were preposterous and insulting, but he had jabbed his finger at a number of weaknesses in the UN system, which required reform: the UN's inability to stop wars involving 123 countries since 1945, its exclusive Permanent Membership (a reality of nuclear power), its powerlessness to act and its inconvenient location, suggesting that it was the turn of the East to host world meetings.

Supporters of Model 3 believe that what is needed is a new world institution, not strengthened international institutions. They see world law being enforced through a World Constitutional Convention which would draft a constitution for the world and present it to the nation-states. The governments of nation-states would be called upon to send delegates to the World Constitutional Convention. If necessary, world constitutionalists would operate independently of nation-states and their governments, for they would represent the nation-states' peoples, not the nation-states. Just as the US Constitution began "We the people", not "We the states", so the World Constitutional Convention's world constitution would begin "We the people of the world".

There have been a number of constitutional conventions over the years which can act as precedents for a World Constitutional Convention. The United States was first. The Annapolis Convention (1786) proposed the Philadelphia Convention (1787), which drafted the United States Constitution for the states to ratify. In France, the National Convention (20 September 1792) convened to write a Republican Constitution after the French monarchy was suspended. The Convention abolished the monarchy the next day. During the American Civil War, the Missouri Constitutional Convention (1861-1863) established Missouri's provisional government. In Canada, the Quebec Conference met in 1864 and the London Conference of 1866 followed soon after. In Australia, there were four constitutional conventions: in 1891, 1897, 1973 and 1998. In the Philippines, a Philippine Constitutional Convention met in 1935 to create the autonomous Commonwealth of the Philippines under the US Tydings-McDuffie Act, and in 1971 to draft a revised constitution that replaced the US-organized constitution of 1935. In Germany the Parliamentary Council (*Parlamentarischer Rat*, 1948) drafted the Basic Law of the Federal Republic to be ratified by the *Länder*.

In Northern Ireland, a Constitutional Convention (1975-1976) failed to find a solution to the status of Northern Ireland. In Scotland, a Scottish Constitutional Convention (1989) produced a plan for Scottish devolution. The European Convention (2001) drafted the Constitution for Europe, for it to be approved by the European Council and ratified by member states. Constitutional conventions have also been used by states of federations, including individual states of the United States, to create, replace or amend their own constitutions.

The American Constitutional Convention of May 1787 consisted of 55 delegates, who met in the Pennsylvania State House, Philadelphia (now called

Independence Hall). The Convention's aim was "to render the Constitution of the Federal Government adequate to the exigencies of the Union".

The main reason for the 1787 Convention was that the articles of Confederation (1781) required the unanimous consent of all 13 states before the US Government could take action. The system was cumbersome and unworkable. George Washington was elected president of the Convention. The Convention established the principle of a national authority with a bicameral Congress, equal representation in the Senate and proportional representation in the House of Representatives. This plan was sent to a committee of detail, which listed 18 specific powers of Congress, including the power "to make all laws". In ten days it achieved a charter of government. The plan was returned to the Convention, which approved the draft constitution and sent it to a committee of style. The convention approved the final draft and adopted it on 17 September.[5] Article 5 established that further conventions could be called for proposing amendments to the Constitution. Amendments could also be made on a vote by two-thirds of each house of Congress.

Just as the American Constitutional Convention approved the principle of a national authority, so a World Constitutional Convention could approve the principle of a supranational authority. Every state except Hawaii has made applications for an Article-V convention, mostly in the 20th century. There is no official record of how many applications have been made, but one count suggests there have been 567.[6]

The European Convention had its origin in the European Council conference for Heads of State held in Nice in December 2000. It was agreed that there should be a "broader and deeper debate" on the future of the EU before the European Council met in Laeken the following year. In Laeken the European Council made a declaration committing the EU to greater democracy, transparency and efficiency, and setting out the process by which a constitution could be written. There was to be a convention which would produce a draft constitution that would be handed over to the Intergovernmental Conference expected to be held in 2004.

The European Convention was established with 105 members drawn from the national parliaments of member states and candidate countries, the European Parliament, the European Commission and representatives of heads of state and governments. It was chaired by former French president Valéry Giscard d'Estaing. The Convention met for the first time in February 2002, and there was a plenary session once or twice a month. It deliberated in public in the European-Parliament building in Brussels. The draft was unveiled on 28 October 2002. In a speech in Bruges on 2 October 2002 Giscard d'Estaing, the President of the Convention, had said: "I see [the Union] as being a Union of European States closely co-ordinating their policies and administering certain competences, along federal lines."

The word "federal" originally appeared in Article I-1. It was swiftly removed and replaced by the word "Community", but it was clear that greater integration would be achieved by the Treaty establishing a Constitution for Europe. The opening words of the Constitution are: "Reflecting the will of the citizens and States of Europe to build a common future, this Constitution establishes the European Union, on which the Member States confer competences to attain objectives they have in common. The Union shall co-ordinate the policies by which the Member States aim to achieve these objectives, and shall exercise on a Community basis the competences they confer on it."[7] In other words, there was to be a union of European States which, while retaining their national identities, would closely co-ordinate their policies at a European level and administer certain common competences on a federal basis.

Just as the European Convention established the European Union, so a World Constitutional Convention could establish a World State.

Supporters of Model 3 say that a World Constitutional Conference could draft a world constitution. A World Constitutional Conference may, indeed, be a good method of bringing a World State into being. However, it is only a method. To follow a similar procedure to the one that took the European Convention from the Treaty of Nice to Laeken and thence to the draft Constitution would require the nation-states to accept it, just as the European states had to accept the European Convention. UN member governments have always put their "overriding vital interests" first. We are left with a (for now) unanswered question: How could the nation-states be induced to accept a World Constitutional Conference?

Philosophical Summary

What can the Universalist proposing a World State take from our consideration so far of a supranational authority that would implement international law to guarantee peace?

Views from the past regarding a supranational authority that works by binding arbitration of a council. A permanent assembly of princes or delegates to arbitrate international disputes. International law can keep peace. Settling disputes between nations by international arbitration. A perpetual alliance of European states to establish a congress that would arbitrate disputes and enforce decisions by armed action.

The goals of a supranational authority: peace, sharing natural resources and energy, solving environmental problems, tackling disease and famine, avoiding financial crisis, redistributing wealth. Eight models for a supranational authority. Spreading a world community is gradualist and too *status-quo*. Sticking with the UN and strengthening great-power agreement has failed to prevent wars. A World Constitutional Convention is a method for arriving at a World State, so long as nation-states can be induced to entertain it.

To sum up, the philosopher devising a World State can distil from international law:

binding arbitration of a council or assembly of delegates;
perpetual alliance of states to establish a congress that will arbitrate disputes and enforce decisions by armed action;
goals of peace, sharing natural resources and energy, solving environmental problems, disease, famine and financial crisis, redistributing wealth;
eight models for a supranational authority;
spreading a world community is gradualist and too *status-quo*;
sticking with the UN and strengthening great-power agreement has failed to prevent wars;
a World Constitutional Convention is a method for arriving at a World State, so long as nation-states can be induced to agree to it.

What would induce the nation-states to agree to a convention? Does reforming the UN hold the key?

5

Models of a Supranational Authority: Reforming the UN

The first three models were all relatively close to the *status quo*. The next two attempt to reform the UN, each in a quite different way.

Model 4: Revising the UN Charter to Strengthen International Law

We have noted some of the weaknesses of the UN. Its Charter has proved itself unable to prevent wars, as we saw when we considered Model 2, whose supporters prefer to work within the existing system.

Reforming the UN Charter, a (perhaps deliberately) vague document in places whose loose wording allows room for interpretation and inclusiveness and broadens the chances of international agreement, is an arduous task. This task was undertaken in the 1950s when Grenville Clark, a Harvard-educated lawyer and Harvard friend of Roosevelt, and Louis Sohn, a Harvard Professor in international law and friend of Dean Rusk, co-authored *World Peace Through World Law* (1958).

The book was reprinted in 1960 and amended to include provisions for an Outer Space Agency. This second edition of the book set out detailed proposals for revision of the UN Charter. Its call for disarmament must be understood within the historical context of its time. The British Foreign Secretary Selwyn Lloyd had proposed "comprehensive disarmament" in the UN on 17 September 1959, and the Soviet leader Nikita Khrushchev had called for "general and complete disarmament" in the UN next day, 18 September 1959. On 1 December 1959 the US and Soviet Union, and ten other major countries, agreed to the Antarctic Treaty, which banned all weapons and military activities from Antarctica.

President Kennedy created the US Arms Control and Disarmament Agency, with the aid of Republican John McCloy. On 20 September 1961, the Soviet Union and US issued a "Joint Statement of Agreed Principles for Disarmament Negotiations", which came to be known as the McCloy-Zorin Agreement. It aimed to negotiate a "general and complete disarmament". Kennedy spoke on 25 September 1961 before the UN General Assembly and said: "Mankind must put an end to war – or war will put an end to mankind."[1] The Cuban crisis of

1961, when the Soviet Union, still ruled by Khrushchev, was caught on film sending missiles by ship to Cuba and President Kennedy successfully ordered Khrushchev to remove them from Cuba, put an end to all talk of disarmament.

A third edition in 1966 included a proposed Treaty Establishing a World Disarmament and World Development Organization (see Model 5.) In 1973, *Introduction to World Peace Through World Law* appeared after Clark's death, with an updating essay 'Two Alternative Plans', by Sohn and essays by others.

These various editions and versions are all important, and in what follows I regard the evolving work as a whole.

The fundamental premise of the Clark-Sohn book is President Eisenhower's statement on 31 October 1956, the first day of the Suez crisis during which Britain, France and Israel invaded Egypt, a sovereign nation-state, and a week before the Hungarian uprising against the USSR, which was crushed by Soviet tanks: "There can be no peace without law." He meant the "law" of a World Authority that could be uniformly applied to all nations – Britain, France, Israel and the Soviet Union – and forbid violence.

The principles behind the book were:

(1) that only enforceable world law can preserve peace, which meant that all nations must completely disarm, and adopt and uphold a law against violence on a world-wide basis;
(2) the world law against international violence must be stated in statutory form and forbid the use of force by any nation against any other for any cause except self-defence;
(3) world judicial tribunals should interpret and apply the world law, and there should be organs of mediation and conciliation to set up peaceful means of adjudication and adjustment in place of violence;
(4) there should be a permanent world police force which should suppress any violation of the world law against international violence;
(5) the complete disarmament of all nations (rather than mere "reduction" or "limitation" of armaments) is essential for lasting peace, and should be conducted in a simultaneous and proportionate manner, with verified stages and inspections;
(6) the vastly different economic condition of differing regions should be equalised, to remove a major cause of instability of conflict; and
(7) common natural resources, such as outer space and the oceans, should be managed equitably.

There were supplementary principles:

(1) all nations must actively participate in the world peace authority, which should be universal, and any nations that for whatever reason opt out must abolish their armed forces, so that the constitutional document creating the world peace organization will have a majority of all nations and peoples of the world;
(2) the world law should apply to all individuals as well as nations;
(3) the basic rights and duties of all nations to maintain peace should be stated in the constitutional document, which should also set out the powers of the new world organization;
(4) the powers of the world organization should be restricted to the maintenance of peace, and all other power should be with the nations and their peoples;
(5) to be acceptable, the peace plan must demonstrably be seen to be capable of preventing war while safeguarding the powers of nation-states.

The main features of the revision of the UN Charter are:

(1) virtually all nation-states of the world (192 within the UN in 2009 and various related and disputed territories) should have Permanent Membership of the new world organization before the revision of the UN Charter takes effect, and the revised Charter would require ratification by five-sixths of all nation-states;
(2) the General Assembly should have its powers, composition and method of voting revised, with the four largest nations having 30 representatives, the 10 next largest 12, the 15 next largest 8, the 20 next largest 6, the 30 next largest 4, the 40 next largest 3 and the smallest nations 1, making a total in 1970 of 744 representatives from 143 nations;
(3) the Security Council would be abolished and replaced by an Executive Council, composed of 17 Representatives elected by the General Assembly (the four largest nations having Permanent Representation, five of the 10 next largest having seats in rotation, and the eight chosen by the General Assembly from the representatives of other nation-states), and this veto-less Executive Council would decide whether

each stage of the disarmament process was satisfactorily completed;

(4) the Economic and Social Council (and the Trusteeship Council, recently recommended for abolition) would be continued, but with larger and different composition;

(5) the disarmament process would involve a step-by-step elimination of armaments over a six-year period, and the UN Peace Force would take possession of arms handed over;

(6) military forces would be completely eliminated, and breaches of the enforced peace would be suppressed by a World Police Force, which would have a strength of 200,000-400,000, as determined from year to year by the General Assembly, and a Peace Force Reserve would have a standing strength of 300,000-600,000 as determined by the General Assembly;

(7) the adjudication or settlement of international disputes should be conducted by the Judicial and Conciliation System, under which the International Court of Justice would have the authority to decide on the interpretation of the revised Charter and the regional UN courts would introduce enforceable world law regarding world peace, while a World Conciliation Board would mediate and conciliate in disputes, which could then be placed before the International Court of Justice or the World Equity Tribunal;

(8) enforcement would involve prosecution in UN regional courts of individuals who have violated disarmament provisions, following investigation by a UN civil police force of 10,000 working under the UN Attorney-General, and there should be penalties for violation of Charter regulations;

(9) a World Development Authority would grant interest-free loans to assist the economic and social development of underdeveloped areas, and the World Development Commission would be supervised by the Economic and Social Council;

(10) a UN Ocean Authority should be established, with a structure similar to that of the Outer Space Authority;

(11) the United Nations Environment Protection Authority would be set up with an intergovernmental Council representing developed and developing nations, and a five-member Environment Commission to co-ordinate national and international environment programs;

(12) a United Nations Revision System would raise funds to pay for the

new world institutions (UN Peace Force, the Inspection Service, the World Development Authority, the Nuclear Energy Authority, the Outer Space Authority, the Ocean Authority, the Environment Protection Authority, the World Equity Tribunal and the World Conciliation Board), especially for the UN Peace Force which was expected to cost $12 billion annually in 1970, while the World Development Authority was then expected to need $75 billion to even out economic disparities between nations and regions;

(13) the privileges and immunities of UN personnel should be set out in the constitutional document, and safeguards against abuse of privileges and immunities should be in the Treaty;

(14) the limitation of the authority of the new UN organizations should be defined with great precision, and guarantees should be given against violation by the UN and included in the constitutional document of individual rights;

(15) ratification of the revised Charter should be by five-sixths of the world's nations, including all the four nations with the largest populations and at least six of the ten next largest nations, the aggregate of the populations of the ratifying nations equalling at least five-sixths of the total world population, and each nation's ratification should be by its own constitutional processes;

(16) amendments to the revised Charter should be by a vote of two-thirds of all General Assembly Representatives or of a General Conference held for the purpose of amendment, and ratification should be by four-fifths of the member nations, including 10 of the 14 member nations entitled to 12 or more Representatives in the assembly;

(17) the existing UN organs and agencies should be strengthened, and thus the Executive Council which should replace the Security Council would be veto-less; and the International Court of Justice should have enlarged jurisdiction and greater authority.

It must be stressed that the above scheme was last updated in the early 1970s. Since then the composition of the four largest nations in the world has changed. In 1970 they were the People's Republic of China, India, the Soviet Union and the United States. The break-up of the Soviet Union means that Indonesia is now the fourth-largest nation in the world in terms of population, and the Russian Federation is therefore outside the top four. This anomaly will have to be addressed. It would be bizarre to give non-nuclear Indonesia Permanent Representation on the Executive Council and to bar the nuclear Russian Federation, which holds over half the nuclear warheads in existence, from having Permanent Representation, and the same applies to barring the Russian Federation from being among the four Permanent Members in ratification. The Clark-Sohn plan states that the UN Trusteeship Council should continue, but this was recommended for abolition as part of UN Secretary-General Kofi Annan's reform plan as the newly independent 11 trust territories had been dissolved.

The two co-authors, Clark and Sohn, print the existing UN Charter down the left-hand side of each page and their proposed text for revising each Article and Chapter alongside it on the right-hand side, with "comment" beneath each Article. The detail fills more than 367 pages.

To taste the flavour of their amendments, it is worth giving their proposed text for the areas I picked out in ch. 4. Their version of point 1 of the purposes of the United Nations (see pp80-81) is: "To maintain international peace and security, and to that end: to abolish all national military forces and, through a United Nations system of inspection and a United Nations military force, to take effective measures for the enforcement of disarmament, for the prevention and removal of threats to the peace, for the suppression of acts of aggression or other breaches of the peace, and for ensuring compliance with this revised Charter and the laws and regulations enacted thereunder; and through United Nations agencies and tribunals, to bring about by peaceful means, and in conformity with the principles of justice and international law, adjustment or settlement of international disputes or situations which might lead to a breach of the peace."

The proposed revision of point 1 of the principles of the United Nations (see p81) is: "All nations shall be equally entitled to the protection guaranteed by this revised Charter, irrespective of size, population or any other factor; and there are reserved to all nations or their peoples all powers inherent in their sovereignty, except such as are delegated to the United Nations by this revised Charter, either by express language or clear implication, and are not prohibited by this revised Charter to the nations." In other words, all nation-states would retain their sovereignty under the revised UN Charter.

The proposed text for the revised Article 41, which is cited as justifying sanctions (see p83), omits "and it may call upon the Members of the United Nations to apply such measures". The revised UN Charter has strengthened this Article, which no longer depends on a "call" to UN Members. The revised UN Charter would be stronger in enforcement and penalties, and so it would not be necessary to "call" on Members who take measures. These would be mandatory.

The proposed text for the revised UN Charter's Article 42, which provides for the use of armed force by the UN (see p84), is: "Should the General Assembly or the Executive Council in the circumstances defined in paragraph 2 of Article 39, consider that measures provided for in Article 41 would be inadequate or have proved to be inadequate, it shall direct such action by air, sea, or land elements of the United Nations Peace Force as may be necessary to maintain or restore international peace and security or to ensure compliance with this revised Charter and the laws and regulations enacted thereunder. Such action may include demonstrations, blockade, and other operations; but any such action shall be taken pursuant to the procedures and subject to the limitations contained in Annex II." Annex II (several pages long) is about the United Nations Peace Force.

So Model 4 removes the right to violence (except in the case of self-defence) from nation-states but leaves all their other powers intact. The proposed text for the revised UN Charter has been in the public domain since 1960, and 50 years have now passed.

I can legitimately ask, why has it not been taken up? Undoubtedly the US-Soviet arms reduction programs owe much to its call for disarmament, but the Cold War continued for 30 years after the Clark-Sohn plan first appeared, and fear of the nuclear Soviet Union, and security considerations, no doubt prevented the implementation of the plan during those years.

It could be that its legalistic approach has not captured the imagination. Its law-based proposal was both conservative and radical: law and order in the world is a conservative theme, yet giving up national sovereignty to world institutions is a radical change. The mixture of conservative and radical outlook may have proved confusing. Lawyers offering side-by-side charters can split hairs in their wording, inviting a contrast between a shade of emphasis in the UN Charter and a slightly different shade of emphasis in their proposed text. The result may appear over-legalistic, like the text of the European Constitution, which is in places unreadable and therefore has not inspired the European people. The simplicity and directness of the Declaration of Independence, on the other hand, is still inspiring.

Be that as it may, the fact remains that a very full plan for Model 4 has been on the table for 50 years and could easily be brought up to date. It would reassure nation-states that their power would continue, even though they were giving up deciding disputes by resorting to war.

Does Model 4 guarantee perpetual peace? We are back to my conclusion regarding Model 2 (see p85). Except for the one area of abolishing violence, the *status quo* is preserved. And the UN remains an essentially inter-national body attempting to fulfil a supranational role. Does the supranational authority of Model 4 go far enough? Should there be a supranational authority that is external to the inter-national UN?

Model 5: A Treaty for a New Organization to Exist Alongside, and Strengthen, the UN

In the 1966 3rd edition of their *World Peace Through World Law*, Clark and Sohn offered an alternative to reforming the UN Charter: a Draft Treaty that would create a new organization that would exist alongside the UN and strengthen it – the World Disarmament and Development Organization.

In this alternative plan, the UN – with the Security Council still intact – would continue to exercise the limited powers under the existing Charter and would receive additional powers under the proposed Treaty. The Treaty would supplement the existing machinery of the UN. Much of the proposed text in the revised UN Charter could be shifted into the Treaty, giving the same disarmament plan and abolition of violence we encountered in Model 4. Features (1)-(17) of Model 4 therefore also apply to Model 5. Thus, all nations would be members of the new organization.

The Draft Treaty is some 120 pages long with 114 Articles. Article 1 states:

"The purposes of the World's Disarmament and World Development Organization are:

1. To bring about and maintain a permanent state of universal and complete national disarmament under effective international control;
2. To establish effective institutions for the maintenance of peace and to provide reliable procedures for the settlement of all international disputes by peaceful means; and
3. To provide adequate machinery and resources to mitigate the immense disparities in the economic condition of various regions of the world which endanger international peace."

The relationship between the UN and the new organization would be a close one, for the Treaty provides:

(1) that all the new organizations should consult with the United Nations' organs and agencies on all matters of mutual interest;
(2) that annual and special reports on the Organization should be made to the UN;
(3) that persons authorised by the General Assembly should have the right to take part, without vote, in the deliberations of the General Conference of the Organization, and that persons authorised by the Security Council and the Economic and Social Council of the UN should take part, without voting, in the deliberations of the Executive Council and the World Development Authority;
(4) the General Assembly and other organs of the UN may make recommendations to the Organization; and
(5) all sanctions should be initiated by the UN through its General Assembly or Security Council, or by the General Conference of the Organization, which would support the UN in such measures.

The new Organization's institutions would have the words "United Nations" before them. Thus the Peace Force would be called the "United Nations Peace Force". The United Nations would remain as a world forum for debate, but the World Disarmament and the World Development Organization would have financial, judicial and military powers which the United Nations now lacks – which the framers of the UN Charter did not give it.

Model 5 recognises that the United Nations has always lacked a standing world police force; a judicial system with compulsory jurisdiction over international disputes; and a revenue system. Supporters of Model 5 claim that the UN has done useful work to keep world peace, that it should not be abolished, but that it should be supplemented so it can maintain peace more effectively.

Supporters of Model 5 claim that although the world disarmament and World Development Organization's living alongside the existing UN would be an awkward arrangement, it would be worth putting up with some awkwardness if it was effective in enforcing and keeping world peace.

So Model 5 has the same features as Model 4, from which it differs in one respect: instead of revising the UN Charter, it creates a new organization to exist alongside it, and the 17 features would therefore be within the new organization rather than within a revised UN Charter.

Model 5 is therefore as much a part of the *status quo* as Model 4, and the same doubts apply. Why has it not been taken up when it has been on the table for 50 years? The same answers apply as on pp98-99. As with Model 4, the *status quo* is preserved except for the one area of abolishing violence. Again, the UN remains an essentially inter-national body attempting to fulfil a supranational role. Again, does the supranational authority of Model 5 go far enough? Should there be a supranational authority that is elsewhere than alongside the inter-national UN?

Philosophical Summary

What can the Universalist proposing a World State take from our consideration of reforms to the UN?

Eisenhower's "There can be no peace without law" – the world law of a supranational authority. World law must be enforceable. Judicial tribunals should enforce world law. A permanent world police force. Complete disarmament of all nations. Evening up disparities between regions. Managing humankind's common natural resources, including outer space and oceans. All nation-states should participate. Nations' rights and duties should be in a revised Charter/Treaty. Nations retain their powers except for the right to go to war.

The General Assembly should be elected. The Security Council should be replaced by a veto-less Executive Council. The Economic and Social Council should continue. A six-year disarmament process. A UN revenue system. A World Disarmament and Development Organization should exist alongside the UN. The relationship between the two bodies.

To sum up, the philosopher devising a World State can distil from UN reform:

revising the UN Charter preserves the *status quo* except for going to war;
world law must be enforceable;
judicial tribunals to enforce the law;
a permanent world police force;
complete disarmament of all nations;
evening up disparities between regions;
humankind's common natural resources should be managed, including outer space and oceans;

all nation-states and individuals should participate in world law;
nations' rights and duties should be in a revised Charter/Treaty;
nations retain their powers except for the right to go to war;
the General Assembly should be elected;
the Security Council should be replaced by a veto-less Executive Council;
the Economic and Social Council should continue;
there should be a six-year disarmament process;
there should be a UN revenue system;
as an alternative there could be a World Disarmament and Development Organization, which would exist alongside the UN.

Before we consider a supranational authority that is elsewhere than alongside the UN, we must consider an attempt in our own time to bring in a New World Order of global governance that could become a World State.

6

Models of a Supranational Authority: Global Governance

The New World Order is a more radical model as it would subsume nation-states and absorb them into a world government.

Model 6: *Élite*s' Secretive World Government through Exclusive Groups

The New World Order was made possible by *élite*s who have operated for nearly 250 years. In 1776 Mayer Amschel, a Frankfurt Jew,[1] became court agent for the Elector, William IX, Landgrave of Hesse-Cassel, who hired out 16,800 Hessian troops to fight for Great Britain during the American Revolution. When Napoleon invaded Germany William fled, leaving Mayer Amschel to guard $3 million[2] buried in his garden. William gave a power of attorney to Carl Friedrich Buderus von Carlshausen, finance officer to William IX, who made Amschel his banker to collect the interest on royal loans. Amschel came to be known after the red shield or "rotschildt" that hung over the door in the house at the prosperous end of Jew Street in the ghetto where his ancestors lived in Frankfurt.[3]

Mayer Amschel Rothschild had five sons who had banks in London, Paris, Frankfurt, Vienna and Naples. When he died in 1812, he was the richest man ever to have lived,[4] with $3.5 million,[5] and he passed his fortune down through his male descendants.[6]

His eldest son Nathan speculated on the outcome of the Battle of Waterloo in 1815.[7] His selling caused a price collapse. He then bought the market and government bonds, and owned the Bank of England. By 1820 he increased the fortune to $7.5 billion, and may have increased it to $100 billion by 1840.

All Mayer Amschel Rothschild's sons were linked to their governments. By the time Nathan's son Lionel had bought the Suez Canal for Disraeli in 1875[8] the Rothschilds had become the richest family ever, with more wealth than all the crowned heads of Europe put together and 42 great country houses throughout Europe. The Rothschilds financed railroads, the new railway system across the United States, and, having attempted and failed to establish an American Central Bank during the Civil War, created the US Federal

Reserve System in October 1914. This was a Rothschild-controlled central-banking system for the US. Rothschilds' movements of gold from the US to Europe triggered the crash and Depression of the late 1920s.[9]

The Rothschilds' *protégé* in the late 1860s was the American oil magnate John D. Rockefeller, who had German blood. He was descended from a Hessian mercenary (Roggenfelder, which means "rye fields" in German)[10] who had Turkish ancestry and fought for the British army during the Revolutionary war – one of the 16,800 sent by William IX. This Roggenfelder deserted when offered land in New Jersey and changed his name to Rockefeller.[11] In 1870 his descendant John D. Rockefeller incorporated Standard Oil of Ohio with Rothschilds' financial help via their agent, Jacob Schiff.[12] By 1879 Rockefeller controlled 90 per cent of all the refined oil sold in the US. He owned 20,000 oil wells and had 100,000 employees, with branches in Western Europe and China. Rockefeller's wealth rose from £200 million to £1 billion by 1911,[13] when he shed 37 subsidiaries and created 34 companies.[14] Like Mayer Amschel Rothschild, he had five sons: John III, Nelson, Laurance, Winthrop and David.

The German-American-Turkish Rockefellers funded the Kaiser during the First World War and had links with Ottoman oil. In 1914 Standard Oil loaned the Turkish Government $35 million and were permitted to drill for oil in Ottoman territory, sometimes alongside the British. Rockefellers gave the Kaiser $300 million[15] to finance the First World War, and they supplied the Germans with oil. In 1925 Rockefellers struck a deal with Stalin whereby they had half the oil produced in the Soviet Union in return for funding Stalin's Five-Year Plans.[16] In due course "Rockefellers" supplied Hitler with oil via Standard Oil of New Jersey though Spain. They funded part of Hitler's war effort, giving the Nazis $25 million in 1939.[17]

By the time John D. Rockefeller died in 1937, the Rockefellers owned a known fortune of at least $5 billion[18] and owned 20 per cent of American industry. In 1940 the Rothschilds were estimated as being worth $500 billion.[19]

The Rothschilds and Rockefellers were the two wealthiest families in the world in the 1950s, and both families set themselves to continue their dynastic policy of working for global governance and a world government – controlled by their own interests. Their agenda was to add to their wealth by cornering the Earth's natural resources and then selling them.

At this point I shall start placing inverted commas round the family names "Rothschilds" and "Rockefellers". By doing so I seek to make it clear that I am not referring to particular individuals but to a particular emphasis of a commercial pattern – in the case of "Rothschilds" a commercial drive associated with their 19th-century financial dominance and imperialism, and in the case of "Rockefellers" a commercial drive associated with their 20th-century acquisition of oil and shaping events through revolutions.

In 1954 "Rothschilds" and "Rockefellers" co-founded the secretive Bilderberg Group, which was named after the Hotel de Bilderberg in Oosterbeek, Holland, where the Group first met. The Group worked for the unification of Europe, which began to happen with the 1957 Treaty of Rome. The annual meeting of the Bilderberg Group still takes place, and the most prominent attender of the Group during the last 55 years has been David Rockefeller, now in his eighties. The meetings are attended by the most powerful men in the world, all handpicked: the Presidents of the IMF, World Bank and Federal Reserve, chairmen of 100 of the most powerful corporations in the world, Vice-Presidents of the US, directors of the CIA and FBI, Secretaries-General of NATO, US Senators and members of Congress, European Prime Ministers and leaders of opposition parties, pro-world politicians, top editors and CEOs of leading newspapers. They meet to establish a consensus between America and Europe on which forthcoming policy can be based. Bilderberg recommendations have a habit of being implemented during the following year: the 1989 fall of Thatcher and the invasion of Iraq (which Donald Rumsfeld promised the Bilderberg meeting held at Chantilly, Virginia on 30 May-2 June 2002 would not take place until the following year) are two of many such recommendations.[20]

They meet under the Chatham House Rule under which participants are free to use the information received, but the identity of the speakers and the location of the forum in which it was conveyed must not be revealed. Future presidents and prime ministers turn out to have been attenders of the Bilderberg Group's meetings. The agenda of the Bilderberg Group is confidential, and an aura of secrecy and deception surrounds their discussions. The hotel is taken over, the delegates arrive secretly, troops surround the hotel, helicopters hover, a security cordon is thrown round the hotel and no parking is allowed within half a mile. An open body having a straightforward meeting does not resort to such secretive practices.

In the early 1970s David Rockefeller created the Trilateral Commission to bring together about 250 members from the US, Europe and Pacific nations (particularly Japan). This group meets annually, and the G7 industrial powers are represented.[21]

It has been reckoned that these *élite*s have around 6,000 sympathisers, who covertly run a world of more than 6 billion people by undertaking advance planning and active discussions of population reduction programs. These are all "Rockefellerite" in inspiration. In 1952 John D. Rockefeller established a Population Council to urge "zero population growth". In 1971 the secretive "Rockefellerite" Club of Rome, which first met on David Rockefeller's private estate in Bellagio, Italy in 1968, published a report, *Limits to Growth*. In 1972 Laurance Rockefeller issued a report on population growth. The 1980 *Global 2000 Report to the President* was built on "Rockefellerite" policies. It states: "The world's population would reach 10 billion by 2030." Its accompanying *Global Future* made recommendations and declared "that global population would eventually stabilise at 8 billion". There was some ambiguity. If read in one way, the Report seemed to be implying that humankind should be reduced by 2 billion people.[22] The "Rockefellerite" 1974 Kissinger Report had referred to "useless eaters"[23] of the Third World: Africans and Asians who are not productive, do no work and consume the Earth's food. The *Global 2000 Report* implies that they are the ones who should be reduced, and that reduction will take place by contrived wars, diseases (like AIDS) and famine.

Meanwhile the US military and arms industry, given the go-ahead by Congress and financed by borrowings from the *élite*s' banks, dominated American life. In 1961 Eisenhower gave this warning at the end of his presidency: "We have been compelled to create a permanent armaments industry of vast proportions. Added to this, three and a half million men and women are directly engaged in the defense establishment. We annually spend on military security more than the next income of all the United States corporations. This conjunction of an immense military establishment and a large arms industry is new in the American experience. The total influence – economic, political, even spiritual – is felt in every city, every State house, every office of the Federal Government....We must guard against the acquisition of unwarranted influence, whether sought or unsought, by the military-industrial complex. The potential for the disastrous rise of misplaced power exists and will persist."[24] In an earlier draft he referred to the "military-industrial-congressional complex".[25] Eisenhower was referring to the *élite*s of the Syndicate (see p109) and expressing fears first uttered by the Founding Fathers that the republic's values could be corrupted.

During the Cold War, the *élite*s sold arms to both sides – both the Soviet and

US Governments – and made a fortune out of funding the production of stockpiles of nuclear weapons. From a high of 69,401 nuclear weapons in 1985, in 2009 there were about 8,200 active nuclear warheads. In total there were 23,574 nuclear warheads in the world. In 2009 Russia had about 12,987 nuclear weapons, the US 9,552, France 300, Israel 200, the UK 225, China 176, Pakistan 90, India 75, and North Korea 2.[26] Many of these weapons of mass destruction were bought with money borrowed from these *élite*s, who increased their wealth at the expense of taxpayers saddled with paying for their governments' borrowing.

Out of this view of the world grew the New World Order. The concept of a "new world" was first used in this sense in modern times by the US President Woodrow Wilson in an address to Congress outlining Fourteen Points on 8 January 1918: "We wish her [Germany] only to accept a place of equality among the peoples of the world – the new world in which we now live – instead of a place of mastery".[27] The term grew out of the thinking of Adam Weishaupt, founder of the Bavarian Order of the Illuminati in 1776, the reverse of whose seal displayed a pyramid under which was the Latin tag *Novus Ordo Seclorum* (*Seculorum*), "New Secular Order" or "New Order of the Ages". Benjamin Franklin incorporated the seal of the Illuminati as the reverse of his two-sided design for the Great Seal of the United States, which was adopted in 1782.

The pyramid and Latin tag were placed on the US one-dollar bill by Henry A. Wallace, the US Secretary of Agriculture from 1933 to 1940 who was in charge of presenting the New Deal. In 1933 or 1934 Wallace drew President Roosevelt's attention to the pyramid and tag, which he translated as "the New Deal of the Ages".[28] *Novus Ordo Seclorum* echoes a phrase of the epic poet Virgil's, adapted from lines 5-8 of the 'Fourth Eclogue', "*Magnus ab integro saeclorum nascitur ordo*", "The great order of the ages is born afresh". (Virgil, an epic poet who wrote of war, nobly longed for and dreamed of a new era of peace that would benefit humankind, just as I, who have written two epic poems about war, long for and dream of a new era of peace that will benefit humankind in this work.)

The phrase "New World Order" was taken up by Hitler who was quoted as saying during the Second World War: "National socialism will use its own revolution for the establishing of a new world order."[29] He told Hermann Rauschning, the President of the Danzig Senate: "Yes, we are barbarians. We want to be barbarians. It is an honourable title. *We* shall rejuvenate the world.

This world (or the present world) is near its end. It is our mission to sack it (or cause unrest)."[30] He saw himself as standing for a new world order.

Nelson Rockefeller called for World Federation in *The Future of Federalism* (1962), claiming that events demanded "a new world order" as the old order was crumbling. In October 1967 Richard Nixon echoed this call in *Foreign Affairs*, the Council on Foreign Relations Journal (October 1967 issue). Nixon wrote of nations' evolving regional approaches and of the evolution of a "new world order".

New York Governor Nelson Rockefeller was quoted by AP (on 26 July 1968) as pledging that "as President he would work toward international creation of a 'new world order'".

On 30 January 1976 a new "Rockefellerite" document, *The Declaration of Interdependence*, signed by 32 Senators and 92 Representatives, stated: "We must join with others to bring forth a New World Order....To establish a New World Order of compassion, peace, justice, and security, it is essential that mankind free itself from the limitations of national prejudice, and acknowledge that...all people are part of one global community".[31]

Much was made of the New World Order during the First Iraq War. On 11 September 1990, Bush Sr said, that "a New World Order can emerge" that could "shape the future for generations to come". Secretary of State James Baker said that "it would set an extremely unfortunate precedent for the New World Order" if aggression were rewarded and that "if we really believe that there's an opportunity here for a New World Order,...we can't start out by appeasing aggression". President Bush made a number of references to the New World Order in January 1991. In an interview he said on 7 January, "I think what's at stake here is the New World Order. What's at stake here is whether we can have disputes peacefully resolved in the future by a reinvigorated United Nations." On 9 January he said: "[The Gulf crisis] has to do with a New World Order. And that New World Order is only going to be enhanced if this newly activated peace-keeping function of the United Nations proves to be effective." On 16 January he said: "When we are successful, and we will be, we have a real chance at this New World Order, an Order in which a credible United Nations can use its peace-keeping role to fulfil the promise and vision of the UN's founders."

On 6 February 1991 Bush was asked by a reporter: "Can you give us a definition of a New World Order, and if it depends on the collaboration between the Soviet Union and the United States?" Bush replied: "Well, it doesn't depend entirely on it, but it would be greatly enhanced by a Soviet Union that goes down the line with its commitment to market reform, to private ownership of land, to a free economic system, to a system that resists, and does not use force to assure order amongst the republics, that goes farther down the road with elections, and all the openness that I give President Gorbachev credit for....Now, my vision of a New World Order foresees a United Nations with a revitalised peace-keeping function." It is clear that Bush envisaged the New World Order as a world democracy that would include the ex-Soviet Union.

In August 1991 he wrote: "In the Gulf we saw the United Nations playing the role dreamed of by its founders....I hope history will record that the Gulf crisis was the crucible of the New World Order."[32]

The term "New World Order" at present has two meanings: American superpowerdom after the Cold War, when the world became unipolar rather than bipolar and there was no more balance of power, just one superpower; and a conspiracy among megabillionaires' families, led by "Rothschilds" and "Rockefellers", under which their Syndicate – in its dictionary sense of "a combination of individuals or commercial firms to promote some common interest"[33] – corner all the world's natural resources including gas and oil, convey them to ports through pipelines and sell them to increase their profits in the post-arms-race world.

There is evidence that the commercial *élite*s were involved in engineering both the US invasion of Afghanistan in 2001 and the US invasion of Iraq in 2003. In both countries pipelines were involved: the Trans-Afghan pipeline and the abortive attempt to reconstruct the Kirkuk-Haifa pipeline, which has not been implemented due to the instability in Iraq. Both "Rothschilds" and "Rockefellers" professed to be aghast at George W. Bush's American-supremacist role which cut across their plans for a New World Order. "Rothschilds"' associate George Soros called Bush's pre-emptive military action "pernicious", and Senator Jay Rockefeller called for an inquiry into the poor quality of American intelligence.[34]

Elsewhere[35] I have described in some detail how Freemasonry may have reached America with the 1607 voyage to Jamestown; how Freemasonry gave the Founding Fathers the idea of federalism through Anderson's *Constitutions* (1723); and how Freemasonry came to be enmeshed in the American State, and eventually in the New World Order in this second meaning.

The Syndicate have found another way to make money: by shifting to a global currency. On 7 September 2009 the Geneva-based UN Conference on Trade and Development called for a global currency. To progress towards it, the organization wants to eliminate all national currencies and have three regional currencies, the euro for the European Union, the "amero" for a similar American Union and a new currency not yet given a name for an Asia-Pacific Union. The world would be split into three giant regions, each with its regional currency.

In the meantime, the Syndicate have made a killing out of the credit crunch. On 11 September 2008, the seventh anniversary of 9/11, there was a massive withdrawal of funds from the American banking system. Between 9 a.m. and 11 a.m. $550 billion was withdrawn, and the Treasury spent another $105 billion in propping the currency up, making a total loss of $655 billion. Then the Treasury stopped trading for the day.[36] If it had not done so, there would have been a cascade and $5.5 trillion would have haemorrhaged by close of business. The US economy would have collapsed that same evening and the world economy the next day. The Treasury, Federal Reserve and President Bush agreed that the raid should be kept secret to avoid panicking Americans.

A massive hole had to be plugged as swiftly as possible, and on 23 September 2008 Congress agreed to make available $700 billion "to buy toxic assets from many banks". European and Asian governments also had to make funds available for banks. In all, $3 trillion were transmitted from the Western (American and European) and Eastern governments to Syndicate banks, which shored up the financial system in preparation in preparation for going over to the three currencies.

Who was responsible for the withdrawal, which involved multiple central banks? One can only study the facts. Of 192 UN nations at the time, "Rothschilds" owned or controlled 187 central banks. The only central banks in the world they did not then control were those in Iran, Sudan, Cuba, Libya and North Korea. In 2001 they did not own the central banks of Afghanistan and Iraq, but following the Anglo-US invasions of those two nation-states in 2001 and 2003, they do now.[37]

There seems little doubt that the Syndicate have planned to reshape the world and reduce its population to a "sustainable" figure by encouraging local wars, spreading disease and exploiting famine so that it can control the world and loot the Earth's natural resources for the benefit of its own select band of relatively few oligarchs – not for the benefit of the many people of the world. The world crises of the early 21st century have advanced their cause. The

2007-2009 financial crisis has strengthened world calls for a World Treasury[38] (or proper World Bank), and the possibly engineered outbreak of swine flu and fear of an ensuing pandemic has strengthened calls for a World Health department.

The *élite*s have manipulated Western political life and have delivered the regional and Union structure we encountered in Model 1. The changes mixing nation-states listed on p77 may have happened anyway but have been accelerated by the *élite*s. They have operated in great secrecy and with lack of openness. All European nation-states have lost over 80 per cent – and following the ratification of the Lisbon Treaty, nearly 100 per cent – of their law-making power to the EU without their peoples having a true say. A referendum promised to the British people never happened. The methods of the Syndicate may be effective in the long run, but using secrecy, deviousness and deception to advance their ends has tarnished their work. Many feel that they have intrigued a world which will be dictatorial rather than democratic.

Is Model 6 a desirable model? No, it is insufficiently open and too controlled by *élite*s. One way to circumvent self-interested *élite*s is to give the regions more power by strengthening democracy. International politics have gone wrong, with secret bodies and self-interested *élite*s exploiting world natural resources and energy, and a reform of global governance is now pressing. A Universalist initiative is needed to refocus on the interests of humankind.

Model 7: Democratizing the UN and making Global Governance Accountable

In 1995 the Commission on Global Governance released its recommendations for the strengthening of global governance, which "does not imply world government or world federation". It has been said that the difference between "world government" and "global governance" is the difference between "rape" and "date-rape".

Global governance is founded on the belief that the world is run on "a set of core values that can unite people of all cultural, political, religious or philosophical backgrounds". These core values are: "respect for life, liberty, justice and equity, mutual respect, caring and integrity". The machinery of global governance would be a General Assembly of the People and a Forum of Civil Society. Global revenue would be raised by taxation on the global commons, especially taxes on airline tickets, ocean maritime transport, ocean fishing,

Antarctica, geostationary satellites and use of the electromagnetic spectrum.

This perspective on global governance was taken up by *The Charter for Global Democracy* (also known as Charter 99)[39], a grassroots movement with initial support from 60 countries that aimed to place democratic reform of global governance at the top of the international political agenda prior to the Special General Assembly of the UN in 2000, also known as the UN Millennium Assembly. The Charter was addressed in the form of a letter to Representatives of the Millennium Assembly. It said:

"There have been well-meaning and sometimes eloquent calls for world government; calls which pointed to the unfairness, inequality and injustice of the present distributions of wealth, power and policy-making – which mean that today one in five of us lives in absolute poverty; calls which emphasised the dangers to peace and even to human survival. If only we could work as one world, then we could solve the world's problems together....But during the 1990s, demands for international government have taken on a new energy and precision."

Initiatives in the 1990s included: the Commission on Global Governance to draw up a framework for global politics; the Earth Summit in Rio, Agenda 21, The Earth Charter, the Real World Coalition, Earth Action's Call for a Safer World, the One Planet Initiative, Citizens' Public Trust Treaty, Global Coalition World Democracy 2010, which aimed to bring in global democracy and sustainable development; the Hague Agenda for Peace which sought to replace the causes of war with a culture of peace; the campaign against landmines, which changed international law; international conferences at New York, Vienna, Cairo, Copenhagen, Beijing and Istanbul on gender, family and social rights; the Inter-Parliamentary Union's 1997 Universal Declaration on Democracy, which has been endorsed by most parliaments in the world; Jubilee 2000, which sought to cancel the poorest countries' unpayable debts; the International Commission on Rights and Responsibilities, which attempted to codify human duties and responsibilities; the International Criminal Court, which was created at Rome in 1998 to reinforce international criminal law; and the Human Development Report, 1999, which called for more democratic global governance.

The Charter continued: "In addition, a growing scholarly literature on all aspects of globalization has begun to explore how governments can regulate and democratize international affairs. There are now detailed, practical measures which set out an ambitious agenda for democracy in international decision-making, now increasingly known as 'global governance'. We believe that there is a profound and important reason for this historic shift. It is that in many ways we now have world government.

"It is not to be found at the United Nations. Rather, the UN has been sidelined, while the real business of world government is done elsewhere. Global policies are discussed and decided behind closed doors by exclusive groups, such as the G8, OECD, the Bank for International Settlements, the World Bank, the International Monetary Fund, the World Trade Organization and others. These agencies are reinforced by informal networks of high officials and powerful alliances. Together they have created what can be seen as dominant and exclusive institutions of world government. All too often they are influenced by transnational corporations which pursue their own world strategies.

"These agencies of actual world government must be made accountable. If there are to be global policies, let them be answerable to the peoples of the world.

"We call on you, therefore, to start the new century by initiating the process of democratic global governance following three fundamental principles: openness and accountability; environmental sustainability; and equality and justice."

The Charter goes on: "The first aim is to make the already existing processes of world administration and governance accountable. We want to know what decisions are being taken and why. We want the decision-takers to know they are answerable to the public in every country which feels the breath of international bodies. Then we want all decisions to be compatible with public criteria of environmental sustainability.

"Finally, if most ambitiously, we want them to be compatible with the principles of equality, human rights and justice, including social and economic justice.

"What we want from the Millennium Assembly and Member States is decisive action to put these principles into practice. We do not think they will be easy to achieve. We do not have all the answers. But we believe the difficulties can and must be overcome. In our era everyone is linked through our shared environment, trade and communications. We live together as neighbours, and as neighbours we must respect the rights of all persons to address common problems. A joint effort of learning and negotiation, of trial and error, will be needed.

"Many vital issues can best be tackled effectively at a global level, such as the environment, biodiversity and climate change; international security and disarmament; international trade, finance and labour fights; epidemics; communications; and international crime.

"The first question is where should we start? We believe that the answer has to be at the United Nations. The inadequacy of the UN is well known. All around we see the principles of the UN subverted, sidelined and suppressed. Since the UN Charter was signed, more than 30 million people have been killed in war, most of then unarmed civilians; millions more people have been slaughtered in genocide and ethnic conflict; over 100 million people have fled their homes due to conflict or persecution, with over 20 million remaining as refugees today; Permanent Members of the Security Council have armed belligerents and engaged in war; governments have invested more in preparing for war than in strengthening peace; human rights have been violated with little redress.

"Nevertheless the United Nations as an institution can hardly be blamed for the appalling behaviour of its member states. Without the UN, wars would have been even more frequent; they would have gone on longer; there would have been a greater number of victims, and many more refugees living without hope. The UN is the only arena in which all countries sit side by side. For all its weakness, it retains an unmatched legitimacy in world affairs.

"The UN's founding Charter mandates you to achieve international co-operation in solving international problems of an economic, social, cultural or humanitarian character and to be a centre for harmonising the actions of nations (Article 1).

"We therefore call on you to create effective mechanisms to hold every agency of actual world government to account. These include international economic alliances, military alliances, the central banking system and agencies for environmental, financial, social, sporting or other activity. All should have to answer regularly for what they have done and intend to do, for their impact on the world community and for their adherence to the UN Charter and international law. We want action to start the process now.

"The creation of democratic global governance may be complicated. But the need for it is simple and urgent. Global problems will only get worse if international decision-making is left in the hands of the present undemocratic, exclusive institutions. Therefore we will continue to press for action and public support around the world.

"World-wide campaigns have led to the end of *apartheid* in South Africa, to the Statute for an International Criminal Court, to the ban on landmines and some debt-reduction for the world's poorest countries. The time has come to make democratic reform of international affairs our priority, both as an end in itself and as a means of solving many serious social and economic problems. Many reforms are needed."

The Charter then becomes more specific: "The following 12 points are a summary of the many demands and proposals being made across the world for better international governance. As an urgent first step we call on you to set in motion a rigorous process to hold all agencies of global governance to account and democratize international decision-making according to the principles set out in this letter.

"*Strengthen democratic accountability and participation in international decision-making:*

1. Give the UN General Assembly powers to scrutinize the work of UN agencies and other agencies of global governance; create a UN Parliamentary Assembly and an annual Forum of Civil Society; open international institutions to increased participation by civil society and elected representatives from member countries; bring the WTO (World Trade Organization) into the UN system and strengthen the co-operation between all international groupings under the UN system.
2. Create within the UN system an accountable, equitable and effective mechanism to monitor, supervise and regulate transnational corporations and financial institutions; and require transnational companies to adhere to an international code of conduct covering agreed principles concerning human rights, the environment and core labour standards.
3. Give UN institutions an additional and independent source of revenue such as taxation of foreign exchange transactions, aircraft and shipping fuels, arms sales and licensing use of the global commons.

Maintain international peace and security:

4. Reform the UN Security Council to open all decision-making to public scrutiny; phase out the single-country veto and Permanent Membership; establish equitable representation from each region of the world; set up a high-level early-warning system; and provide effective authority to mediate and intervene in disputes at an early stage, within national boundaries where necessary.

5. Establish a permanent, directly recruited UN Rapid Reaction Force to hold the peace in a crisis, police gross violations of human rights and support multilateral defence against aggression and genocide.
6. Make the UN register of arms mandatory; ratify and implement the Landmine Ban Treaty; outlaw all weapons of mass destruction; initiate programs to control the arms trade, convert the arms industry to peaceful production and cut military spending world wide; strengthen accountability to the UN of all international military action; and reduce the size of national armies as part of a multilateral global security system.

Uphold fundamental human rights:

7. Strengthen world citizenship based on compliance with and respect for the Universal Declaration of Human Rights and all international instruments on Human Rights, including the six core treaties on economic, social and cultural rights; civil and political rights; racial discrimination; discrimination against women, children's rights, torture, and the Conventions on genocide, refugees and labour standards.

Strengthen justice under international law:

8. Ratify the Statute of the International Criminal Court; accept compulsory jurisdiction of the International Court of Justice, the International Criminal Court and the UN Human Rights Committee; increase the Courts' powers of enforcement; open the ICJ to individual petition and protect the judicial independence of the ICC.

Promote social progress and better standards of life:

9. Establish a strong UN institution for Economic and Environmental security to promote international prosperity, protect the global commons and secure reasonable development.
10. Establish an International Environmental Court to enforce international treaties on the environment and protect the global commons.
11. Declare climate change to be an essential global security interest and establish a high-level international urgent action team to assist the UN Conference of the Parties on Climate Change to set up a scientifically based global ceiling on greenhouse gas emission, to allocate national shares of permissible emissions based on convergence to equal *per capita* rights, and to work with governments, companies, international agencies and NGOs (non-governmental organizations) to cut

emissions of greenhouse gases to a sustainable level.

12. Make poverty reduction a global priority: secure universal access to safe drinking-water, health care, housing, education, family planning, gender equality, sustainable development and economic opportunities, and strengthen the capacity of development agencies to eliminate malnutrition, preventable diseases and absolute poverty through conservation and equitable sharing of global resources. Cancel the unpayable debts of the poorest nations and institute measures to prevent severe debt burdens from ever building up again."

The Charter proposes a directly elected UN. We have already seen that the UN has weaknesses. The world is run by megabillionaires and power-brokers, allegedly in the interests of economic growth and progress. The borderless Earth seen by astronauts has no elected law-makers, no compulsory judging or mediation, no enforceable revenue source, and no penal, rehabilitating or incentive system other than superpower-sponsored trade bans (sanctions) or war. Article 2 and other Articles of the UN Charter allow sovereign nations to use force if they claim it is for self-defence. The UN spends less than a cent for each dollar (one per cent) spent on war industries. A directly-elected UN has been long overdue. If *The Charter for Global Democracy* were implemented, the UN General Assembly would become the "UN Parliamentary Assembly".

The Charter for Global Democracy calls not just for the democratizing of the UN, but also for the accountability and openness of all the institutions of global governance: the G8, OECD, the Bank for International Settlements, the World Bank, the International Monetary Fund and the World Trade Organization and all the agencies of the UN. By implication, it would include the institutions of the New World Order that I have dealt with earlier in this chapter, which have been so surrounded by secrecy and deception.

So does Model 7 remove the right to violence of nation-states? It has to be said that it does not. Democratizing the UN is a step forward, but directly elected representatives of nation-states in a UN Parliamentary Assembly operating the existing UN Charter can still go to war too readily, and making the G8, the trade and banking organizations and institutions of the New World Order accountable will not by itself remove their secrecy, if they are minded to continue to act by stealth. Under Model 7 there is no supranational authority except directly elected public opinion. We encountered electing a UN General

Assembly in Models 4 and 5.

Does Model 7 guarantee perpetual peace? No, for apart from direct elections and scrutiny the *status quo* is preserved.

Philosophical Summary

What can a Universalist proposing a World State take from our look at global governance?

The New World Order would subsume nation-states. *Élite*s, the most prominent of whom are "Rothschilds" and "Rockefellers", run the world through exclusive groups (the Bilderberg Group, Trilateral Commission). The *élite*s are secretive and lack openness. Population reduction. The New World Order as American superpowerdom, and as a conspiracy by *élite*s to corner and then sell the world's natural resources. The Syndicate's common purpose. A global currency, via three union currencies. Moves to a World Treasury and World Health authority via a possibly contrived credit crunch and massive withdrawal, and a pandemic. The Syndicate plan to reshape the world by reducing its population through local wars, disease and famine. The *élite*s have manipulated Western political life.

Global governance is founded on core values. A General Assembly of the People. Global revenue from taxation. Earth Charter, One-Planet initiatives. Democratizing the exclusive groups. Openness and accountability. Reforming the United Nations so the General Assembly scrutinizes UN agencies and other agencies, and creates a Parliamentary Assembly. Make the UN system accountable, give it Revenue. Scrutinize the Security Council. A UN Rapid Reaction Force. Register arms. A Universal Declaration of Human Rights. Promote prosperity. Enforce treaties. Poverty reduction. A directly elected UN. A borderless Earth.

To sum up, the philosopher devising a World State can distil from global governance:

the New World Order subsumes nation-states;
*élite*s run the world through exclusive groups;
the *élite*s are secretive and lack openness;
population reduction;
the New World Order as American superpowerdom;
the New World Order as a conspiracy by *élite*s to sell the world's natural resources;

the Syndicate's common purpose;
a global currency, via three union currencies;
moves to a World Treasury and World Health authority;
the Syndicate reshape the world by reducing the world's population through local wars, disease and famine;
the *élite*s have manipulated Western political life;
global governance is founded on core values;
another General Assembly of the People;
global revenue from taxation;
Earth Charter, One Planet;
democratizing the exclusive groups, more openness and accountability;
reforming the UN so the General Assembly scrutinizes UN agencies and exclusive groups and creates a Parliamentary Assembly;
making the UN system accountable, giving it revenue;
scrutinizing the Security Council;
a UN Rapid Reaction Force;
registering arms;
a Universal Declaration of Human Rights;
promoting prosperity;
enforcing treaties;
poverty reduction;
a directly elected UN;
a borderless Earth.

We have looked at global governance in our time, and have concluded that democratizing the UN and making global governance accountable, while steps in the right direction, are simply not enough. The UN would remain an essentially inter-national body attempting to fulfil a supranational role. A more radical approach needs to be adopted. There must a supranational authority with the legal clout to enforce peace and disarmament. It is now time to construct my blueprint for a World State.

PART THREE

THE STATECRAFT OF WORLD GOVERNMENT: A BLUEPRINT FOR A WORLD STATE

7

The Ideal Form of World State

In Part Two we have been looking at eight models for a world government, none of which have measured up to a supranational authority capable of preventing war by enforceable means and of maintaining world peace. On pp73-74 I established a World State's goals: (1) peace between nation-states and disarmament; (2) sharing natural resources among, and solving energy supply to, all humankind; (3) solving environmental problems such as global warming; (4) ending disease; (5) ending famine; (6) solving the financial crisis; (7) redistributing wealth to eliminate poverty. Of these we have been particularly concerned with bringing peace between nation-states.

Tinkering with the *status quo*, reforming the UN and pursuing existing models of global governance with loose associations of nation-states and federal regional Unions are all, for various reasons, unsatisfactory. They do not abolish war, they leave nation-states in charge of war, and where organs of global governance have evolved they have a disturbing lack of openness and incline to downright deception.

I can eliminate all eight models, which means we are left with a more radical alternative: to go a little further towards supranationalism than the eight models, but not so far towards it that the nation-state system is completely abolished for a fundamentally new system; and to devise a supranational authority with as little surrender of sovereignty on the part of nation-states as possible. I need to employ statecraft, "the art of conducting the offices of state" (*Concise Oxford Dictionary*) – by devising a completely new World State. I need to draw on what statecraft I can muster to offer a blueprint for a World State that will achieve the goals I have set.

Having summarised all the points we have gleaned at the end of each chapter, I can now review them. They represent the sum total of the wisdom of the past regarding the dream of world government. I can then incorporate the key points into my own model for the future. For convenience I reproduce the six Philosophical Summaries of the essential facts so far:

1\.

government progresses from tribe to complex organization;

government progresses from small locality to more global extent;
splinter groups resist global government;
progression towards a World State is inevitable (Wendt);
Hitler's world-government organization in Nuremberg;
the quality of a world government depends on its incumbents.

2.
cosmic unity should be reflected in a oneness of humankind;
a universal monarch can bring peace;
international law to make peace;
forming a federation of states by social contract;
morally perfect states will not happen;
a universal republic gives more security than a monarchy;
there should be a federation of free states;
a universal republic should replace sovereign states;
a federation of all humanity;
the atomic bomb has increased the urgency for permanent peace;
movements of world federalists want a world government;
federal regions like the EU are a step towards world government;
many world leaders have called for a world government.

3.
history is teleological and approaches its goal, an end-point which will last for a while and not forever;
the purpose of history is to achieve a World State that enshrines freedom for a while;
history progresses towards liberal democracy, the institutionalization of freedom;
humankind evolves to egalitarian unity in a World State;
during their evolution to unity, human beings live within rising and falling civilizations;
all civilizations flow into, or beneath the influence of, a world-wide civilization for a while;
the system under which humankind has been living is outmoded and collapsing;
capitalism has been weakened by the financial crisis;
socialism has been weakened by the fall of Communism;

we live under a mixture of watered-down capitalism and socialism;
totalitarianism is finished;
the nation-state subdivides and segregates humankind and has been weakened by interdependence and regional administration;
nationalism (fidelity to the nation-state) has been weakened;
colonialism (running territories in empires) is defunct;
self-determination has weakened;
internationalism (co-operation between nation-states for the prevention of war) has weakened before the defiance of outmoded states and needs to be replaced;
collective security has weakened as it is based on weakened nation-states;
superpowerdom (the dominance of one nation-state) belongs to the old order;
organized religions segregate parts of humankind;
there should be a Universalist religion;
a Copernican perspective of a World State is ahead, and will replace the Ptolemaic conception of the nation-state.

4.
binding arbitration of a council or assembly of delegates;
perpetual alliance of states to establish a congress that will arbitrate disputes and enforce decisions by armed action;
goals of peace, sharing natural resources and energy, solving environmental problems, disease, famine and financial crisis,
redistributing wealth;
eight models for a supranational authority;
spreading a world community is gradualist and too *status-quo*;
sticking with the UN and strengthening great-power agreement has failed to prevent wars;
a World Constitutional Convention is a method for arriving at a World State, so long as nation-states can be induced to agree to it.

5.
revising the UN Charter preserves the *status quo* except for going to war;
world law must be enforceable;
judicial tribunals to enforce the law;
a permanent world police force;

complete disarmament of all nations;
evening up disparities between regions;
humankind's common natural resources should be managed, including outer space and oceans;
all nation-states and individuals should participate in world law;
nations' rights and duties should be in a revised Charter/Treaty;
nations retain their powers except for the right to go to war;
the General Assembly should be elected;
the Security Council should be replaced by a veto-less Executive Council;
the Economic and Social Council should continue;
there should be a six-year disarmament process;
there should be a UN revenue system;
as an alternative there could be a World Disarmament and Development Organization, which would exist alongside the UN.

6.
the New World Order subsumes nation-states;
*élite*s run the world through exclusive groups;
the *élite*s are secretive and lack openness;
population reduction;
the New World Order as American superpowerdom;
the New World Order as a conspiracy by *élite*s to sell the world's natural resources;
the Syndicate's common purpose;
a global currency, via three union currencies;
moves to a World Treasury and World Health authority;
the Syndicate reshape the world by reducing the world's population through local wars, disease and famine;
the *élite*s have manipulated Western political life;
global governance is founded on core values;
another General Assembly of the People;
global revenue from taxation;
Earth Charter, One Planet;
democratizing the exclusive groups, more openness and accountability;
reforming the UN so the General Assembly scrutinizes UN agencies and exclusive groups and creates a Parliamentary Assembly;
making the UN system accountable, giving it revenue;

scrutinizing the Security Council;
a UN Rapid Reaction Force;
registering arms;
a Universal Declaration of Human Rights;
promoting prosperity;
enforcing treaties;
poverty reduction;
a directly elected UN;
a borderless Earth.

These points can be considered as I make my statement of the ideal model of the World State, and our consideration will then draw on the collective wisdom of the past.

The ideal form of World State is one that delivers the seven goals I have listed on pp73-74. We are seeking a model for the most desirable kind of supranational authority, i.e. the one that can best achieve the seven goals. We have considered loose and more tightly centralised federal models – federal models like the EU – and have concluded that a more radically different model is best suited to achieving these goals. The federal arrangements for regional government are an intermediate stage to a more radical model.

Bearing this in mind, I can now select the more radical points from our six lists. These are:

progression towards a World State is inevitable (Wendt);
the quality of a world government depends on its incumbents;
international law to make peace;
forming a federation of states by social contract;
a universal republic should replace sovereign states;
a federation of all humanity;
movements of world federalists want a world government;
the purpose of history is to achieve a World State that enshrines freedom for a while;
during their evolution to unity, human beings live within rising and falling civilizations;
all civilizations flow into, or beneath the influence of, a world-wide civilization for a while;
the system under which humankind has been living is outmoded and

collapsing;
the nation-state subdivides and segregates humankind and has been weakened by interdependence and regional administration;
superpowerdom (the dominance of one nation-state) belongs to the old order;
world law must be enforceable;
a permanent world police force;
complete disarmament of all nations;
evening up disparities between regions;
humankind's common natural resources should be managed, including outer space and oceans;
all nation-states and individuals should participate in world law;
the General Assembly should be elected;
the Security Council should be replaced by a veto-less Executive Council;
there should be a six-year disarmament process;
binding arbitration of a council or assembly of delegates;
perpetual alliance of states to establish a congress that will arbitrate disputes and enforce decisions by armed action;
goals of peace, sharing natural resources, solving environmental problems, disease, famine and financial crisis, redistributing wealth;
a World Constitutional Convention is a method for arriving at a World State, so long as nation-states can be induced to agree to it;
the *élite*s are secretive and lack openness;
the New World Order as a conspiracy by *élite*s to sell the world's natural resources;
a global currency, via three union currencies;
moves to a World Treasury and World Health;
global governance is founded on core values;
another General Assembly of the People;
global revenue from taxation;
democratizing the exclusive groups, more openness and accountability;
reforming the UN so the General Assembly scrutinizes UN agencies and exclusive groups and creates a Parliamentary Assembly;
scrutinizing the Security Council;
a UN Rapid Reaction Force;
registering arms;
a Universal Declaration of Human Rights;

promoting prosperity;
enforcing treaties;
poverty reduction;
a directly elected UN;
a borderless Earth.

So what can I distil from this collective wisdom of the past regarding the creation of a World State?

Model 8: A World Commission, World Parliamentary Assembly, World Senate, World Judicial Tribunals, World Armed Force, World Council of Ministers, World President, World Leaders' Guidance Council, World Bank and World Court of Justice, all above the UN

I have said (on p122) that I am devising a supranational authority with as little surrender or sovereignty on the part of nation-states as possible. I want to be clear on what I am not distilling or proposing. I am not proposing:

- A United States of the World as a reflection of the United States of America, in which a federal world government is in charge and all nation-states, perhaps grouped into 50 regions, are reclassified as states, like the states of the US. The nation-state may be in decline and of the old order, but this would be a drastic change, in which everything would be fundamentally new, both at the federal level and at the local/regional level. Such a system could not be brought in abruptly without unsettling all the world's citizens. Such a United States of the World would not involve "as little surrender of sovereignty on the part of nation-states as possible". It is more extreme – more a "fundamentally new system" – than the model I have set out to propose.
- A United States of the World in the sense of Lenin's phrase in his writings,[1] a "dictatorship of the proletariat" with all nation-states grouped into regions as "Soviets" (Lenin's totalitarian conception). Following the fall of the Berlin Wall, Communism has died in the West, and although it lingers on in the East in China and in the nation-states surrounding it, to group regions into Soviets would be both anachronistic and undesirable. This concept is no longer an option.
- The New World Order of the Syndicate in which the regions and Unions

of global governance – the 13 listed on p161 – would be linked, and their leaders would control the world's natural resources on behalf of the Syndicate, who would only allow a veneer of democracy to co-exist with its multinational corporations. I rejected this as undesirable when I considered model 6.

So, in our distilling of the six lists I am steering clear of the above impractical (or impracticable) or unsuitable possibilities.

The model of a supranational authority I am proposing and recommending should have a *partial* federal level that can be effective in a limited way in implementing the seven goals I listed on pp73-74, including the enforcing of peace and disarmament by international law; while preserving the local/regional level in all other respects, so world citizens can experience continuity despite the structural change.

Focusing on key points I can summarise the six lists in the following 17 points, which offer a model of a supranational authority and World State that achieves the seven goals. I should point out that in contrast the 17 features of the revision of the UN Charter on pp94-96 focused on nation-states. All of the following 17 points are taken from the six lists and our previous investigation, and I have added some embellishment:

(1) A supranational authority above the UN should form a partial federation of all humankind, a partial federal association of all nation-states. This would be set up by a World Constitutional Convention on a US initiative that would be supported by the UN.

(2) The authority would be given power to use international law to make peace and create a borderless Earth.

(3) The authority would form a world government that would enforce peace and complete disarmament, which would be achieved in a phased process over a period of time. Its remit would be to focus on the seven goals. At the supranational level it would consist of an administration or World Commission that would propose laws (like the EU Commission); a directly elected World Parliamentary Assembly (a General Assembly of the People) operating within the UN as a lower house (like the House of Representatives) and a World Senate operating at a supranational level as an upper house, that would together pass the laws; and a World Armed Force (or Rapid Reaction

Force) of 200,000-400,000 and a reserve of 300,000-600,000, that would enforce laws. A World Leaders' Guidance Council of elders would give guidance, and a World Court of Justice would arbitrate on disputes and enforce supranational law.

(4) At the inter-national level the UN General Assembly would be turned into a World Parliamentary Assembly (or General Assembly of the People) that would be largely chosen on the basis of population percentages. The four largest countries – China, India, the EU (following ratification of the Lisbon Treaty and excluding the UK and France, both Permanent Members of the UN Security Council), and the US (which will eventually be grouped with Canada and Mexico as North America) – should each have 30 members; the three Permanent Members of the UN Security Council not included in these four (the Russian Federation, the UK and France) should each have 15 members; the 10 largest countries in the world after the four largest 12, the 15 next largest 8, the 20 next largest 6, the 30 next largest 4, the 40 next largest 3; the 49 smallest nations 1. Two seats would be allocated to Puerto Rico and Palestine, the non-UN-member states with the largest populations, which would have associate status until they become independent. There would be a total of 816 representatives (with the prospect of 850 when all dependent and disputed territories become independent and are allowed 1 member in their own right). All these members would be directly elected, from 192 UN member nations and (when they become independent) non-UN-member dependent and disputed territories.

At the supranational level the World Senate would be chosen on a regional basis. The largest and most populated continents and nation-states would be zoned (north, south, east, west). There would be 46 electoral zones or constituencies in all, each of which would elect two senators. As in the American system, both the lower house and the Senate would pass the laws, and the smaller membership of the Senate would permit more extended debate than could be expected in the Assembly. There would be less party control in the Senate. (See ch. 8 for details.)

Universal democracy would be implemented in the directly-elected World Parliamentary Assembly when it has replaced the UN General Assembly, and in the upper-house directly-elected World Senate.

(5) The weakened nation-state system would continue, and would continue to use the UN in the same way as at present. The UN would refer intractable conflicts up to the new authority, the World Commission, and a supranational Universal Declaration of Human Rights would be passed by the World Parliamentary Assembly and World Senate to protect the perpetuation of the freedom of all individuals at the supranational level.

(6) The directly-elected UN General Assembly would be phased in. The Security Council would become a vetoless Executive Council of 17. Five representatives would represent each of the Permanent Members, 5 of the next 10 largest nation-states would have rotational representation (so that all 10 are represented, but only 5 at any one time), and the other 8 would be chosen by the World Parliamentary Assembly from representatives of other nation-states. The activities of the Executive Council would be scrutinized by directly elected UN Assembly members.

(7) The authority's world laws would be enforceable by World Judicial Tribunals, which would be under the World Court of Justice, following investigation by a civil police force of 10,000 working for the World Commission.

(8) The authority would carry out work to achieve all its goals: besides bringing peace and complete disarmament, it would begin a phased redistribution of humankind's natural resources and energy supply to even up the disparities between regions, work to ease environmental problems such as global warming and manage common natural resources including outer space and oceans; end disease and famine; and solve the world's financial crisis. A minimum standard of living would be guaranteed to all humankind on a phased basis, and a World Development Authority would grant interest-free loans to assist the economic and social development of under-developed areas.

(9) The authority would be funded by phased taxation from all nation-states and would be accountable.

(10) All nation-states and individuals should participate in, and be bound by, the world law of the authority set up by a World Constitutional Convention at US and UN instigation.

(11) The laws proposed by the World Commission and passed by the World Parliamentary Assembly and World Senate would be binding, and the

arbitration of disputes and enforcement carried out by World Judicial Tribunals would be supported by armed action carried out by the World Armed Force (or Rapid Reaction Force).

(12) Nation-states represented at the UN General Assembly before its transformation into the World Parliamentary Assembly should be persuaded to agree to a World Constitutional Convention on a five-sixths' vote: five-sixths of the world's nations, including the four largest countries listed in (4), the three Permanent Members of the UN Security Council separate from the four listed in (4) (the Russian Federation, the UK and France), and at least six of the ten next largest countries in the world, the aggregate of the populations of the voting nations equalling at least five-sixths of the total world population.

(13) To ratify the authority once the World Constitutional Convention has set it up, the UN General Assembly should vote by five-sixths of the world's nations on the same basis as (12). above. Further amendments should be by four-fifths of the directly elected World Parliamentary Assembly and two-thirds of the World Senate.

(14) The secretive *élite*s should be democratized; some delegates to the Bilderberg Group and Trilateral Commission meetings, and to those of other agencies, should be directly elected and these two *élite* organizations should submit their agendas and decisions to a World Openness Committee.

(15) There would be no population reduction by devious means (contrived wars, diseases and famines). The authority would conduct a phased redistribution of the Earth's natural resources and energy supply so that they are spread among all humankind.

(16) There should be a World Council of Ministers drawn from the directly elected World Parliamentary Assembly. These Ministers, working under the chairmanship of their World President, or World-Lord, who should be directly elected like the US president, should undertake the government of the world government's departments. The organs of global governance should be restructured to be under the control of the authority. There should be a World Treasury with one global currency, and a World Health department under the World Council.

(17) Life within the weakened nation-states would continue, and the UN would be an intermediary body charged with resolving conflicts. Initially the supranational authority would share the UN buildings one

day, and later two days, a week and an appropriate number of UN administrative staff would be seconded to a supranational level to get the new authority up and running. It is anticipated that the volume of the work of the UN, an association of nation-states, would be reduced once the supranational authority was established and more and more UN administrative personnel were seconded to fill supranational positions. The UN would refer upwards to the World Commission all disputes it could not resolve by peaceful discussion in the World Parliamentary Assembly, and the upper tier of world government, consisting of the World Commission, the World Senate, World Judicial Tribunals, the World Armed Force, the World Council of Ministers and their World President or World-Lord, would come into force and enforce peace and complete disarmament.

I have taken the jumbled jigsaw pieces on the list, each of which bears a fragment of the whole, and have rearranged them to show an ordered picture which I have embellished here and there. One piece that was missing from the six lists was the World Openness Committee, which I have introduced to complete the picture. I have also introduced the context, that the authority would be above the UN.

Before we look at the 17-point supranational authority in greater detail, a few general observations are in order. For a start, it must be conceded that although President Obama, leader of the sole superpower since 1989, has said that the world has ceased to be unipolar and has become multipolar with potentially several centres of power including China and India, the United States is still so powerful (and recently quasi-imperial) that the supranational authority could not come into being without American instigation. The authority can therefore be seen as the expression of a stage of the North-American civilization, which I have shown elsewhere[2] to be in stage 15 out of 61 stages, the stage the Roman civilization was in during the rise of the Roman Empire. Although the post-Obama US does not claim to be imperialistic it would in fact be behind such a supranational authority and World State.

Secondly, the membership of the World Parliamentary Assembly cannot be based solely on population percentages. Otherwise, the nuclear Russian Federation which at the time of writing has 12,987 nuclear warheads would have less membership than non-nuclear Indonesia, which has replaced it in the top four most-populated nations following the break-up of the USSR. However,

Indonesia slides down to fifth when the EU is included as one nation-state following the ratification of the Lisbon Treaty. (See pp138 and 245.) Permanent Membership of the existing UN Security Council must be taken into account in the voting described under (4), and in establishing the basis of the membership of the World Commission. For complete disarmament is the new authority's priority, and all nuclear powers must be represented at the highest level so that they fully participate in nuclear disarmament.

The importance of the UN General Assembly votes referred to in (12) and (13) demands that a five-sixths majority should include the four largest countries (China, India, the EU and US) and the three Permanent Members of the UN Security Council not among these, whose status as original nuclear powers should continue to be recognised. Those nation-states with nuclear weapons must be heavily involved in setting up a World Constitutional Convention and ratifying it so that they disarm themselves.

For the basis of membership of the World Commission and World Senate, see ch. 8.

Thirdly, the cost of a world government might seem to be prohibitive in the short and medium terms. The American economy is in debt with financial problems. The dollar has not been strong during the financial crisis, and the Chinese have proposed that the international currency should be BIS (Bank for International Settlements) credits. It has, however, been suggested that China could go bust. There are massive economic and social divisions between world citizens. Like America, Europe has no savings and is in debt. Some ex-Soviet nation-states had little or no pension provision, and were offered financial inducements to join the EU. These have been paid for by Germany, France and the UK. A quarter of the Indian population do not have electricity and therefore do not use light bulbs. There is a similar imbalance in China. Money has to be pumped into India and China to improve standards of living. All world citizens cannot be brought up to a minimum standard of living in one go. The process can be started in principle, and can only be phased. It may take decades before parity in the standard of living of world citizens is achieved.

In view of the financial crisis the world government should be established within the UN in an interim capacity, and staffed by UN personnel who would be seconded to the supranational authority. Initially, therefore, setting-up costs of the new authority would be kept to a minimum.

Without financial inducements many leaders of sovereign nation-states may not agree to vote for the UN to set up a World Constitutional Convention to establish a federal World State without financial inducements. How can such inducements be afforded in the early-21st-century's financial climate?

There may have to be a massive devaluation, whereby a new global currency is created, a new Earth dollar that is worth, say, 10 old dollars, a move linked to "quantitative easing" (or printing money) that at a stroke would write off nine-tenths of the previous global debt. This would mean that the entire foreign currency market would vanish overnight. The average daily turnover in global foreign exchange markets is estimated at £3.98 trillion[3] (against a daily stock-market turnover of about $100 billion). A new global currency would therefore involve a massive loss of business in the financial sector. I am not suggesting that this is a good way of proceeding. I am merely pointing out how the system of global governance could escape from the legacy of debt if such a scheme were applied to the whole world on the same day, and start afresh.

Finally, the supranational authority would be Universalist. It would embody a form of political Universalism. The aim of political Universalism is to construct a World State, a federal association of all nation-states under a supranational world government. This is what Model 8 would achieve.

Would Model 8 achieve the goals a supranational authority would need to achieve in order to solve the old order's problems, the goals listed on pp73-74 and 122 including bringing peace between nation-states and complete disarmament? Yes, it would. Model 8 escapes the difficulties associated with all the other models, which were too *status-quo* and insufficiently radical, and its regime of international law does offer the prospect of world peace. Let us see in greater detail how.

Philosophical Summary

But first, a brief reminder of the proposed partial supranational authority:

it is not a United States of the World on the lines of the USA;
it is not Lenin's United States of the World;
it is not the New World Order's federal Union;
17 points on the World Parliamentary Assembly, World Commission, World Senate and other supranational institutions;
sharing the UN in the short term to cut costs.

These are the points I will now amplify.

8

The Structure of the New World State

I now come to the structure of the 17-point supranational authority, a concept that we saw (on pp15-16) Wendt urged. The actual structure of a World State will of course be determined by the World Constitutional Convention.

The proposals which I shall now set out really amount to one model for such a structure, a model that the World Constitutional Convention can either implement or vary depending on the thinking of the experts on the Convention. In making these proposals I am pointing a way forward, proposing a direction. It will be for the rank and file of Convention members to consider my proposal, flesh out the details and come up with the best-possible structure that will achieve the seven goals listed on pp73-74 and 122.

It is best to begin with an overview, with the diagram/flow chart on p143. This shows three different levels. The existing levels, the national and inter-national levels, are the levels of nation-states and of the UN, which is an association of nation-states. The supranational level is a level above nation-states and the UN.

I shall start with the existing inter-national level.

The Inter-national Level

International affairs are at present conducted by the UN General Assembly and Security Council, and a number of inter-national agencies which are offshoots from the General Assembly.

World Parliamentary Assembly

I have said that the UN General Assembly should become a lower house, the directly-elected World Parliamentary Assembly which would be involved in passing supranational laws proposed by the World Authority. The Assembly should be chosen on the basis of an initial allocation of 816 seats, along criteria stated by Clark and Sohn in *World Peace Through World Law* and modified to take account of, and adjust for, nuclear influence and Permanent Membership of the Security Council, as proposed in (4) on p130.

I can now set out the structure of the representation on the World Parliamentary Assembly. The mathematics looks like this:

Countries		Members		Seats
4	x	30	=	120
3	x	15	=	45
10	x	10	=	120
15	x	8	=	120
20	x	6	=	120
30	x	4	=	120
40	x	3	=	120
49	x	1	=	49
+2	x	1	=	2
				Initial total 816

In future

+26	x	1	=	26
+8	x	1	=	8
				Eventual total 850

I can now flesh out these figures, using the UN-sourced world population percentages in the Appendix. (See pp245-255.) These are based on 1 July 2009 estimates by the UN Department of Economic and Social Affairs – Population Division.[1] The alphabetical letter at the beginning of each line below corresponds to the alphabetical letters against the relevant countries in the Appendix. The "largest" and "next-largest" countries mean "most populated". The representation in the World Parliamentary Assembly, on the basis of the 2009 criteria, looks as follows:

Letter on pp245-255	Countries	No. each	Seats
A.	The 4 largest countries: China, India, the EU (on the basis of 27 members including Bulgaria and Romania, excluding the UK and France, see B), the US.	30 each	120
B.	3 Permanent Members of the Security Council: the Russian Federation, the UK, France.	15 each	45

C.	The 10 largest countries after the 4: Indonesia, Brazil, Pakistan, Bangladesh, Nigeria, Japan, Mexico, Philippines, Vietnam, Ethiopia.	12 each	120
D.	The 15 next-largest countries: Egypt, Iran, Turkey, Democratic Republic of Congo, Thailand, Myanmar (Burma), South Africa, South Korea, Ukraine, Colombia, Tanzania, Argentina, Kenya, Sudan, Algeria.	8 each	120
E.	The 20 next-largest countries: Canada, Uganda, Morocco, Iraq, Nepal, Peru, Venezuela, Malaysia, Afghanistan, Uzbekistan, Saudi Arabia, North Korea, Ghana, Yemen, Taiwan, Mozambique, Australia, Syria, Côte d'Ivoire, Sri Lanka.	6 each	120
F.	The 30 next-largest countries: Madagascar, Cameroon, Angola, Chile, Kazakhstan, Burkina Faso (formerly the Republic of Upper Volta), Niger, Malawi, Cambodia, Ecuador, Guatemala, Mali, Zambia, Senegal, Zimbabwe, Chad, Cuba, Tunisia, Dominican Republic, Guinea, Haiti, Rwanda, Bolivia, Serbia, Belarus, Somalia, Benin, Azerbaijan, Burundi, Switzerland.	4 each	120
G.	The 40 next-largest countries: Honduras, Israel, Tajikistan, Papua New Guinea, Togo, Libya, Paraguay, Laos, Jordan, El Salvador, Nicaragua, Sierra Leone, Kyrgyzstan, Turkmenistan, Eritrea, Singapore, Norway, United Arab Emirates, Costa Rica, Croatia, Central African Republic, Georgia, New Zealand, Lebanon, Bosnia and Herzegovina, Republic of the Congo, Moldova, Liberia,	3 each	120

	Panama, Uruguay, Lithuania, Mauritania, Armenia, Albania, Kuwait, Oman, Jamaica, Mongolia, Namibia, Lesotho.		
H.	The 49 next-largest countries: Republic of Macedonia, Botswana, Gambia, Guinea-Bissau, Gabon, Qatar, Trinidad and Tobago, Mauritius, Swaziland, East Timor, Djibouti, Fiji, Bahrain, Guyana, Bhutan, Comoros (an island nation in the Indian Ocean), Equatorial Guinea, Montenegro, Solomon Islands, Suriname, Cape Verde, Brunei, Bahamas, Belize, Iceland, Maldives, Barbados, Vanuatu (an island nation in the South Pacific), Samoa, St. Lucia, São Tomé and Principe (an island nation in the Gulf of Guinea), Federated States of Micronesia, St. Vincent and the Grenadines, Grenada, Tonga, Kiribati (formerly known as the Gilbert Islands, in the Pacific Ocean), Antigua and Barbuda, Andorra, Seychelles, Dominica, Marshall Islands, St. Kitts and Nevis, Liechtenstein, Monaco, San Marino, Palau (an island nation in the Pacific Ocean), Tuvalu (formerly known as the Ellice Islands, in the Pacific Ocean), Nauru (formerly known as Pleasant Island, in the South Pacific), Vatican City.	1 each	49
I.	2 non-UN-members with largest populations: Puerto Rico, Palestine	1 each	2
		Initial total	816
J.	26 dependent territories outside the UN and not yet independent with associate status until they become independent: Macau, Western Sahara, Netherlands	1 each	26

	Antilles, Guam, US Virgin Islands, Aruba (an autonomous region of the Netherlands in the Caribbean), Jersey, Northern Mariana Islands (a commonwealth in political union with the US, in the Western Pacific), Isle of Man, American Samoa, Bermuda, Guernsey, Greenland, Cayman Islands, Faroe Islands, Turks and Caicos Islands, Gibraltar, British Virgin Islands, Cook Islands, Anguilla, Montserrat, St. Helena, Falkland Islands, Niue (a self-governing nation in free association with New Zealand, in the South Pacific), Tokelau, Pitcairn Islands – seats held in reserve for when they become independent.		
K.	8 disputed territories not on the UN-based list: Kashmir, Abkhazia, Nagomo-Karabakh, Kosovo, Transnistria, South Ossetia, Chechnya, Tibet.	1 each	8
		Eventual total	850

It must be stressed that this is a flexible list. There would be movement within it. For example, as more nation-states enter the EU, those that enter would lose their individual representation, leaving a vacancy in their group for a country in the group below it to be promoted. Associate dependent territories in J and K obtaining independence will have one member each and those passing within another nation (as Hong Kong did when it became a part of China) would lose their independent representation. The 850 seats is a maximum that would not be reached immediately. There is scope for future developments within the designation of an eventual tally of 850 seats, and there is no reason why there should not in due course be 850 seats or more if changes to national arrangements in the coming years require such an increase.

Offshoots

All the offshoots from the UN General Assembly would continue to operate: the Economic and Social Council, the International Criminal Court, the

International Court of Justice and the UN organs (UNDP, UNHCR, UNICEF and UNEP) and specialised agencies (FAO, UNESCO, WHO and WTO). (See pp194 and 195-200.)

Of these, the International Court of Justice, based in the Peace Palace at The Hague, Netherlands, the primary judicial organ of the UN, would continue to settle legal disputes submitted to it by nation-states and give advisory opinions on legal questions placed before it by the replacement for the UN General Assembly, the World Parliamentary Assembly. Like the tripartite Assembly/Executive Council/Secretary-General, the International Court of Justice would continue to resolve legal problems arising from conflicts in the first instance.

World Political Parties

All members of the World Parliamentary Assembly would belong to one of the world political parties. There would be a World Centre/Right Party, a World Socialist Party and a Liberal Centrist Party. In addition, no doubt, there would be a World Green Party, a Far-Left Party, a Far-Right Party and a Party for Worldsceptics. Different world parties would have different views on the management of world natural resources and energy supply, and on the level of world taxation and redistribution.

UN Executive Council

The UN Security Council would continue to operate as a vetoless Executive Council. It would continue to have 5 Permanent Members and 12 Non-Permanent Members elected for two-year terms. The World Parliamentary Assembly would make recommendations as does the UN General Assembly, and the Executive Council would decide as does the Security Council. The UN Secretary-General and his Secretariat would continue to implement.

This tripartite UN structure would continue to field all conflicts requiring resolution in the first instance. Only the intractable problems on which the Executive Council could not reach agreement would be passed up to the supranational level. The UN Peacekeeping Forces would continue to operate under the Executive Council as under the Security Council in containable conflicts that do not require the involvement of the supranational level.

The UN Executive Council's (ex-Security Council's) 17 representatives would be elected by the World Parliamentary Assembly. Five representatives would represent each of the Permanent Members, 5 of the next 10 largest nation-states would have rotational representation (so that all 10 are represented, but only 5 at any one time), and the other 8 would be chosen by the World Parliamentary Assembly from representatives of other nation-states. This veto-less Executive Council would decide whether each stage of the disarmament process was satisfactorily completed.

It is important to stress that, from the point of view of the nation-states, life under the UN, and their experience of the UN and the inter-national level, would go on pretty much as before except that the UN General Assembly would operate as a directly elected Parliament. Life within each nation-state or regional grouping, whether loose, or tight (like the EU following the ratification of the Lisbon Treaty), would go on just the same, and nation-states would continue to pursue their self-interest within their implementing of the supranational authority's seven goals. Civilizations would carry on progressing through their various stages. At the inter-national level, the life of civilizations would continue.

There would be just one fundamental change, that from time to time the supranational tier would come into play. When a nation-state or civilization had a conflict that the UN could not deal with and might lead to war, as has happened in the case of conflicts involving 123 countries since 1945, the conflict would be referred to the supranational level whose higher tier would enforce peace and impose a settlement just as if two American states had had a disagreement and had gone to court and been bound by the court's legal ruling.

The Supranational Level

The supranational level would provide the context within which the nation-states and their civilizations operate.

The executive, the World Commission – the supranational authority's equivalent of the European Commission – would propose laws, monitor the implementation of all directives and world policies, and represent the World Authority in the international institutions of global governance (the G8, OECD, the Bank for International Settlements, the World Bank, the International Monetary Fund, the World Trade Organization and all the agencies of the UN). The World Commission's proposals would all relate to the achievement of the goals listed on pp73-74 and 122, including the enforcement of peace and disarmament, while guaranteeing the security of nation-states.

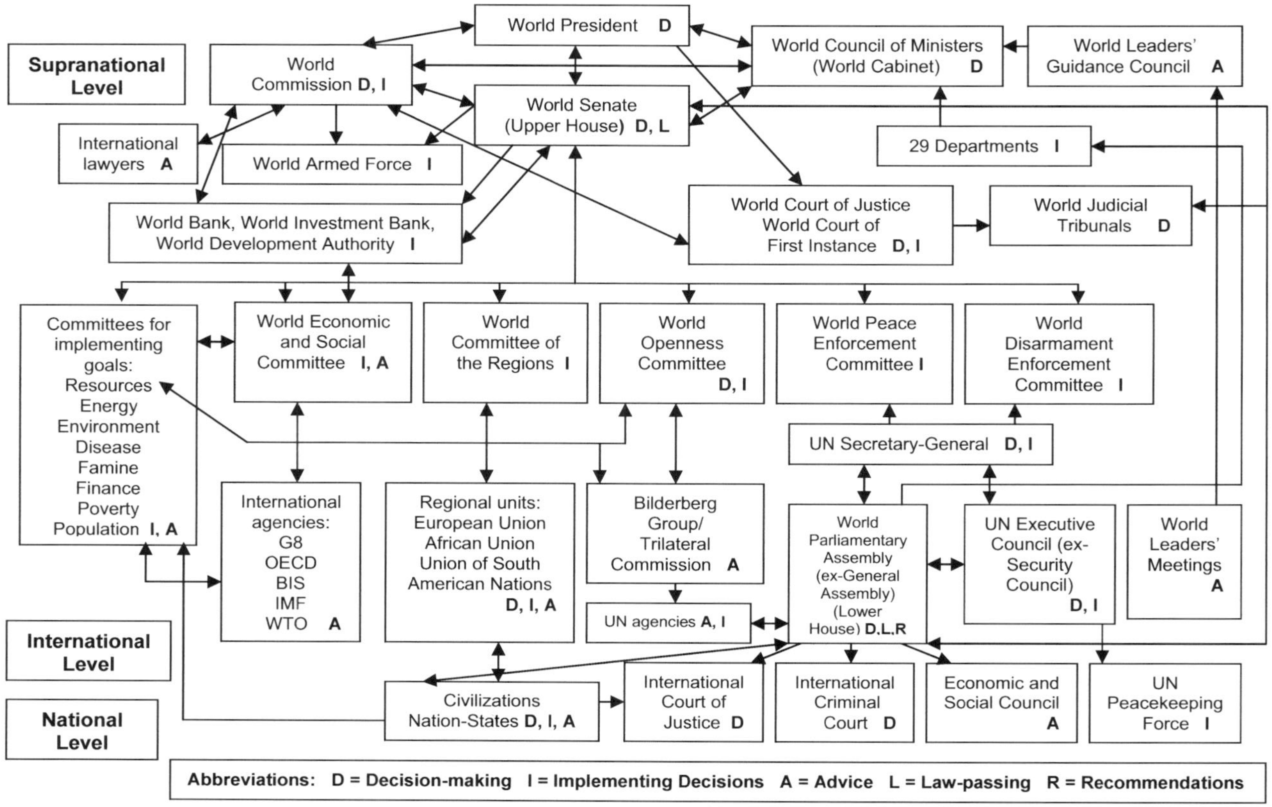

Diagram/Flow Chart of the Supranational Authority: The Structure of the World State

World Commission

The World Commission should be composed of 27 members, about the maximum number that can comfortably sit round a table and take part in world-authority meetings to enforce peace and conduct a world government. The 27 World-Commission representatives should be appointed on the basis of taking into account: regional representation; population percentages; topographical extent; Permanent Membership of the UN; and possession of nuclear warheads to be disarmed.

The data for these criteria can be found in the Appendix. The world population percentages for each nation-state are on pp245-255, and historical movements of percentages are on pp244-245. A fundamental approach to regions is on p244: Asia has 56.6 per cent of world population; Europe 12 per cent; North America 5.1 per cent; Latin America and the Caribbean 8.6 per cent; Africa 14.3 per cent; the Middle East and North Africa 3 per cent; and Oceania/Australia 0.5%. As we shall shortly see, I have broken these regions up into smaller representational denominations. (I have done likewise in arriving at different representational regional zones or constituencies for the World Senate, below.)

There are different schools of thought regarding regions. Sometimes Central America is linked to the Caribbean to form a region, and this region is distinguished from South America. The "Rockefellerite" Club of Rome, one of the undemocratic international agencies, put forward 10 regions in 1973.[2] (See p262.) These 10 zones, identified during the Cold War, included "centrally-planned Asia", meaning Communist Asia (Mongolia, North Korea, North Vietnam and China).

China's emergence as the most populated nation with industrial and nuclear power, has required a rethinking of regional zones. It must not be forgotten that the main object of the World Commission is to deliver world peace through international law, and so it must include representation from all the nation-states that have been party to recent wars and conflicts. A balance has to be struck between representing the entire population of the world (as in the World Parliamentary Assembly) and representing the most powerful nation-states that need to sit round a table in order to deliver world peace and disarmament with the greatest degree of effectiveness.

The principle should be that members of the World Commission should be nominated by the governments or organizations of the countries/regions on the basis of no more than one member per region (as distinct from nation-state). I am basing my regions on the regions in the list on pp256-258, but have varied some regions to achieve a scheme that works in relation to delivery of the seven goals (taking into account the list on pp258-261).

I propose that the 27 members of the World Commission should be drawn up on the basis below. I have given reasons for my proposal in brackets. In the table below (and in the table on pp147-148) the abbreviation R means that there are regional considerations for the nomination; PM means Permanent Member of the UN; and N means that there are nuclear/disarmament considerations behind the nomination; wpp means world population percentage. The number 1 means one member to be nominated by a particular nation-state. Thus 1 China means one member nominated by China. My proposed members are as follows:

1	China (PM, N, wpp 19.5%)
1	Communist Asia (Mongolia, North Korea, N, Laos, Vietnam)
1	Russian Federation (PM, N, largest country in world)
1	Central Asia (ex-USSR)
1	Canada (topographical size) and Greenland
1	USA (PM, N)
1	UK (PM, N)
1	France (PM, N)
1	Western Europe including Germany (R)
1	Eastern Europe (R)
1	Central America and Caribbean (R)
1	North-East South America (including Brazil, N, R)
1	South-West South America (including Argentina, R)
1	Northern Africa (R)
1	Southern Africa (R)
1	Arab Middle East (R)
1	Israel (N)
1	Iran (N?)
1	Pakistan (N)/Afghanistan (R)
1	India (N, wpp 17.23%)
1	West-Central and South-East Asia (Bangladesh to Cambodia, R)
1	East Asia (Japan, South/North Korea, Philippines, R)
1	Indonesia (wpp 3.39%)/Malaysia
1	Australia/Oceania (R, wwp 0.5%)

1	UN (secondment of executive expert)
1	World Bank (secondment of expert)
1	Agencies of global government (secondment of expert)
27	Total

The allocation of governments'/agencies' nominations is a balance between regional representation, population percentages and world influence. It can be criticised from a number of angles.

Have I not been too generous to the Russian Federation and the ex-USSR? I would say that the territory covered by the Russian Federation and the ex-USSR states east of the Caspian and in Eastern Europe is perhaps four times as large as India.

Have I not been too ungenerous to the US, the sole superpower? The principle has been one member per region, and there are certainly two regions (East/West) within the US. However, Canada only has one member and has larger territory. Australia is nearly as large as the US and has to share one member with Oceania (including New Zealand).

Have I not given too much weight to nation-states with nuclear weapons? I would say that a World Commission committed to complete disarmament cannot have under-representation from the powers that have produced nearly 24,000 nuclear warheads which are still in storage throughout the world, whose co-operation it needs.

Is it right to include Israel, the Middle East and Iran and thus allocate three members to the Middle-Eastern region, the same number as Central and South America? I would say that the greatest threat to world peace is in the Middle East, where the World Commission needs to influence Islamists in Iraq, Palestine, Israel, Iran, and of course in Central Asia (Afghanistan and Pakistan).

Is it right to subordinate North Korea to one of three Communist-Asian nation-states? I would say that North Korea needs steadying, and that it would be wrong to allocate one seat to it for breaking rules but equally wrong to ignore it and isolate it.

Similar "cons" can be raised about each nation-state listed as nominating a member to the World Commission and I would say that for each "con" there is a "pro" that gives each listed nation-state a better right to nomination than the right of any other nation-state or region I have not included on the list.

There may be arguments about the detail of my list, which can easily be corrected, but the important thing is: the principle behind the choice of nominating countries/regions/agencies is right. In principle, I have put forward a workable list. In the interests of administrative efficiency, the representation on the World Commission should not be increased beyond 27.

World Senate

The World Senate would be a directly elected upper house, like the American Senate. The relationship between the World Commission and the World Senate would be like that of the European Commission and the European Parliament – only there would be a bicameral system, one chamber (the World Parliamentary Assembly) being at inter-national level and the higher chamber (the World Senate) being at supranational level and dedicated to implementing the seven goals of the supranational authority by passing the appropriate laws to bring in and enforce a peaceful world.

The World Senate would be elected on a basis of regional zones, with weight being given to more scrupulously defined regions than the ones that would nominate the World Commission. The criteria would include regional representation, population percentages, topographical area, possession of nuclear weapons to be disarmed, political clout and environmental considerations.

I propose that there should be in the first instance 46 zonal constituencies, each of which would elect 2 Senators, making a total of 92 seats. I have based these regional zones on the lists of regions on pp256-258 and 258-261, which include countries in each region. The numbers in what follows refer to the number of zonal regions or constituencies, each of which would have 2 Senators.

4 China: East, West, North (including Mongolia), South (PM, N, wwp 19.5%)
3 Russian Federation: East, Central, West (PM, N)
2 Central Asia: North-Central (including Kazakhstan), South-Central (including Pakistan)
3 Canada: East, West, North (including Greenland and Arctic)
4 USA: East, West, North, South, including dependent territories (PM, N)
1 UK (PM, N)
1 France (PM, N)

4	Europe: 2 North-Western, (including Scandinavia, Germany), 1 Eastern, 1 Southern (i.e. Northern Mediterranean – Spain, Italy, Greece/Aegean)
1	Central America, including Mexico
1	Caribbean
3	South America: North-East (Brazil, Bolivia, Paraguay), South (Argentina, Chile, Uruguay and Antarctica), North-West (Peru, Ecuador, Colombia, Venezuela, North Coast)
4	Africa: North, East, West (including Atlantic Ocean), South (NB Middle Africa distributed among these 4)
2	Middle East: Northern (including Turkey, Iraq), Southern (including Egypt, Saudi Arabia)
1	Israel
1	Iran
3	India, North (including Nepal), Central, South (including Sri Lanka, Maldives and Indian Ocean)
2	East-Central Asia (Bangladesh, Myanmar/Burma, Thailand, Laos, Vietnam, Cambodia)
1	South-East Asia (Malaysia, Indonesia, wpp 3.39%)
2	East Asia (Japan, North/South Korea, Philippines)
2	Australia: East, West
1	Oceania (New Zealand, islands and dependent territories)
46	Total

Again, there may be disagreements regarding the detail and the number of seats allocated to a particular region, bearing in mind its population or topographical size. But I have said enough to demonstrate that 92 Senators can fairly represent all the nation-states and regions in the world. If this scheme were implemented there would be scope for 4 more zones to even up unfair allocations where regions feel hard-done-by, which would eventually give a Senate of 50 zones and 100 Senators.

The Senators would work closely with the World Commission, and with the World Parliamentary Assembly. The Assembly would send up to the World Commission matters beyond its competence, conflicts which would require enforcement, and the Commission would pass its proposals to the World Senate for them to become law. It is envisaged that some Senators would be experts in international law.

As in the case of the American system, each party would select a Senate leader who would appoint members of his or her party to Senate committees. These would include a World Committee of the Regions, a World Economic and Social Committee, a World Peace Enforcement Committee and a World Disarmament Enforcement Committee which would liaise with the World Commission, the World Court of Justice and the Assembly.

There would also be World Committees to implement the remaining six of the seven goals: a World Resources Committee, a World Energy Committee, a World Environmental Committee, a World Disease Committee, a World Famine Committee, a World Finance Committee, a World Poverty Committee and a World Population Committee.

World Openness Committee

The Senate Committees would include the very important World Openness Committee, which would review the position of the agencies and scrutinize all world personnel for any relationship with "Rockefellers" and "Rothschilds" and their self-interested world agendas. In view of the enmeshing of the New World Order, the Syndicate and Freemasonry, this Openness Committee would be alert to undue Freemasonic influence and would particularly look for any hidden links to élitist agencies which might suggest that a candidate for world officialdom would be linked to their known wish to control the Earth's natural resources and energy supply, and effect population reduction by violent means, which would be a crime under World Authority international law.

Working in conjunction with the World Resources Committee, this Openness Committee would co-control the return of all privately-owned energy to the people of the Earth, including all Russia's oil and gas which was acquired by "Rockefellers" in the early 1990s for about one-tenth of its market value.[3] Multinational corporations would be permitted to continue conveying energy, but would have to surrender private ownership to the World Authority.

Under this scrutinizing regime "Rothschilds" would be free to continue to control 187 world central banks, but any manipulation of candidates, officials or policies would be identified and exposed as a breach of international law for which there would be severe penalties. The World Openness Committee would also receive advance copies of all agendas of meetings of agencies such as the Bilderberg Group and the Trilateral Commission, and all minutes made of their meetings. It would be a legal requirement that two representatives of the

Senatorial World Openness Committee should attend all meetings of these groups and report back to the World Commission, to ensure that the work of all agencies was transparent.

Quite simply, the Syndicate would be excluded from decision-making and would be subject to investigation by the civil police and to law enforcement.

World Council of Ministers

Vetting by the World Openness Committee would also apply to the World Council of Ministers, the world Cabinet, which would be drawn from the directly-elected World Parliamentary Assembly.

There would be 29 Departments, and therefore 29 World Ministers, the absolute maximum number that can comfortably sit round a Cabinet table and take part in high-level World-Authority meetings.

Unlike the EU, where the Council of Ministers is an assembly of national Ministers, the World Council of Ministers would comprise ministers of world Departments:

- World Finance;
- World Treasury;
- World Peace;
- World Disarmament;
- World Resources;
- World Environment;
- World Climate Change;
- World Health (ending disease);
- World Food (ending famine, crop-growing programs);
- World Regions, Communities and Families;
- World Work and Pensions;
- World Housing;
- World Economic Development;
- World Regional Aid and International Development (ending financial crises);
- World Poverty (eliminating poverty);
- World Population Containment (not reduction);
- World Energy Regulation;
- World Transport (world aviation, roads and rail);
- World Law;
- World Oceans;

- World Space;
- World Education;
- World Citizenship (law and order);
- World Culture and History;
- World Sport;
- World Unity in Diversity;
- World Dependent Territories;
- World Foreign Policies (liaising with nation-states' Foreign Ministers); and
- World Human Rights and Freedom (guaranteeing individual freedoms, including freedom from population reduction under the new system).

All these Departments would work closely with Senatorial Committees operating within their field.

World President

The World Council of Ministers would meet as the world Cabinet under the leadership of the World President, who would be elected every four years like the President of the United States.

The World President would be nominated by one of the world parties. There would be several candidates, one for each party, and each would be vetted by the World Commission and the Senatorial World Openness Committee for any links to élitist agencies that might suggest that a candidate would be likely to pursue élitists' agenda regarding world natural resources, energy supply and population reduction rather than a philanthropic agenda.

There would be a world election campaign involving visits to the main regions and television coverage of speeches that would go out to the whole world. There would be a world ballot involving polling stations in key cities and rural areas, postal voting and online voting.

The successful World President would be sworn in by the World Commission and a judge from the World Court of Justice. The President would lead the world Cabinet to achieve the seven goals, paying attention to the democratic sway of the electorate. He could stand for a second term and serve if elected.

World Guidance Council

A World Guidance Council of elder statesmen and distinguished world figures would assemble every three months, or more frequently if a crisis demanded, to give advice to relevant members of the World Commission, World Senators and World Council of Ministers. These wise elders would be chosen on merit and expertise, with consideration being paid to regional representation, population percentages and political clout, on the recommendation of the World Commission, World Senate and World Council of Ministers.

World Leaders' Meetings

In addition to these guidance meetings, sometimes there would be a business meeting involving World Leaders of nation-states in key regions or their foreign ministers.

There would in particular be a Regional Leaders' meeting for the leaders of the 13 main regions: North America; Europe; Japan; Oceania; China; Tibet; the Russian Federation; South America; Islam; Africa; India; South-East Asia; and Central Asia. There would be regular live link-ups between the World President and the Regional Leaders. There would be smaller groups of Regional Leaders, on the lines of the G4 and G8.

An appropriate member of the World Commission would be present at all meetings of World Leaders, along with the Minister of the appropriate department and a Senator. These meetings of World Leaders would be like the European-Council meetings.

World Banking

The World Bank would be overhauled to operate at a supranational level. It would continue to make loans to poorer countries for capital programs to reduce poverty. The World Investment Bank would also be overhauled to streamline a new supranational role.

Through these world banking institutions the supranational authority/World Commission would carry out work to achieve all its goals. Besides bringing peace and complete disarmament, it would begin a phased redistribution of humankind's natural resources and energy supply to even up the disparities between regions; work to ease environmental problems such as global warming and manage common natural resources including outer space and oceans; end disease and famine; and solve the world's financial crisis. A minimum standard of living would be guaranteed to all humankind on a phased basis, and a World Development Authority would grant interest-free loans to assist the economic and social development of under-developed areas.

International Lawyers

An executive of international lawyers would help the World Commission, World Senate and World Parliamentary Assembly turn the Commission's proposals into international laws. This executive would liaise with the World Peace Enforcement Committee and the World Court of Justice.

World Court of Justice

The World Court of Justice would have 25 judges. These would be chosen on the same basis as the World Commission excluding representation from the World Bank and agencies of global governance.

The Court's primary function would be to hear actions brought by the World Commission against a nation-state for breaking a directive. One of its briefs would be to rule against self-interested *élite*s' use of the world's natural resources and energy supply. It would also rule on conflicts, fulfilling a role of conflict resolution by ordering a nation-state to desist from actions that could result in war. It would hear cases regarding conflicts between nation-states referred up to the Assembly and brought by the World Commission before the Court.

It would rule on legal disputes between member states and between the World Commission and institutions and agencies. It would further disarmament. It would hear complaints against actions taken by a world institution. It would interpret world law at the request of national courts, and respond to direct petitions. It would establish rules and world law for all world citizens without having to resort to their nation-states. It would be responsible for making sure that all world law was upheld.

World Court of First Instance

A World Court of First Instance would exist alongside the World Court of Justice to ease the World Court of Justice's workload. This Court would hear actions brought by citizens and companies against the World Commission for its deeds or failure to act, and would hear actions for damages against the World Commission.

World Judicial Tribunals

There would be a substructure of World Judicial Tribunals under the World Court of Justice, which would further take pressure off the World Court of Justice. These Tribunals would hear cases in which world laws needed to be enforced.

The supranational authority's world laws would be enforceable by these World Judicial Tribunals, following investigation by a civil police force of 10,000 working for the World Commission.

World Armed Force

The World Armed Force or Rapid Reaction Force of 200,000-400,000 would be at the service of the World Commission, the World President, the World Senate and the World Court of Justice. The World Armed Force would be used to enforce laws for the World Commission just as the UN's Peacekeeping Force has been used to enforce laws for the Security Council. There would be a reserve force of 300,000-600,000.

The supranational tier, then, is above the inter-national tier in which associations of nation-states try to keep the peace between nation-states. I have said that from the perspective of nation-states, life under the UN, which would in turn be under the supranational institutions, would be little different from now. Civilizations would go on rising and falling.

Civilizations would all flow into one world-wide civilization in the sense that they would all be under the technical rule of the World Commission, World Senate and World Parliamentary Assembly, World President and World Council of Ministers, but the supranational structure would be sufficiently remote to allow civilizations to continue as before at the lower inter-national level.

Sovereignty

So what would happen to the sovereignty of nation-states under a World Commission, World Senate and Assembly, World President and World Council of Ministers? Clearly, by nominating representatives to the World Commission and electing members of the World Senate and its lower house, the Assembly, at the inter-national level, nation-states would be accepting the authority of the Commission and the new supranational structure and would all be giving up some sovereignty together with giving up their right to fight wars and stockpile nuclear warheads. But it would only be a relatively small amount of sovereignty that would be given up: just enough to secure the achievement of the seven supranational goals.

The structure I have described does not envisage a world government with total sovereignty and control over all our lives. It merely envisages a world government that would operate at a supranational level and permit the inter-national level to continue pretty much as before except for the seven areas relating to the seven goals – only there would now be more democracy and an end to some of the élitist abuses of global governance. My structure assumes that all nation-states would participate in world elections, no matter whether they are democracies or dictatorships. There is thus no need to exclude those listed on pp231-235 and 235-242 as "Partly Free" and "Not Free". The dictatorships would soon be under pressure as their oppressed peoples would experience voting in world elections and would acquire a taste for democracy. To embark on such a scheme can only be good for the spreading of world democracy.

I am proposing a structure that would have no adverse impact on individual liberty outside the achievement of the seven goals, and which would bind all humankind together in an awareness of its unity. I have proposed a structure for a political Universalism that would unite humankind as all-embracingly as did the vision of St. Augustine's *City of God*. The upper tier guarantees that life can continue in the two lower tiers without the upper tier's impacting on it except in the areas of the seven goals listed on pp73-74 and 122, progress in each of which would benefit humankind. Conversely, the upper tier would only be federal in respect of the areas of the seven goals

Location

The location of the supranational tier of government would initially be in the UN, on a rotational basis. Thus the UN General Assembly would continue to meet while the World Parliamentary Assembly was being set up and elected. And once elected the new Assembly would carry on in the same UN chamber, replacing the General Assembly. There would be plenty of room as the UN General Assembly has 1,321 seats and can accommodate 1,898 personnel in all.[4] No doubt a chamber within the UN could be found for the World Senate in the short-term on a similar, shared basis, even if this had to be within the main UN building in Vienna. Such a chamber would only need to accommodate 92 Senators and officials.

Offices within, or near, the UN would be provided on a cost-conscious basis for the embryonic World Commission of 27 Commissioners nominated by governments and regions as I have proposed. Initially its location would be in New York, but there would be scope for the Commission to be elsewhere if accommodation were prepared. London would make a good venue as English is the world's administrative language and Great Britain governed a quarter of the world in the early 20th century. The UK has acted as a bridge between the US and Brussels/Europe, and its location would address Gaddafi's complaint about jetlag.

Eventually a purpose-built site could be found to house all the buildings of the world government. Such a site might be found on the fringe on Docklands, London's Manhattan, where a cluster of high-rise buildings could be located. After the 2012 London Olympics, the site of the Olympic village could be dedicated to the world government if the Olympic stadium could be relocated elsewhere. That is not a proposal, just a thought with Athens in mind, where stadia built for the 2004 Olympics are now standing in near-dereliction. If the world government is to be accommodated outside the US and not in London, then Hamburg may provide a venue. It should not be accommodated in Brussels, which is already too crowded from hosting the complex of EU buildings.

Funding

The change-over from the UN General Assembly to a World Parliamentary Assembly would be accompanied by another long overdue reform. All the agencies listed on pp194 and 195-200 would be streamlined and the 18 separate budgets of the 18 agencies under the Economic and Social Council would be converted into one centralised UN budget.

There would be one budget for the entire UN and all its committees, agencies and operations. This budget would be funded from the nation-states' governments' taxation revenues. The budget would be reduced to take into account that the upper tier would be taking over work previously attempted by the UN, and this reduction would allow existing UN funds to be diverted to the supranational levels higher tier.

The funding of the setting-up of the supranational level would therefore be partly covered by these diverted UN funds and partly by (initially) new money made available on a cost-conscious basis by nation-states' governments' taxation revenues. Eventually this new money would be recouped from, and offset against, and more than covered by, the peace dividend, savings from reductions in military expenditure. The amounts contributed from these taxation revenues would reflect each nation-state's involvement in the world government, and would be *pro rata* in relation to the number of seats in the World Parliamentary Assembly and World Senate, and the extent of the representation within the World Commission and World Council of Ministers, that the nation-state had been allocated. The bigger the involvement, the more money to be contributed; the smaller the involvement, the less funding.

It must be emphasised that all nation-states would be able to cut their defence budgets dramatically as the World Commission would have abolished war and the need for expenditure on arms. The amount saved would be nearly $1.5 trillion a year and additional savings from the cost of renewing deteriorating nuclear weapons. (See p165.) Most nation-states would therefore be able to divert some of this saved military expenditure into funding for the supranational tier – and still be in surplus as savings on military expenditure would far outweigh contributions to the funding of the World Commission and the new world structure.

Timescale

As to the timescale of the introduction of the world government, this could begin immediately on the cost-conscious basis of sharing the UN building in New York. Two sets of world elections could be organized as soon as world parties have come into being and candidates have come forward.

That will only happen when there is a Declaration of Intent regarding a forthcoming world government. The US President should go to the UN General Assembly and make a declaration of such an intent, and of his intention to organize a World Constitutional Convention if the UN General Assembly approve it. Such an announcement would be followed by a mobilising of democratic activity throughout the world, during which new political parties would be thrown up.

The point I am making is that the new structure could be implemented relatively quickly on a cost-conscious short-term basis. There is no question of having to wait a decade or a generation to start. There may not be a truly fair redistribution of wealth for more than 100 years, long after the lifetime of all reading these words when they first appear. But the point is, that goal can only be achieved after a lengthy process, and a start can be made before the exact details are known as to how world poverty can be eliminated.

The structure I have proposed draws on, and blends, aspects of the US, British and European systems to create a new and distinct model that can assume its own legal personality and distinctive characteristics. It would be looser than a

United States of the World and would not seek to control every facet of life within the nation-state. It would allow civilizations to continue within a new Era of Peace. Billions of dollars spent on armaments and war could be diverted to advance the progress of all humankind.

My new, moderately radical and distinct model offers the prospect of a realisation of the dream of a politically-unified known world that has fascinated thinkers since Western philosophy began with the Presocratic Greeks.

Philosophical Summary

A brief reminder of the points I have covered:

World Parliamentary Assembly – 816/850 seats;
offshoots;
elected political parties;
UN Executive Council of 17;
World Commission of 27;
Elected World Senate of 92 seats in 46 zones;
World Openness Committee to control the Syndicate;
World Council of Ministers – 29 Departments;
elected World President;
World Leaders' Guidance Council;
World Leaders' Meetings;
international lawyers to advise World Commission;
World Court of Justice – 25 judges;
World Court of First Instance;
World Judicial Tribunals;
World Armed Force;
sovereignty;
location of World Authority/world government;
funding;
timescale;
a blend of US, British and European systems.

The supranational level can influence the inter-national fate of the world until the 22nd or 23rd century.

9

Peering into the Future: A Glimpse of the World State

We have considered a two-tier structure for bicameral World State with an executive and other bodies. It is now time to look forward and to consider what will happen in the coming years if the supranational authority is *not* set up.

The Future without a Supranational Authority

My study of the rise and fall of civilizations[1] focuses on the inter-national level, not the supranational level. As I said on pp4 and 42, it shows 25 civilizations passing through 61 similar stages, after which a civilization passes into another civilization just as in 642 the Egyptian civilization passed into the Arab civilization and acknowledged Allah in place of Ra and the pantheon of Egyptian gods. Civilizations rise and fall and pass away, but there are always civilizations.

In my study I show the North-American civilization to be the youngest. It was founded by early settlers, most notably those who founded the Jamestown Settlement of 1607. This civilization is currently in stage 15, a quarter through, at the same stage the Roman civilization was in during the rise of the Roman Empire.

The North-American civilization through the US, now the sole superpower following the fall of the Berlin Wall and the demise of Soviet Communism, is set to control the world's regions, which are gathering themselves into regional Unions: a European Union, an African Union, a Union of South American Nations, a soon-to-be American Union and a soon-to-be Pacific Union (or Asia-Pacific Union). These Unions will be like provinces, federal regions above nation-states but all linked to America as the Roman provinces were linked to Rome, only on a looser basis. The President of the EU and the President of the African Union (at the time of writing Gaddafi) will not be governors of provinces in the tight way that Roman governors were governors of Roman provinces.

Many of these regions reflect the stage their civilizations are in. In my study, in stage 43 "a civilization loses its national sovereignty to a secularising conglomerate". The following are stage-43 civilizations/regions:

- The European civilization, which is just entering this stage. After the American occupation of Germany in 1945, US investment since the Marshall Plan and extensive US military influence in Europe during the Cold War, Europe acquired a legal personality following ratification of the Lisbon Treaty and the new European constitution. This ratified EU is a conglomerate in which the Christian religion will be secularised under Brussels' multi-cultural approach.
- The Japanese civilization, which has also been in stage 43 since the American occupation of 1945 and US financial investment. Japan is now a unified conglomerate of 47 prefectures or provinces, and rose to be an economic semi-superpower that looked towards America, its imperial Shinto religion secularised, during the third quarter of the 20th century.
- The Oceanian civilization, which has been in stage 43, under secularising Western rule, for much of the 20th century, and is now passing into a more federal stage.
- The Chinese civilization, which has been under foreign Marxian influence and in stage 43 since 1949, and may soon pass into a more federal stage.
- The Tibetan civilization, which is under Chinese foreign influence and has also been in stage 43 since 1951.

Many of the recently-formed regions are further advanced in my rise-and-fall pattern. In my study, stage 46 is "a further attempt at counter-thrust under foreign federalist influence". The following are stage-46 civilizations/regions:

- The Byzantine-Russian civilization, which passed into the Russian Federation in 1991, having been influenced by the EU and US capitalism, and is now in stage 46.
- The Andean and Meso-American civilizations, which are currently in stage 46. Their nation-states are already linked through the Organization of American States (OAS) and 34-state Free Trade Area of the Americas (FTAA), which was set up in 2005 as a stepping-stone to an American Union. There has been heavy investment from the US.
- The Arab civilization, which has entered stage 46. Its nation-states have been linked through the Arab League of 1945 and there has been heavy post-colonial oil revenue investment from the US/West. A federal Union

is in the process of being born.

- The African civilization, which has entered stage 46. The Organization of African Unity (OAU) became the African Union in 2002, with Western investment.
- The Indian civilization, which has been a federation since 1947, with 28 states and 7 union territories, all federally-linked, and US-Western investment. It has a constitution that is quasi-federal and provides for a unitary state with subsidiary federal features. India joined the South Asian Free Trade Area (SAFTA) in 2004.
- The South-East-Asian civilization, which has had US/Western investment since c.1950. Its nation-states have been linked through the Southeast Asia Treaty Organization (SEATO) and the Association of Southeast Asian Nations (ASEAN). Ten countries are set to pass into an Asian Economic Community in 2010. Federal linkage is growing.
- The Central-Asian civilization, which has been under Soviet-Chinese federal control of Mongolia and much of Central Asia.

To sum up, the US will have a co-ordinating impact on: Europe; Japan; Oceania; China; Tibet; the Russian Federation; South America; Arab Islam; Africa; India; South-East Asia; and Central Asia. In other words, on all the world's regions. There will be 13 regional Unions in all to be co-ordinated, including North America. All these Unions will eventually be democracies, elected by their own regional peoples.

We are thus approaching a time in which the US as sole superpower marshals a regional world. Global governance will continue during the 21st century, regional associations will increase.

At present the Syndicate, the network of *élite*s who control global governance behind the scenes, have a major influence in controlling natural resources, including oil and gas, as we have seen. The *élite*s would continue to drive political events to suit their commercial interests. Just as the political invasions of Afghanistan and Iraq have resulted in attempts to implement oil and gas pipelines across Afghanistan and Iraq – notably, the Trans-Afghan pipeline in Afghanistan and an abortive attempt to revive the Kirkuk-Haifa pipeline across Iraq (which had not been started by 2010 because of the instability in Iraq) – that have furthered the *élite*s' self-interested, Mafia-like ambition to own and sell the world's natural resources, so, if there is no supranational authority, there will be further actions involving the Middle East and the Caspian to corner oil and gas in a productive region. More local wars can be expected.

For this reason it is likely that if there is no supranational authority in 2050 the War on Terror will still be continuing in some form. In the late 1990s bin Laden is thought to have bought several nuclear-suitcase bombs from the Chechen Mafia.[2] The West entered Afghanistan to expel the Taliban who had allowed al-Qaeda to use it as a base, and to train Afghans to prevent al-Qaeda from returning. The US and British leaders wanted a strategy for an early exit. However, al-Qaeda sought to regroup alongside the Taliban in Afghanistan. The Afghanistan terrain makes the Afghans insuperable in their home country, as British armies discovered in the 19th century and the Soviet army in the 20th century. For 300 years there has been a long civil war between two groups of Pashtuns, the Durranis (ruled by President Karzai and supported by a Tajik army) and the Ghilzai (who ran the Taliban and were ousted by the US invasion of 2001). Bin Laden's successors will continue bin Laden's drive to revive the Caliphate in Baghdad.[3] It is likely that the war in Afghanistan and the Middle East will drag on for more than a generation in some form while Western troops search for al-Qaeda's weapons and disrupt further plans for the Caliphate to attack the West.

Unless the Islamic regime falls, Iran will have nuclear weapons and billions of dollars will be spent on a combined US-Russian missile shield. Israel will still be guarding her borders. There will be a rise in federalism and regional Unions. The US, the sole superpower, will have a struggle to maintain its world position as India and China, whose populations are each nearly one-fifth of the world population, increase their economic influence.

In November 2009 the Indian Prime Minister Manmohan Singh was reported as visiting the White House and seeking to spend $90 billion on the latest US weapons system to defend itself against Chinese expansion.[4] The prospect loomed of a confrontation between the two nuclear states, India and China.

Even with a program of containment the world's population will increase from 6.789 billion on 6 October 2009 to 9.4 billion, and perhaps 10.5 billion by 2050.[5] Both figures are UN estimates. The population of Asia will be up from 4.054 billion (2008) to 5.628 billion (2050) according to another UN estimate[6] which puts the world population in 2050 at 8.909 billion. Africa's population will nearly double from 0.973 billion (2008) to 1.766 billion (2050). During the same period the population of Europe will decline from

0.732 billion (2008) to 0.628 billion (2050).

The increased world population in Asia and Africa will not be matched by a comparable increase in Asia's and Africa's share of the world's wealth and natural resources following the 2008-2009 financial crisis. This will mean that there will be a shortage of food and water. Oil and gas will be increasingly scarce.[7] By 2030 some oil will have dried up (according to the UK Energy Research Centre) [8] and some gas will be in shorter supply. US natural gas may dry up in 30-50 years.[9] The power behind world governments, the "New World Order" of "Rockefellers" and "Rothschilds", who have cornered almost all the central banks and whose multinationals control the oil and gas pipelines, will compound the energy shortage. As energy prices rise, so will their profits. The West will struggle not to be dependent on Russia for energy.

During this difficult time there will be heavy Syndicate (and therefore Freemasonic) influence behind the US world presence as it copes with federalism and the economic Unions that will take place: in addition to the European Union and African Union, there will be an American Union, a Pacific (or Asia-Pacific) Union and a Middle-Eastern Union. A Union of some description will cover each of the thirteen regions I listed on p161.

In some places, the Syndicate will achieve a New-World-Order clampdown, and will appear to be a dictatorship behind the US presidency. Global governance will continue to be secretive and undemocratic, even tyrannical. Policies of population reduction will continue to be pursued to achieve a "sustainable Earth" through local wars, diseases and famines. Under American leadership there will be a Syndicate-controlled world. The rich will become richer and the rest of humankind will buy their natural resources.

Eventually the Syndicate's New World Order may seek to federate the world – link all regional Unions – under itself, using the US Government as a front. Such a supranational, federal Syndicate would dominate the agencies of global governance, which would be beyond the reach of electorates of individual countries and therefore beyond democratic accountability. The governing of all nations would be subsumed under a Syndicate framework of supervision. A nation-state whose interests conflict with other nation-states and which complains it has less freedom than before will be without redress for the greater good of the whole, the welfare of the larger entity.

Long before 2050 failing energy and food, water shortages and failure to contain the increasing world population will create a "perfect storm": food and water riots, migrations by the starving and the spreading of chaos. The regional Unions will have created a borderless Earth, and mass migrations will never have been easier. It is likely that Europe will suffer from migrating Islamic hordes moving west from Central Asia in search of food, water and energy.

By 2050 many of the stage-46 federations will have moved into stage 47, notably South America, India, South-East Asia and Central Asia. In my study, in this stage "economic decline and inflation will lead to class conflict and pave the way for foreign occupation". Such occupations can be expected in Eastern parts of the world from c.2050 onwards. The stage-15 US and stage-43 China, Japan and Europe are the likely occupiers. If there is no supranational authority the Americans, supported by the Syndicate, will occupy South America and (perhaps supported by Europe) India, Tibet and (perhaps supported by Europe and Japan) Central Asia. Japan will occupy South-East Asia. There will be a clash of civilizations as the Arab civilization comes into conflict with the West. The Arab civilization will fall under foreign occupation. By 2100 it is likely that Americans and Europeans will be occupying Islam.[10]

These are the parameters of what will happen if events take their course, and civilizations continue to rise and fall at the inter-national level without the restraint of a US-set-up and -influenced supranational authority. The North-American civilization will build a loose form of a latter-day Roman Empire from the 13 regions and the Unions that will eventually include all of them, and cope with opposition from the Arab Islamic world in an ongoing clash of civilizations. The 13 regions and the Unions that will eventually include all of them will form associations of nation-states while spending vast sums on defence. Economic decline, inflation and foreign occupation await our world if it is left to the mercy of rising-and-falling civilizations.

The Future with a Supranational Authority: Peering into Paradise

Even within these parameters, the abolition of war and implementation of disarmament would make an enormous saving. From 2001 to 2008 the War on Terror cost between $700 billion (according to the Congressional Research Service)[11] – excluding the cost of oil for the US troops amounting to nearly $3 trillion – and $2,324.7 billion (according to Homeland Security Market Research).[12] Some private analysts put the cost at $4 trillion, and have costed the War in Iraq at over $3 trillion.[13] The wars in Afghanistan and Iraq have helped to push the American national debt to over $11 trillion (or according to Obama's federal budget $12.7 trillion) by October 2009[14] and the UK national debt to £800.8 billion by July 2009.[15] In 2007 the EU member states' military spending has been estimated to have been $285 billion.[16] In 2008 alone, global military spending by nation-states totalled $1.4727 trillion, including NATO spending of $1.0498 trillion, some 70 per cent.[17]

To this must be added the future cost of renewing deteriorating nuclear weapons and replacing military equipment. It has been estimated that for the UK to replace the *Trident* nuclear missile system and build two large aircraft carriers would cost £130 billion, and the cost of replacing nuclear weapons could be expected to run to many trillions of dollars.

These vast amounts of taxpayers' money or borrowings are available to be diverted to more peaceful uses, such as implementing the seven goals. The saving would wipe out the consequences of the 2008 financial crisis, which has cost the world many trillions of dollars, far more than the $3 trillion of bank bail-outs. The abolition of defence spending would release nearly $1.5 trillion *each year* (the military expenditure by nation-states and NATO added together) to raise the standard of living across the world for a while to the benefit of all humankind.

The immediate creation of a supranational authority would ease the coming economic decline and inter-national problems.

America is already considering a world that is at peace and disarmed. On 24 September 2009 Obama laid before the UN General Assembly a picture of a harmonious world in which no country would ride roughshod over another: "No one nation can or should try to dominate another nation. No world order that elevates one nation or group of people over another will succeed." This suggests that America would not seek to control a World State. National power would no longer be about military prowess or economic pride, but the inter-connected and co-operative values and image a nation projects to the world, in the tradition of Woodrow Wilson. Obama took this approach to the Arab world (in his speech in Cairo) and to China, and appears to have jettisoned the previous policy of containment of China. My supranational authority and level would achieve this stated goal of America's.

If the supranational authority is set up soon and begins to make a huge defence saving, how will the world look in 2050?

I assume that the 13 Regions and the Unions that will eventually include all of them can be converted into elected democracies quite rapidly by 2020 at the latest. The same potential forces and patterns I have described when projecting the future without a supranational authority would continue to be present at the inter-national level but there would be a better outcome for the world in 2050.

There would be no continuation of the War on Terror after a peace accord covering the entire Middle East, including Iraq, Afghanistan, Iran and Israel, although the World Armed Force may still be patrolling parts of West Asia, coping with outbreaks of insurgency. Internecine wars would be at an end for a while. Bin Laden and al-Qaeda would be disarmed along with the nine nation-states that between them (as we saw on pp106-107) hold 23,574 nuclear warheads. There would be a borderless world and free movement of peoples subject to local restrictions to prevent any one city or region from being swamped. There would be free trade.

The world's population would rise despite a containment policy, and there would be no population reduction by war, disease or famine. The defence saving would be available to feed the increased population. The diversion of these defence funds would ensure that there would be no food shortage, and every world citizen would have access to drinking-water. In a redistribution of wealth out of saved defence spending there would be a minimum standard of living for all, basic accommodation and access to utilities and energy. Clearly, this would take time to achieve in parts of Asia and Africa.

There would be a global policy to convey natural resources and energy to all humankind, and the Syndicate's profit-making role in dispensing natural resources and energy, and the role of multinationals, would be carefully monitored, regulated and controlled. The Four Horsemen of the Apocalypse – conquest, war, famine and disease – would cease to ride. There would be no spreading of man-made diseases like AIDS or viruses like H1N1, the swine-flu virus, that can start a pandemic. The world would become more multipolar with India and China having more influence.

With political Universalism focusing on the 13 regions listed on p161 would come religious Universalism. All religions would draw together. There would be unity in diversity as the common essence of Christianity, Islam, Buddhism, Hinduism, Taoism and other world religions would be emphasised, but in local, regional cathedrals, temples and mosques traditional differentiation and diversity would continue. There would be environmental Universalism as the supranational authority would treat the Earth as one planet and would come up with unified solutions for global agricultural and climate problems. Space exploration on a cost-conscious basis would determine whether it would be possible to colonise the nearest stars.

The supranational pattern would be superimposed on the inter-national pattern which would continue below it. The savings from abolishing military expenditure would slow the pace of economic decline. Foreign occupation would be averted for the time the world was under the supranational authority. The world would be governed by the liberal democracy dreamt of by Kant and Hegel. Education and culture would thrive, along with the arts. There would be money, goods and services for all. There would be sweeping, unified policies and plans to benefit the world. National governments would appear as parochial as local parish councils.

For a while there would be a kind of paradise under a *Pax Americana*, and there would be a new Golden Age of the kind that flourished under Augustus's peaceful Roman Empire where one world-wide religion co-existed with local cults which reflected it.

The World President would be based near the World Commission, the World Senators and the World Council of Ministers, initially in New York, but in due course perhaps in London. The British Royal Family might see fit to vacate Buckingham Palace for him, and live on in their other palaces: Windsor Castle, Kensington Palace, Sandringham and Balmoral. He would have regular live link-ups with the Regional Leaders and World Leaders. His success would be measured by his implementation of the seven goals.

I glimpsed him in 1966. I ended my poem 'Archangel' on my visits to China and Soviet Russia during the height of the Cold War that year with a vision I had in Moscow's Cathedral of the Archangel. I saw world elders near a Leaders' Hall in an unknown location. They did not resemble World Commissioners or World Senators, but rather the elders of the World Leaders' Guidance Council in a place that might be Rome, and a "World-Lord":

"Indifferent tsars and tyrants,
Compassionate inquisitors;
Can nothing bring together
Enslaving Leader and Saint?
As I stared at the murals' centre
In this Cathedral-tomb,
The Archangel became a Shadow
With a sword and wings outstretched,
And I saw in the second icon
The future of the West,

From the Atlantic to the Urals:
Into the People's Square
From the Cathedral gates,
File in the morning rush-hour
An *élite* of self-made Saints
Each still on the last hour's quest.
They reach the central banner
In the forum of statues and graves,
The great mazed *mandala*
Under which the supplicants wait;
Decades of contemplation
Show in their white-haired peace
As, trusting to perfect feelings,
They value each equal they greet;
Until, whispering on silence,
They glide to the Leaders' Hall,
Their hearts, with a World-Lord's wholeness,
At the centre of life, of all,
Their hearts where all past and future meet."[18]

At the time I located this vision in Europe, foreseeing the end of the Cold War and the reunification of Europe ("From the Atlantic to the Urals"), but the setting I saw led me to speak of the "future of the West", and my glimpse was of peaceful world rulers who have mastered the art of living, and of a "World-Lord".

Peering into the future of the supranational authority, we are peering into a Paradise that would be relatively short-lived but would be the apex of human achievement. It has been estimated that the number of humans who have ever lived is between 100 billion and 115 billion, with 106 billion being a calculation based on 2002.[19] Life for the 6.9 to 10.5 billion living under the World Commission would reach a zenith that has never been, and would never be, surpassed. It must be remembered that the Universalist philosophy which is alert to universal being and universal humankind underpins the Universalist political vision, and that there would also be cultural Universalism: a high cultural style unifying local/regional diversity. Communications, the Internet, peace and high culture would all combine to raise civilization to its highest-ever point. Its Universalism can bring in a new Renaissance in the arts during a Golden Age of peace and prosperity for all humankind which would mark the highest peak of world culture.

It must be stressed that the supranational authority would only last for a while. It is in the nature of institutions to have a limited duration. As with the Roman Empire, there would always be challenges to the World Commission. Terrorism has always been with us in some form. Change is ever pressing. The Roman Empire which seemed so solid was subject to pressure from outside forces, barbarians, and the British Empire on which the sun would never set was always subject to winds of change.

There would come a time when an established supranational authority would be regarded as intrusive and tyrannical. There would be a kind of mass nationalism that would reassert the inter-national level, and the supranational authority and level would be swept away, as was the Roman Empire.

The Roman civilization's stage 15 lasted as we have seen from 341 to 218BC, 123 years. My study shows that the North-American civilization's stage 15 began in 1913 and may be reaching an end in c.2250,[20] after more than 300 years. It must be taken into account that other civilizations' stage 15 lasted longer than the Roman civilization's: for example, the Byzantine-Russian civilization's stage 15 lasted nearly 400 years (from AD c.677 to 1071), the Arab civilization's lasted for 265 years (from c.790 to 1055) and the Chinese civilization's lasted for over 300 years (from c.589 to 907).

The Roman civilization progressed to its Principate and the full glory of the Roman Empire in stage 28, which lasted from 30BC to AD270. America has its stage 28 ahead when a new ruling people will bring in a new Universalist vision like the one that inspired the Principate. Europe's new people were the Humanists whose universalism expressed itself in universal Protestantism. The signs are that America's new people, when its time comes, will be Universalists who follow the Light common to all religions and espouse a World State.

Universalists have already begun to appear. My study shows that in a civilization's stage 17[21] a heretical sect surfaces and that in the North-American civilization the sect will follow Universalism, which is regarded by Christianity as heretical as it draws on the metaphysical Light that is the common essence of all religions. There are already tensions between Christians (both Catholic and Protestant) and New-Age Universalists, who regard Christianity as just one of several religions. There have been parallel tensions between many Christians and globalists who follow the Syndicate's

New World Order and invoke the ideals of the Illuminatist Adam Weishaupt (a Satanist) and of Freemasonry, whose demiurge is Lucifer. ('Yes, Lucifer is God, and unfortunately Adonay [Jehovah] is also God,' Albert Pike, the head of Freemasonry from 1858 to his death in 1891, wrote in 1889 to 23 Freemasonic Supreme Councils.)[22] Universalists distance themselves from globalists. In stage 18 this Universalist sect will be resisted by the orthodox religion – by Christianity.

My study shows that by stage 27 the heresy has been grafted on to the civilization's central idea and has become the religion of the new people. Universalism can be expected to be the American religion of the future: a Universalism of what is common in all higher religions, purged of its corrupting Illuminatist/Freemasonic hangers-on.

But we are now peering into the distant future, and this is best done with the patterns of *The Rise and Fall of Civilizations* ready to hand so that the time-spans of different civilizations can be compared at a glance. For our present purposes, suffice it to say that the North-American civilization's expansive stage 15 may include a supranational authority until c.2250 at the very latest, and possibly until 2150 or (on the Roman analogy) until around 2050 – which would make the supranational authority very short-lived indeed.

To sum up, it might be that the supranational authority would not survive c.2150. Certainly, by c.2250 the North-American civilization would have emerged from stage 15, the stage the Roman Empire was in during its rise, and the supranational authority and level would have disappeared.

The rise and fall of civilizations would have continued uninterrupted at the inter-national level, and the collapse of the supranational authority would bring with it a need to rearm, to spend money on limited wars and defence, and would thus accelerate economic decline and foreign occupation. It is reckless to make historical predictions, but my pattern of rising and falling civilizations allows me to overlay living civilizations on dead civilizations and to see what is ahead for the living civilizations. After the fading and fall of the supranational level, the rise and fall of civilizations would continue at the inter-national level, and it would be clear that the world government had not arrested the course of civilizations, which seemed to flow into it. In fact, they would have carried on unhindered beneath the World State at the inter-national level and would be seen to have resurfaced further on.

I have looked into the future and I have seen what is there: regional Unions, the Syndicate's self-interested New World Order whose goal of a federal tyranny can be firmly shackled, and a new Era of Peace that can bring Paradise on Earth for a while along with a new Golden Age. I have had the vision and have described it, and located it and myself, within the tradition of Plato and Kant. I have seen what I have seen. It is for the political class to implement this universal World State.

Philosophical Summary

A reminder of the two possible destinies of the world:

The future without a supranational authority:

stage-15 US marshalling 5 stage-43 and 7 stage-46 civilizations;
influence of *élites*;
population increase;
economic decline and foreign occupation;
Syndicate federal Union of the world.

The future under a supranational authority:

peace dividend nearly $1.5 trillion a year and the cost of renewing deteriorating nuclear weapons;
economic decline and foreign occupation postponed;
era of peace and prosperity – paradise;
a Renaissance in the arts and a Golden Age, as in Augustan Rome.

I offer a vision of hope: an era of universal peace and prosperity that would be recognised in times to come as humankind's greatest achievement. Humankind now has to have the self-belief to bring the vision into actuality.

Epilogue

Making a Golden Age Happen

In the last two chapters I have set out a conception of a World State that is rooted in the history of the last 5,000 years. I have seen the supranational authority and World State as being *partly* federal in limiting itself to seven goals, and loosely allowing nation-states and civilizations to continue at local, regional level. Such a loose structure would allow a high degree of democracy, with the higher Senate and lower Assembly both directly elected. It would avoid the more drastic United States of the World in which there would be upheavals at the local/regional level, and the New World Order's federal Union of the 13 regions that would be controlled by the Syndicate whose agenda is universal world dominance with very little expansion of democracy.

Such a loose federal model limited at the supranational level to seven goals would leave nation-states and civilizations free to run themselves outside the areas of the seven goals through the democratic process via the World Senate and World Parliamentary Assembly. The loss of sovereignty and disturbance to existing nation-states and civilizations would be minimal. Life outside areas of the seven goals and elections to the Senate and Assembly would continue, allowing nation-states and civilizations the maximum amount of continuity with their local and regional traditions.

They would surrender sovereignty in the areas of the seven goals, but their minimal loss of sovereignty would be amply compensated for by a gain in a share of world sovereignty and a maximal increase in democracy via the directly-elected Senate and Assembly.

Sceptics will say, "It will never happen. Vested interests are too strong. No nation-state's government will vote for a reduction in its own sovereignty." However, all nation-states' governments may see that their compensatory gain in a share of world sovereignty will bring a peace "dividend", a fund previously spent on defence, that can bring prosperity to their peoples. The UN spends less than one per cent of what is spent by the war industries. The institutions of the old order – national parliaments, banks and financial institutions – have so manifestly failed that it may be timely for governments to consider starting afresh and directing their UN General Assembly members to vote accordingly.

Some will say that a legally-based supranational authority would be ignored by indigenous and foreign insurgents such as the Afghan and Pakistani Taliban and al-Qaeda, and that the situation under a supranational level in Afghanistan would be no different from what it is without the supranational level.

That may be true, but under a supranational authority the campaign against the Taliban and al-Qaeda would be directed by the World Armed Force, which would deflect some of the animosity away from the US, British and NATO presence in the region. A world presence might carry more authority among the people in the region who have co-existed with the Taliban and al-Qaeda. Afghanistan-Pakistan is an extreme case. A legally-based supranational authority might not have been ignored in the many other conflicts in the Middle East.

Some will say that all nation-states should act with a strengthened sense of their national interest – what advances it or damages it, what priorities to have and what can be afforded – like Washington, Moscow, Delhi and Beijing, and with less bureaucracy. However, many nation-states have already been subsumed into regions or Unions, and the European nation-states, including the UK, have already given up over 80 per cent of their right to enact laws, and therefore of their sovereignty, to the European Union.

Some contemporary historians and commentators focus on the conflicts between nation-states at the inter-national level rather than at the supranational level. Samuel Huntington focuses on the inter-national clash between civilizations, and Robert Kagan does likewise in *The Return of History and the End of Dreams*. Seeing that international convergence had failed to materialize after the Cold War, he regards Fukuyama's "end of history" as an illusion without considering the legal power to abolish war that a supranational authority might acquire.

Champions of weakened nation-states must face the fact that a future based on even stronger national interests would be worse than Model 1. A UN of even stronger nation-states operating inter-nationally would be powerless to stop another round of local wars in the coming years of the kind that have involved 123 countries since 1945. Strengthening nation-states is a milder variation of the option or model I did not include (see p75), that of abolishing the UN and returning the world to potentially warring nation-states.

It is a condition that the supranational authority would have to be set up, as I have made clear, at the behest of, and initially under the control of, the sole remaining superpower, the US.

America has to be involved as, in terms of the dynamic of history, the supranational level is an expression of stage 15 of a civilization, and of the living civilizations only the North-American civilization is at stage 15. For a supranational level to be brought into existence without America would be like a Roman Empire being brought into existence without Rome. The link between the US and the World State would not be overly visible. However, the World State would not outlast the North-American civilization's stage 15 as the World State would be an objectivisation of that global stage and would end when it ended.

My bicameral supranational system would satisfy humankind's long yearning for universal unity. The Grand Inquisitor in Dostoevsky's *The Brothers Karamazov* rebukes Christ for rejecting the third temptation: "The need of universal unity is the third and last torment of men. Mankind as a whole has always striven to organize itself into a world state....By accepting the world and Caesar's purple, you would have founded the world state and given universal peace."[1] The World State I propose offers universal unity free from the complication of Satan's temptations.

The feeling of world citizens towards each other within the World State would begin to reflect the spirit of St Paul's words in *The Acts of the Apostles* (4:32, 34-5), when interpreted in a Universalist sense: "Now the company of those who believed were of one heart and soul, and no one said that any of the things which he possessed was his own, but they had everything in common....There was not a needy person among them, for as many as were possessors of lands or houses sold them, and brought the proceeds of what was sold and laid it at the apostles' feet; and distribution was made to each as any had need." (This is a modern version of: "And the multitude of them that believed were of one heart and of one soul: neither said any of them that ought of the things which he possessed was his own; but they had all things common....Neither was there any among them that lacked: for as many as were possessors of lands or houses sold them, and brought the prices of the things that were sold, and laid them down at the apostles' feet: and distribution was made unto every man according as he had need.") The World State would endeavour to begin to reflect this spiritual vision of the oneness and harmony of humankind, spread contentment throughout the Earth and turn Universalism into a creed of human love.

My proposal for a World State, which I would like to think crowns the thinking of Kant, Hegel and Fukuyama, is, as I said on pp2-3, a consequence of political Universalism. First came the philosophy of Universalism, then came the need for an expression of political Universalism which proposes a form of government that can enforce peace within the whole of humankind without attacking part of humankind through wars, armies and nuclear warheads. The only such form of government is a World State. At the end of *The Syndicate* I titled the Epilogue "World Government versus Global Democracy". The "World Government" was the Syndicate's self-interested brand of world government. The World State includes both world government as it should be and global democracy, and is a benevolent expression of political Universalism.

History has borne humankind from primitive origins to the threshold of a World State. Along the way, Virgil (in the 'Fourth Eclogue'), and Dante (in *De Monarchia*) dreamt of a new order of world peace, and Milton (in *The Ready and Easy Way to Establish a Free Commonwealth*) dreamt of an ideal republic. Universalist history offers the vision of universal history which was so important to Kant: history that is philosophically serious and also empirical. My vision of a supranational authority that delivers seven goals including peace and disarmament while civilizations continue to rise and fall and nation-states continue their sway at the inter-national level – an authority that enforces international law, democratizes the UN, makes global governance accountable and regulates the *élite*s' exclusive groups – is a vision (in Kant's, Hegel's and Fukuyama's sense of the phrase) of the end-point of world history.

I have had the vision and have communicated what I have seen. It is now for others to take it up and make it happen, construct the details, turn the words on these pages into a structure that straddles the world as the Colossus straddled the harbour of Rhodes. A blueprint is a "detailed plan, especially in the early stages of a project or idea", and it is also "a photographic print of the final stage of engineering or other plans in white on a blue background" (*Concise Oxford Dictionary*). Whether it is early or final, a blueprint is an architect's or engineer's plan for builders. It is now time for the builders to be booked and given the go-ahead, for the benefit of humankind. The old order has collapsed, and is in its death-throes. Humankind is crying out for the supranational structure to be built and for the peace dividend to restore health. It is what the world needs to revive, and its resurgence can bring in a coming Golden Age.

However, a Golden Age cannot happen unless an American, through an act of will, sets the process in motion by addressing the UN and proposing a World Constitutional Convention to create a new supranational system. The US President could do this.

And so my final appeal is to the President of the United States and to the UN. Mr President, and members of the General Assembly, do your duty. Give up a little sovereignty to the supranational level in respect of the seven goals, so there can be universal peace and disarmament on a legally enforceable footing. You will still retain your national or regional sovereignty outside the areas of the seven goals. Have courage and be forward-looking. Bring in the Universalist World State.

Chart of 25 Civilizations and Cultures from One to One

The Fundamental Unity of World Culture

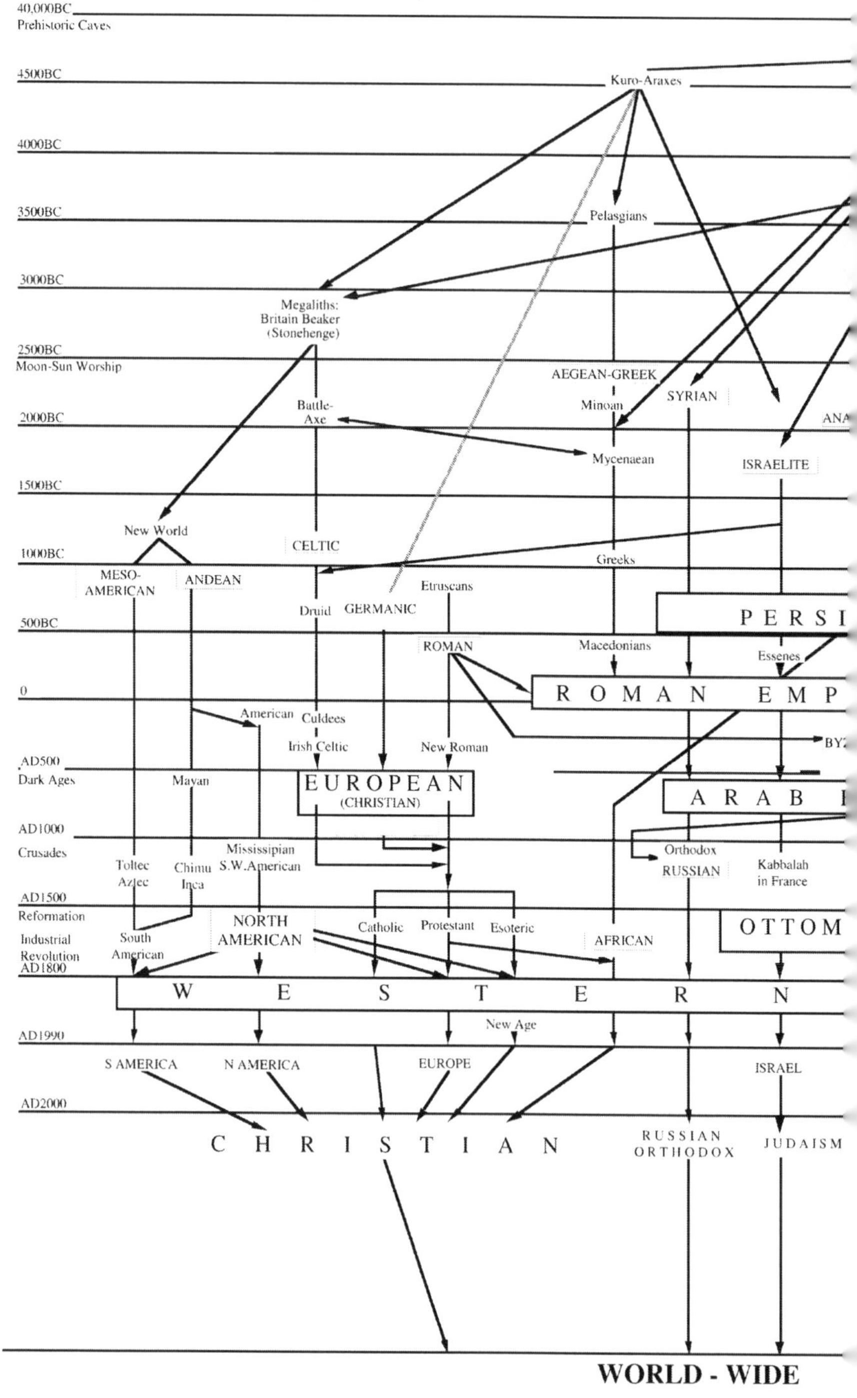

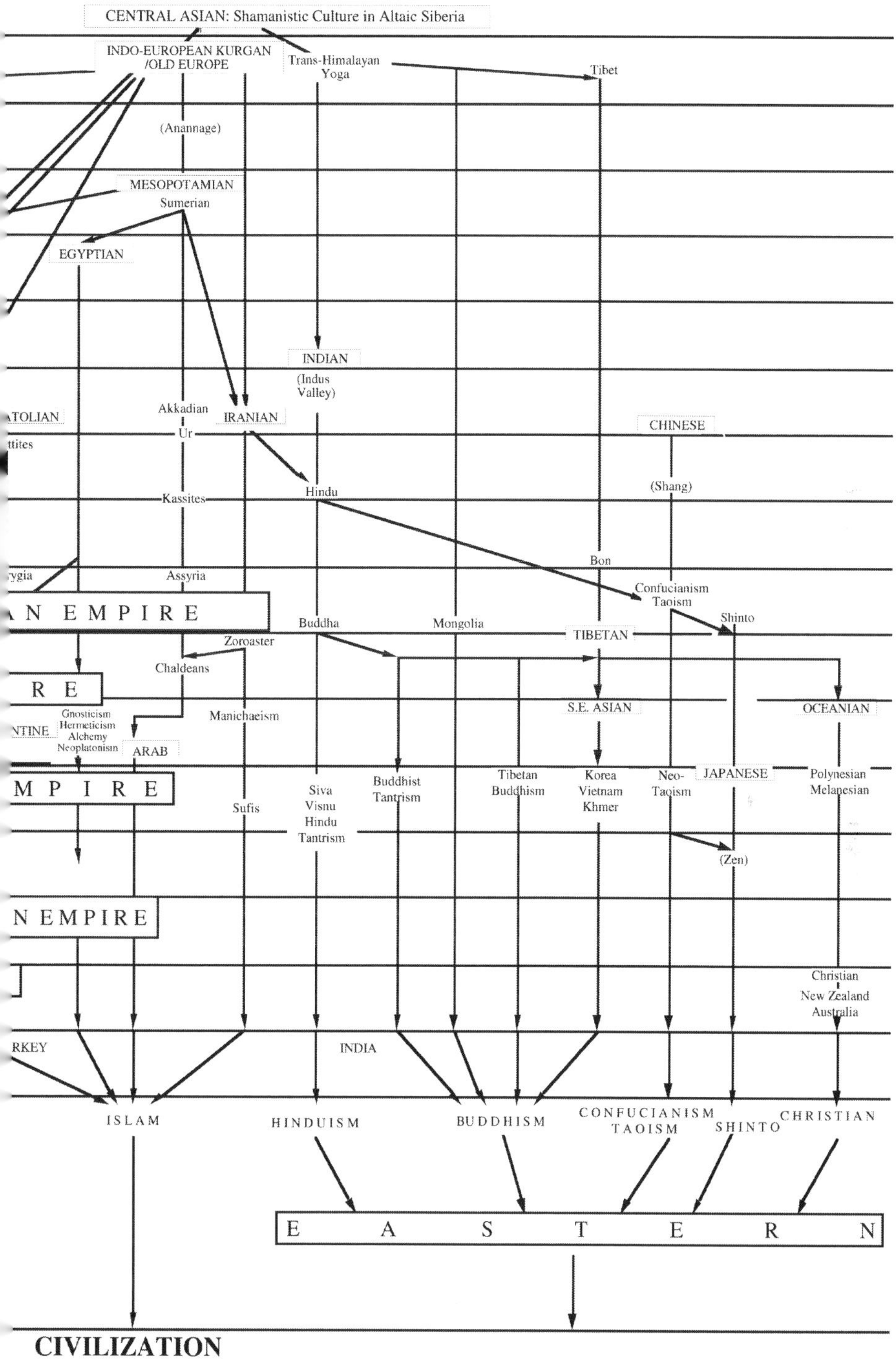

CENTRAL ASIAN: Shamanistic Culture in Altaic Siberia
INDO-EUROPEAN KURGAN /OLD EUROPE
Trans-Himalayan Yoga
Tibet
(Anannage)
MESOPOTAMIAN
Sumerian
EGYPTIAN
INDIAN
(Indus Valley)
ATOLIAN
ttites
Akkadian
Ur
IRANIAN
CHINESE
Hindu
Kassites
(Shang)
Bon
ygia
Assyria
Confucianism Taoism
N EMPIRE
Buddha
Mongolia
Shinto
TIBETAN
Zoroaster
Chaldeans
R E
S.E. ASIAN
OCEANIAN
Gnosticism
Hermeticism
Alchemy
Neoplatonism
NTINE
Manichaeism
ARAB
MPIRE
Siva Visnu Hindu Tantrism
Buddhist Tantrism
Tibetan Buddhism
Korea Vietnam Khmer
Neo-Taoism
JAPANESE
Polynesian Melanesian
Sufis
(Zen)
N EMPIRE
Christian New Zealand Australia
RKEY
INDIA
ISLAM
HINDUISM
BUDDHISM
CONFUCIANISM TAOISM
SHINTO
CHRISTIAN
E A S T E R N
CIVILIZATION

APPENDICES

Data: Facts Relating to the UN, Regions and Nation-States

A. US-Based Documents

1.
Declaration of Independence

July 4, 1776

(See pp25, 40, 41, 42, 58, 98)

When in the course of human events, it becomes necessary for one people to dissolve the political bands which have connected them with another, and to assume among the powers of the earth, the separate and equal station to which the laws of nature and of nature's God entitle them, a decent respect to the opinions of mankind requires that they should declare the causes which impel them to the separation.

We hold these truths to be self-evident:

That all men are created equal; that they are endowed by their Creator with certain unalienable rights; that among these are life, liberty, and the pursuit of happiness; that, to secure these rights, governments are instituted among men, deriving their just powers from the consent of the governed; that whenever any form of government becomes destructive of these ends, it is the right of the people to alter or to abolish it, and to institute new government, laying its foundation on such principles, and organizing its powers in such form, as to them shall seem most likely to effect their safety and happiness. Prudence, indeed, will dictate that governments long established should not be changed for light and transient causes; and accordingly all experience hath shown that mankind are more disposed to suffer, while evils are sufferable than to right themselves by abolishing the forms to which they are accustomed. But when a long train of abuses and usurpations, pursuing invariably the same object, evinces a design to reduce them under absolute despotism, it is their right, it is their duty, to throw off such government, and to provide new guards for their future security. Such has been the patient sufferance of these colonies; and such is now the necessity which constrains them to alter their former systems of government. The history of the present King of Great Britain is a history of repeated injuries and usurpations, all having in direct object the establishment of an absolute tyranny over these states. To prove this, let facts be submitted to a candid world.

He has refused his assent to laws, the most wholesome and necessary for the public good.

He has forbidden his governors to pass laws of immediate and pressing importance, unless suspended in their operation till his assent should be obtained; and, when so suspended, he has utterly neglected to attend to them.

He has refused to pass other laws for the accommodation of large districts of people, unless those people would relinquish the right of representation in the legislature, a right inestimable to them, and formidable to tyrants only.

He has called together legislative bodies at places unusual uncomfortable, and distant from the depository of their public records, for the sole purpose of fatiguing them into compliance with his measures.

He has dissolved representative houses repeatedly, for opposing, with manly firmness, his invasions on the rights of the people.

He has refused for a long time, after such dissolutions, to cause others to be elected; whereby the legislative powers, incapable of annihilation, have returned to the people at large for their exercise; the state remaining, in the mean time, exposed to all the dangers of invasions from without and convulsions within.

He has endeavored to prevent the population of these states; for that purpose obstructing the laws for naturalization of foreigners; refusing to pass others to encourage their migration hither, and raising the conditions of new appropriations of lands.

He has obstructed the administration of justice, by refusing his assent to laws for establishing judiciary powers.

He has made judges dependent on his will alone, for the tenure of their offices, and the amount and payment of their salaries.

He has erected a multitude of new offices, and sent hither swarms of officers to harass our people and eat out their substance.

He has kept among us, in times of peace, standing armies, without the consent of our legislatures.

He has affected to render the military independent of, and superior to, the civil power.

He has combined with others to subject us to a jurisdiction foreign to our Constitution and unacknowledged by our laws, giving his assent to their acts of pretended legislation:

For quartering large bodies of armed troops among us;

For protecting them, by a mock trial, from punishment for any murders which they should commit on the inhabitants of these states;

For cutting off our trade with all parts of the world;

For imposing taxes on us without our consent;

For depriving us, in many cases, of the benefits of trial by jury;

For transporting us beyond seas, to be tried for pretended offenses;

For abolishing the free system of English laws in a neighboring province, establishing therein an arbitrary government, and enlarging its boundaries, so as to render it at once an example and fit instrument for introducing the same absolute rule into these colonies;

For taking away our charters, abolishing our most valuable laws, and altering fundamentally the forms of our governments;

For suspending our own legislatures, and declaring themselves invested with power to legislate for us in all cases whatsoever.

He has abdicated government here, by declaring us out of his protection and waging war against us.

He has plundered our seas, ravaged our coasts, burned our towns, and destroyed the lives of our people.

He is at this time transporting large armies of foreign mercenaries to complete the works of death, desolation, and tyranny already begun with circumstances of cruelty and perfidy scarcely paralleled in the most barbarous ages, and totally unworthy the head of a civilized nation.

He has constrained our fellow-citizens, taken captive on the high seas, to bear arms against their country, to become the executioners of their friends and brethren, or to fall themselves by their hands.

He has excited domestic insurrection among us, and has endeavored to bring on the inhabitants of our frontiers the merciless Indian savages, whose known rule of warfare is an undistinguished destruction of all ages, sexes, and conditions.

In every stage of these oppressions we have petitioned for redress in the most humble terms; our repeated petitions have been answered only by repeated injury. A prince, whose character is thus marked by every act which may define a tyrant, is unfit to be the ruler of a free people.

Nor have we been wanting in our attentions to our British brethren. We have warned them, from time to time, of attempts by their legislature to extend an unwarrantable jurisdiction over us. We have reminded them of the circumstances of our emigration and settlement here. We have appealed to their native justice and magnanimity; and we have conjured them, by the ties of our common kindred, to disavow these usurpations which would inevitably interrupt our connections and correspondence. They too, have been deaf to the voice of justice and of consanguinity. We must, therefore, acquiesce in the necessity which denounces our separation, and hold them as we hold the rest of mankind, enemies in war, in peace friends.

We, therefore, the representatives of the United States of America, in General Congress assembled, appealing to the Supreme Judge of the world for the rectitude of our intentions, do, in the name and by the authority of the good people of these colonies solemnly publish and declare, That these United Colonies are, and of right ought to be, FREE AND INDEPENDENT STATES; that they are absolved from all allegiance to the British crown and that all political connection between them and the state of Great Britain is, and ought to be, totally dissolved; and that, as free and independent states, they have full power to levy war, conclude peace, contract alliances, establish commerce, and do all other acts and things which independent states may of right do. And for the support of this declaration, with a firm reliance on the protection of Divine Providence, we mutually pledge to each other our lives, our fortunes, and our sacred honor.

[Signed by] John Hancock [President]

New Hampshire
Josiah Bartlett, Wm. Whipplt, Matthew Thormton.

Massachusetts Bay
Saml. Adams, John Adams, Robt. Treat Paine, Elbridge Gerry.

Rhode Island
Step. Hopkins, William Ellery.

Connecticut
Roger Sherman, Sam'el Huntington, Wm. Williams, Oliver Wolcott.

New York
Wm. Floyd, Phil. Livingston, Frans. Lewis, Lewis Morris.

New Jersey
Richd. Stockton, Jno. Witherspoon, Fras. Hopkinson, John Hart, Abra. Clark.

Pennsylvania
Robt. Morris, Benjamin Rush, Benja. Franklin, John Morton, Geo. Clymer, Jas. Smith, Geo. Taylor, James Wilson, Geo. Ross.

Delaware
Caesar Rodney, Geo. Read, Tho. M'kean.

Maryland
Samuel Chase, Wm. Paca, Thos. Stone, Charles Carroll of Carrollton.

Virginia
George Wythe, Richard Henry Lee, Th. Jefferson, Benja. Harrison, Ths. Nelson, Jr., Francis Lightfoot Lee, Carter Braxton.

North Carolina
Wm. Hooper, Joseph Hewes, John Penn.

South Carolina
Edward Rutledge, Thos. Hayward, Junr., Thomas Lynch, Junr., Arthur Middleton.

Georgia
Button Gwinnett, Lyman Hall, Geo. Walton.

2.
The North Atlantic Treaty

Washington D.C. – 4 April 1949

(See p62)

The Parties to this Treaty reaffirm their faith in the purposes and principles of the Charter of the United Nations and their desire to live in peace with all peoples and all governments.

They are determined to safeguard the freedom, common heritage and civilisation of their peoples, founded on the principles of democracy, individual liberty and the rule of law.

They seek to promote stability and well-being in the North Atlantic area.

They are resolved to unite their efforts for collective defense and for the preservation of peace and security. They therefore agree to this North Atlantic Treaty:

Article 1

The Parties undertake, as set forth in the Charter of the United Nations, to settle any international dispute in which they may be involved by peaceful means in such a manner that international peace and security and justice are not endangered, and to refrain in their international relations from the threat or use of force in any manner inconsistent with the purposes of the United Nations.

Article 2

The Parties will contribute toward the further development of peaceful and friendly international relations by strengthening their free institutions, by bringing about a better understanding of the principles upon which these institutions are founded, and by promoting conditions of stability and well-being. They will seek to eliminate conflict in their international economic policies and will encourage economic collaboration between any or all of them.

Article 3

In order more effectively to achieve the objectives of this Treaty, the Parties, separately and jointly, by means of continuous and effective self-help and mutual aid, will maintain and develop their individual and collective capacity to resist armed attack.

Article 4

The Parties will consult together whenever, in the opinion of any of them, the territorial integrity, political independence or security of any of the Parties is threatened.

Article 5

The Parties agree that an armed attack against one or more of them in Europe or North America shall be considered an attack against them all and consequently they agree that, if such an armed attack occurs, each of them, in exercise of the right of individual or collective self-defence recognised by Article 51 of the Charter of the United Nations, will assist the Party or Parties so attacked by taking forthwith, individually and in concert with the other Parties, such action as it deems necessary, including the use of armed force, to restore and maintain the security of the North Atlantic area.

Any such armed attack and all measures taken as a result thereof shall immediately be reported to the Security Council. Such measures shall be terminated when the Security Council has taken the measures necessary to restore and maintain international peace and security.

Article 6[1]

For the purposes of Article 5, an armed attack on one or more of the Parties is deemed to include an armed attack:

- on the territory of any of the Parties in Europe or North America, on the Algerian Departments of France,[2] on the territory of or on the Islands under the jurisdiction of any of the Parties in the North Atlantic area north of the Tropic of Cancer;
- on the forces, vessels, or aircraft of any of the Parties, when in or over these territories or any other area in Europe in which occupation forces of any of the Parties were stationed on the date when the Treaty entered into force or the Mediterranean Sea or the North Atlantic area north of the Tropic of Cancer.

Article 7

This Treaty does not affect, and shall not be interpreted as affecting in any way the rights and obligations under the Charter of the Parties which are members of the United Nations, or the primary responsibility of the Security Council for the maintenance of international peace and security.

Article 8

Each Party declares that none of the international engagements now in force between it and any other of the Parties or any third State is in conflict with the provisions of this Treaty, and undertakes not to enter into any international engagement in conflict with this Treaty.

Article 9

The Parties hereby establish a Council, on which each of them shall be represented, to consider matters concerning the implementation of this Treaty.

The Council shall be so organised as to be able to meet promptly at any time. The Council shall set up such subsidiary bodies as may be necessary; in particular it shall establish immediately a defence committee which shall recommend measures for the implementation of Articles 3 and 5.

Article 10

The Parties may, by unanimous agreement, invite any other European State in a position to further the principles of this Treaty and to contribute to the security of the North Atlantic area to accede to this Treaty. Any State so invited may become a Party to the Treaty by depositing its instrument of accession with the Government of the United States of America. The Government of the United States of America will inform each of the Parties of the deposit of each such instrument of accession.

Article 11

This Treaty shall be ratified and its provisions carried out by the Parties in accordance with their respective constitutional processes. The instruments of ratification shall be deposited as soon as possible with the Government of the United States of America, which will notify all the other signatories of each deposit. The Treaty shall enter into force between the States which have ratified it as soon as the ratifications of the majority of the signatories, including the ratifications of Belgium, Canada, France, Luxembourg, the Netherlands, the United Kingdom and the United States, have been deposited and shall come into effect with respect to other States on the date of the deposit of their ratifications.[3]

Article 12

After the Treaty has been in force for ten years, or at any time thereafter, the Parties shall, if any of them so requests, consult together for the purpose of reviewing the Treaty, having regard for the factors then affecting peace and security in the North Atlantic area, including the development of universal as well as regional arrangements under the Charter of the United Nations for the maintenance of international peace and security.

Article 13

After the Treaty has been in force for twenty years, any Party may cease to be a Party one year after its notice of denunciation has been given to the

Government of the United States of America, which will inform the Governments of the other Parties of the deposit of each notice of denunciation.

Article 14
This Treaty, of which the English and French texts are equally authentic, shall be deposited in the archives of the Government of the United States of America. Duly certified copies will be transmitted by that Government to the Governments of other signatories.

Notes

1. The definition of the territories to which Article 5 applies was revised by Article 2 of the Protocol to the North Atlantic Treaty on the accession of Greece and Turkey signed on 22 October 1951.
2. On January 16, 1963, the North Atlantic Council noted that insofar as the former Algerian Departments of France were concerned, the relevant clauses of this Treaty had become inapplicable as from July 3, 1962.
3. The Treaty came into force on 24 August 1949, after the deposition of the ratifications of all signatory states.

3.
Project for the New American Century

Statement of Principles

June 3, 1997

(See p63)

American foreign and defense policy is adrift. Conservatives have criticized the incoherent policies of the Clinton Administration. They have also resisted isolationist impulses from within their own ranks. But conservatives have not confidently advanced a strategic vision of America's role in the world. They have not set forth guiding principles for American foreign policy. They have allowed differences over tactics to obscure potential agreement on strategic objectives. And they have not fought for the defense budget that would maintain American security and advance American interests in the new century.

We aim to change this. We aim to make the case and rally support for American global leadership.

As the 20th century draws to a close, the United States stands as the world's pre-eminent power. Having led the West to victory in the Cold War, America faces an opportunity and a challenge: Does the United States have the vision to build upon the achievements of past decades? Does the United States have the resolve to shape a new century favourable to American principles and interests?

We are in danger of squandering the opportunity and failing the challenge. We are living off the capital – both the military investments and the foreign policy achievements – built up by past administrations. Cuts in foreign affairs and defense spending, inattention to the tools of statecraft, and inconstant leadership are making it increasingly difficult to sustain American influence around the world. And the promise of short-term commercial benefits threatens to override strategic considerations. As a consequence, we are jeopardizing the nation's ability to meet present threats and to deal with potentially greater challenges that lie ahead.

We seem to have forgotten the essential elements of the Reagan Administration's success: a military that is strong and ready to meet both present and future challenges; a foreign policy that boldly and purposefully promotes American principles abroad; and national leadership that accepts the United States' global responsibility.

Of course, the United States must be prudent in how it exercises its power. But we cannot safely avoid the responsibilities of global leadership or the costs that are associated with its exercise. America has a vital role in maintaining peace and security in Europe, Asia, and the Middle East. If we shirk our responsibilities, we invite challenges to our fundamental interests. The history of the 20th century should have taught us that it is important to shape circumstances before crises emerge, and to meet threats before they become dire. The history of this century should have taught us to embrace the cause of American leadership.

Our aim is to remind Americans of these lessons and to draw their consequences for today. Here are four consequences:

- we need to increase defense spending significantly if we are to carry out our global responsibilities today and modernize our armed forces for the future;
- we need to strengthen our ties to democratic allies and to challenge regimes hostile to our interests and values;

- we need to promote the cause of political and economic freedom abroad;
- we need to accept responsibility for America's unique role in preserving and extending an international order friendly to our security, our prosperity, and our principles.

Such a Reaganite policy of military strength and moral clarity may not be fashionable today. But it is necessary if the United States is to build on the successes of this past century and to ensure our security and our greatness in the next.

Elliott Abrams
Gary Bauer
William J. Bennett
Jeb Bush
Dick Cheney
Eliot A. Cohen
Midge Decter
Paula Dobriansky
Steve Forbes
Aaron Friedberg
Francis Fukuyama
Frank Gaffney
Fred C. Ikle
Donald Kagan
Zalmay Khalilzad
I. Lewis Libby
Norman Podhoretz
Dan Quayle
Peter W. Rodman
Stephen P. Rosen
Henry S. Rowen
Donald Rumsfeld
Vin Weber
George Weigel
Paul Wolfowitz

B. The UN

1.
Overview of the UN Structure

(See p82)

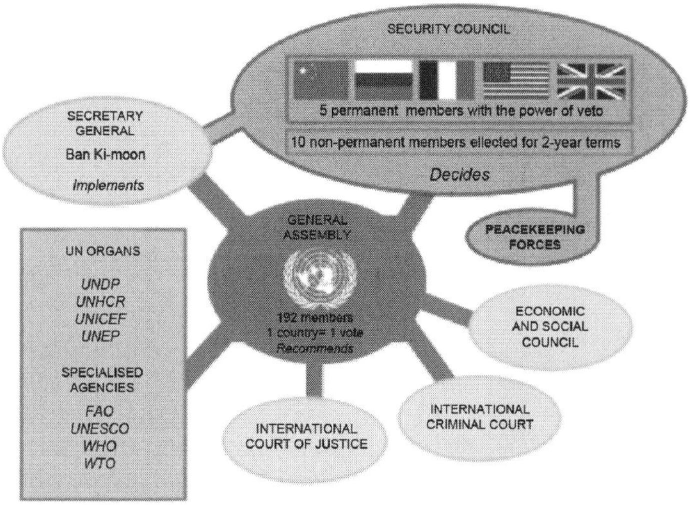

2.
Structure of UN Agencies

(See p142)

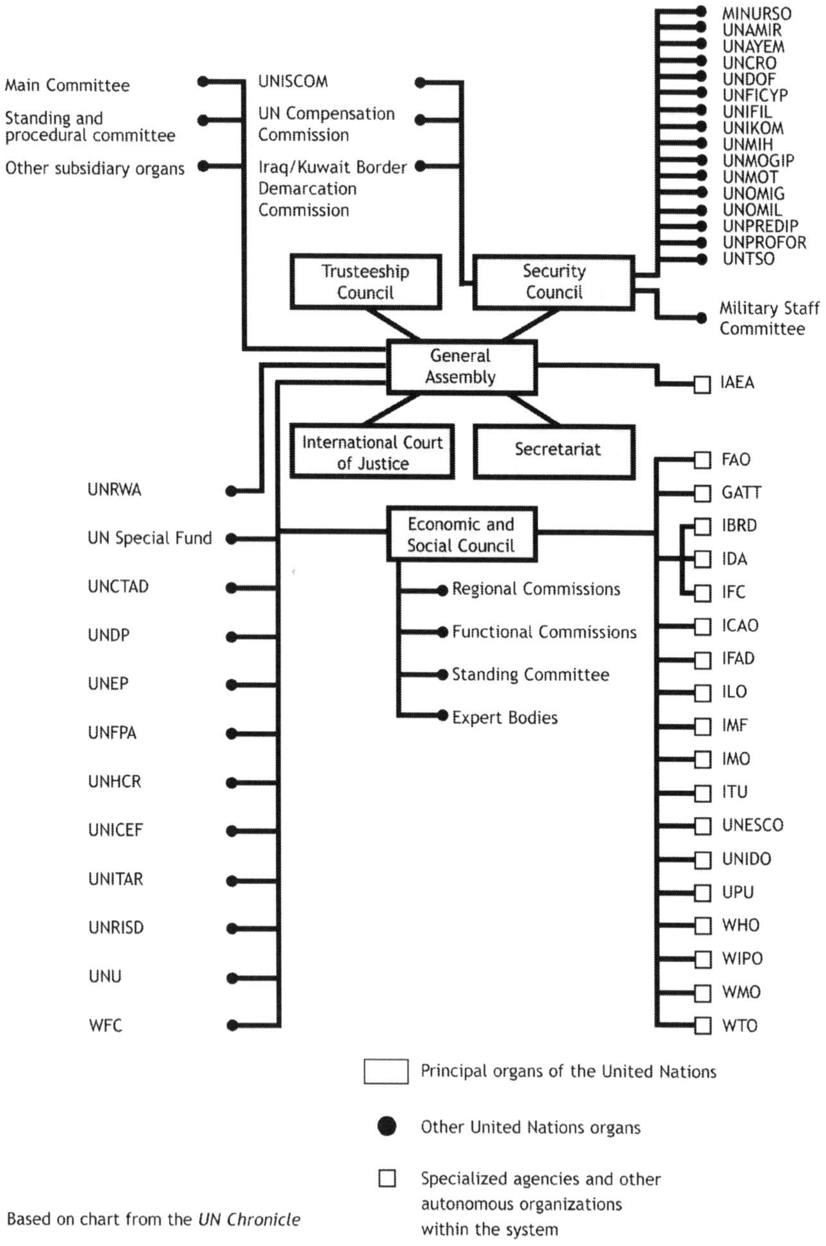

Based on chart from the *UN Chronicle*

3.
UN Organizations
(See p142)

Organizations of the General Assembly

- Main committees
- Other session committees
- Standing committees and *ad hoc* bodies

Some of the Programmes and Funds include:

- Rights Council
- UNCTAD – United Nations Conference on Trade and Development
  - ITC – International Trade Centre (UNCTAD/WTO)
- UNDCP – United Nations Drug Control Programme
- UNDP – United Nations Development Programme
  - UNCDF – United Nations Capital Development Fund
  - UNIFEM – United Nations Development Fund for Women
  - UNV – United Nations Volunteers
- UNEP – United Nations Environment Programme
- UNFPA – United Nations Fund for Population Activities
- UNHCR – Office of the United Nations High Commissioner for Refugees
- UN-HABITAT – United Nations Human Settlements Programme
- UNICEF – Unied Nations Children's Fund
- WFP – World Food Programme
- UNRWA – United Nations Relief and Works Agency for Palestine Refugees in the Near East

Research and training institutes

- INSTRAW – International Research and Training Institute for the Advancement of Women
- UNICRI – United Nations Interregional Crime and Justice Research Institute
- UNITAR – United Nations Institute for Training and Research
- UNRISD – United Nations Research Institute for Social Development
- UNIDIR – United Nations Institute for Disarmament Research (Reports only to the General Assembly)

Other entities

- COPUOS – United Nations Committee on the Peaceful Uses of Outer Space
- JIU – Joint Inspection Unit (oversight body of the United Nations system)
- OHCHR – Office of the United Nations High Commissioner for Human Rights
- UNOPS – United Nations Office for Project Services
- UNU – United Nations University
- UNOOSA – United Nations Office for Outer Space Affairs
- UNSSC – United Nations System Staff College
- UNAIDS – Joint United Nations Programme on HIV/AIDS
- UNRRA – United Nations Relief and Rehabilitation Administration (ceased to exist in 1949)
- UPEACE – United Nations Mandated University for Peace

Organizations of the Security Council

- Military Staff Committee
- Standing Committee and *ad hoc* bodies
- International Criminal Tribunal for the Former Yugoslavia
- International Criminal Tribunal for Rwanda
- 1540 Committee – Committee established pursuant to UN Security Council Resolution 1540 (2004)
- Counter-Terrorism Committee – Committee established pursuant to UN Security Council Resolution 1373 (2001)
- Peacekeeping Operations and Missions
    - MONUC – United Nations Mission in the Democratic Republic of Congo
    - UNAVEM III – United Nations Angola Verification Mission III
    - UNDOF – United Nations Disengagement Observer Force
    - UNFICYP – United Nations Peacekeeping Force in Cyprus
    - UNIFIL – United Nations Interim Force in Lebanon
    - UNMEE – United Nations Mission in Ethiopia and Eritrea
    - UNMIK – United Nations Interim Administration Mission in Kosovo
    - UNMIL – United Nations Mission in Liberia
    - UNMIS – United Nations Mission in Sudan

  - UNMOGIP – United Nations Military Observer Group in India and Pakistan
  - UNMOVIC – United Nations Monitoring, Verification and Inspection Commission
  - UNOMIG – United Nations Observer Mission in Georgia
  - UNOMSIL – United Nations Mission of Observers in Sierra Leone
  - UNSMIH – United Nations Support Mission in Haiti
  - UNTSO – United Nations Truce Supervision Organization
  - UNMIN – United Nations Mission in Nepal
- Former Peacekeeping Operations and Missions
  - ONUMOZ – United Nations Operation in Mozambique
  - UNAMIR – United Nations Assistance Mission for Rwanda
  - UNAMSIL – United Nations Mission in Sierra Leone
  - UNCRO – United Nations Confidence Restoration Operation in Croatia
  - UNIKOM – United Nations Iraq-Kuwait Observation Mission
  - UNMIBH – United Nations Mission in Bosnia and Herzegovina
  - UNMOP – United Nations Mission of Observers in Prevlaka
  - UNMOT – United Nations Mission of Observers in Tajikistan
  - UNSCOM – United Nations Special Commission (Iraq)
  - UNTAET – United Nations Transitional Administration in East Timor
  - UNTAC – United Nations Transitional Authority in Cambodia

Organizations of the Economic and Social Council

Functional commissions

- Commission for Social Development
- Commission on Narcotic Drugs
- Commission on Crime Prevention and Criminal Justice
- Commission on Science and Technology for Development
- Commission on Sustainable Development
- Commission on the Status of Women
- Commission on Population and Development
- Statistical Commission
- United Nations Forum on Forests

Regional commissions

- ECE – United Nations Economic Commission for Europe
- ECA – United Nations Economic Commission for Africa
- ECLAC – United Nations Economic Commission for Latin America and the Caribbean
- ESCAP – United Nations Economic and Social Commission for Asia and the Pacific
- ESCWA – United Nations Economic and Social Commission for Western Asia

Specialized agencies

The specialized agencies are autonomous organizations with the United Nations and each other through the co-ordinating machinery of the Economic and Social Council.

- ILO – International Labour Organization
- FAO – Food and Agriculture Organization
- UNESCO – United Nations Educational, Scientific and Cultural Organization
- WHO – World Health Organization
- World Bank Group
    - IBRD – International Bank for Reconstruction and Development
    - IDA – International Development Association
    - IFC – International Finance Corporation
    - MIGA – Multilateral Investment Guarantee Agency
    - ICSID – International Centre for Settlement of Investment Disputes
- IMF – International Monetary Fund
- ICAO – International Civil Aviation Organization
- IMO – International Maritime Organization
- ITU - International Telecommunication Union
- UPU – Universal Postal Union
- WMO – World Meteorological Organization
- WIPO – World Intellectual Property Organization
- IFAD – International Fund for Agricultural Development
- UNIDO – United Nations Industrial Development Organization
- IRO – International Refugee Organization (ceased to exist in 1952)
- INCB – International Narcotics Control Board
- UNWTO – United Nations World Tourism Organization
- PFII – Permanent Forum on Indigenous Issues

- Sessional and Standing Committees Expert, *ad hoc* and related bodies

Organization of the Secretariat

The United Nations Secretariat is led by the Secretary-General of the United Nations.

- OSG – Office of the Secretary-General
- OIOS – Office of Internal Oversight Services
- OLA – Office of Legal Affairs
- DPA – Department of Political Affairs
- ODA – Office for Disarmament Affairs
- DPKO – Department of Peacekeeping Operations
- OCHA – Office for the Coordination of Humanitarian Affairs
- DESA – Department of Economic and Social Affairs
- DGACM – Department of General Assembly and Conference Management
- DSS – Department of Safety and Security
- DPI – Department of Public Information
- DM – Department of Management
- OIP – Office of the Iraq Programme
- UNSECOORD – Office of the United Nations Security Co-ordinator
- OHRLLS – Office of the High Representative for the Least Developed Countries, Landlocked Developing Countries and Small Island Developing States
- ODC – Office on Drugs and Crime
- UNOG – UN Office at Geneva
- UNOV – UN Office at Vienna
- UNON – UN Office at Nairobi

Related organizations

- IAEA – International Atomic Energy Agency, Reports to the Security Council and the General Assembly
- WTO – World Trade Organization
- ICC – International Criminal Court
- ISA – International Seabed Authority
- ITLOS – International Tribunal for the Law of the Sea

Standby High-Readiness Brigade – the UN's standing military force

UNSOG – Special Operations Group

4.
The UN's 192 Member States*
(See p82)

A

Afghanistan
Albania
Algeria
Andorra
Angola
Antigua and Barbuda
Argentina
Armenia
Australia
Austria
Azerbaijan

B

Bahamas
Bahrain
Bangladesh
Barbados
Belarus
Belgium
Belize
Benin
Bhutan
Bolivia
Bosnia and Herzegovina
Botswana
Brazil
Brunei
Bulgaria
Burkina Faso
Burundi

C

Cambodia
Cameroon
Canada
Cape Verde
Central African Republic
Chad
Chile
China
Colombia
Comoros
Congo (Brazzaville)
Congo (Kinshasa)
Costa Rica
Côte d'Ivoire
Croatia
Cuba
Cyprus
Czech Republic

D

Denmark
Djibouti
Dominica
Dominican Republic

E

East Timor	El Salvador	Estonia
Ecuador	Equatorial Guinea	Ethiopia
Egypt	Eritrea	

F

Fiji	Finland	France

G

Gabon	Ghana	Guinea
Gambia	Greece	Guinea-Bissau
Georgia	Grenada	Guyana
Germany	Guatemala	

H

Haiti	Honduras	Hungary

I

Iceland	Iran	Israel
India	Iraq	Italy
Indonesia	Ireland	

J

Jamaica	Japan	Jordan

K

Kazakhstan	Korea, North	Kuwait
Kenya	Korea, South	Kyrgyzstan
Kiribati		

L

Laos	Lesotho	Liechtenstein
Latvia	Liberia	Lithuania
Lebanon	Libya	Luxembourg

M

Macedonia
Madagascar
Malawi
Malaysia
Maldives
Mali
Malta
Marshall Islands
Mauritania
Mauritius
Mexico
Micronesia
Moldova
Monaco
Mongolia
Montenegro
Morocco
Mozambique
Myanmar

N

Namibia
Nauru
Nepal
Netherlands
New Zealand
Nicaragua
Niger
Nigeria
Norway

O

Oman

P

Pakistan
Palau
Panama
Papua New Guinea
Paraguay
Peru
Philippines
Poland
Portugal

Q

Qatar

R

Romania
Russia
Rwanda

S

St. Kitts and Nevis
St. Lucia
St. Vincent and the Grenadines
Samoa
San Marino
São Tomé and Principe
Saudi Arabia
Senegal
Serbia
Seychelles
Sierra Leone
Singapore
Slovakia
Slovenia
Solomon Islands
Somalia
South Africa
Spain
Sri Lanka
Sudan
Suriname
Swaziland
Sweden

Switzerland
Syria

T

Tajikistan
Tanzania
Thailand
Togo
Tonga
Trinidad and Tobago
Tunisia
Turkey
Turkmenistan
Tuvalu

U

Uganda
Ukraine
United Arab Emirates
United Kingdom
United States
Uruguay
Uzbekistan

V

Vanuatu
Venezuela
Vietnam

Y

Yemen

Z

Zambia
Zimbabwe

* The US Department of State recognised 194 countries in 2009, including Kosovo and Vatican City/The Holy See

5.
The UN Universal Declaration of Human Rights 1948

(Adopted by the UN General Assembly on 10 December 1948)

(See pp30, 33, 116, 118, 131)

PREAMBLE

Whereas recognition of the inherent dignity and of the equal and inalienable rights of all members of the human family is the foundation of freedom, justice and peace in the world,

Whereas disregard and contempt for human rights have resulted in barbarous acts which have outraged the conscience of mankind, and the advent of a world in which human beings shall enjoy freedom of speech and belief and freedom from fear and want has been proclaimed as the highest aspiration of the common people,

Whereas it is essential, if man is not to be compelled to have recourse, as a last resort, to rebellion against tyranny and oppression, that human rights should be protected by the rule of law,

Whereas it is essential to promote the development of friendly relations between nations,

Whereas the peoples of the United Nations have in the Charter reaffirmed their faith in fundamental human rights, in the dignity and worth of the human person and in the equal rights of mean and women and have determined to promote social progress and better standards of life in larger freedom,

Whereas Member States have pledged themselves to achieve, in co-operation with the United Nations, the promotion of universal respect for and observance of human rights and fundamental freedoms,

Whereas a common understanding of thee rights and freedoms is of the greatest importance for the full realization of this pledge,

Now, Therefore THE GENERAL ASSEMBLY proclaims THIS UNIVERSAL DECLARATION OF HUMAN RIGHTS as a common standard of achievement for all peoples and all nations, to the end that every individual and every organ of society, keeping this Declaration constantly in mind, shall strive by teaching and education to promote respect for these rights and freedoms and by progressive measures, national and international, to secure their universal and effective recognition and observance, both among the peoples of Member States themselves and among the peoples of territories under their jurisdiction.

Article 1

All human beings are born free and equal in dignity and rights. They are endowed with reason and conscience and should act towards one another in a spirit of brotherhood.

Article 2
Everyone is entitled to all the rights and freedoms set forth in this Declaration, without distinction of any kind, such as race, colour, sex, language, religion, political or other opinion, national or social origin, property, birth or other status. Furthermore, no distinction shall be made on the basis of the political, jurisdictional or international status of the country or territory to which a person belongs whether it be independent, trust, non-self-governing or under any other limitation of sovereignty.

Article 3
Everyone has the right to life, liberty and security of person.

Article 4
No one shall be held in slavery or servitude, slavery and the slave trade shall be prohibited in all their forms.

Article 5
No one shall be subjected to torture or to cruel, inhuman or degrading treatment or punishment.

Article 6
Everyone has the right to recognition everywhere as a person before the law.

Article 7
All are equal before the law and are entitled without any discrimination to equal protection of the law. All are entitled to equal protected against any discrimination in violation of this Declaration and against any incitement to such discrimination.

Article 8
Everyone has the right to an effective remedy by the competent national tribunals for acts violating the fundamental rights granted him by the constitution or by law.

Article 9
No one shall be subjected to arbitrary arrest, detention or exile.

Article 10

Everyone is entitled in full equality to a fair and public hearing by an independent and impartial tribunal, in the determination of his rights and obligations and of any criminal charge against him.

Article 11

1. Everyone charged with a penal offence has the right to be presumed innocent until proved guilty according to law in a public trial at which he has had all the guarantees necessary for his defence.
2. No one shall be held guilty of any penal offence on account of any act or omission which did not constitute a penal offence, under national or international law, at the time when it was committed. Nor shall a heavier penalty be imposed than the one that was applicable at the time the penal offence was committed.

Article 12

No one shall be subjected to arbitrary interference with his privacy, family, home or correspondence, nor to attacks upon his honour and reputation. Everyone has the right to the protection of the law against such interference or attacks.

Article 13

1. Everyone has the right to freedom of movement and residence within the borders of each state.
2. Everyone has the right to leave any country, including his own, and to return to his country.

Article 14

1. Everyone has the right to seek and to enjoy in other countries asylum from persecution.
2. This right may not be invoked in the case of prosecutions genuinely arising from non-political crimes or from acts contrary to the purposes and principles of the United Nations.

Article 15

1. Everyone has the right to a nationality.
2. No one shall be arbitrarily deprived of his nationality nor denied the

right to change his nationality.

Article 16

1. Men and women of full age, without any limitation due to race, nationality or religion, have the right to marry and to found a family. They are entitled to equal rights as to marriage, during marriage and at its dissolution.
2. Marriage shall be entered into only with the free and full consent of the intending spouses.
3. The family is the natural and fundamental group unit of society and is entitled to protection by society and the State.

Article 17

1. Everyone has the right to own property alone as well as in association with others.
2. No one shall be arbitrarily deprived of his property.

Article 18

Everyone has the right of freedom of thought, conscience and religion; this right includes freedom to change his religion or belief, and freedom, either alone or in community with others and in public or private, to manifest his religion or belief in teaching, practice, worship and observance.

Article 19

Everyone has the right to freedom of opinion and expression; this right includes freedom to hold opinions without interference and to seek, receive and impart information and ideas through any media and regardless of frontiers.

Article 20

1. Everyone has the right to freedom of peaceful assembly and association.
2. No one may be compelled to belong to an association.

Article 21

1. Everyone has the right to take part in the government of his country, directly or through freely chosen representatives.

2. Everyone has the right of equal access to public services in his country.
3. The will of the people shall be the basis of the authority of government, this will shall be expressed in periodic and genuine elections which shall be by universal and equal suffrage and shall be held by secret vote or by equivalent free voting procedures.

Article 22

Everyone, as a member of society, has the right to social security and is entitled to realization, through national effort and international co-operation and in accordance with the organization and resources of each State, of the economic, social and cultural rights indispensable for his dignity and the free development of his personality.

Article 23

1. Everyone has the right to work, to free choice of employment, to just and favourable conditions of work and to protection against unemployment.
2. Everyone, without any discrimination, has the right to equal pay for equal work.
3. Everyone who works has the right to just and favourable remuneration ensuring for himself and his family an existence worthy of human dignity, and supplemented, if necessary, by other means of social protection.
4. Everyone has the right to form and to join trade unions for the protection of his interests.

Article 24

Everyone has the right to rest and leisure, including reasonable limitation of working hours and periodic holidays with pay.

Article 25

1. Everyone has the right to a standard of living adequate for the health and well-being of himself and of his family, including food, clothing, housing and medical care and necessary social services, and the right to security in the event of unemployment, sickness, disability, widowhood, old age or other lack of livelihood in circumstances beyond his control.
2. Motherhood and childhood are entitled to special care and assistance.

All children, whether born in or out of wedlock, shall enjoy the same social protection.

Article 26

1. Everyone has the right to education. Education shall be free, at least in the elementary and fundamental stages. Elementary education shall be compulsory. Technical and professional education shall be made generally available and higher education shall be equally accessible to all on the basis of merit.
2. Education shall be directed to the full development of the human personality and to the strengthening of respect for human rights and fundamental freedoms. It shall promote understanding, tolerance and friendship among all nations, racial or religious groups, and shall further the activities of the United Nations for the maintenance of peace.
3. Parents have a prior right to choose the kind of education that shall be given to their children.

Article 27

1. Everyone has the right freely to participate in the cultural life of the community, to enjoy the arts and to share in scientific advancement and its benefits.
2. Everyone has the right to the protection of the moral and material interests resulting from any scientific, literary or artistic production of which he is the author.

Article 28

Everyone is entitled to a social and international order in which the rights and freedoms set forth in this Declaration can be fully realized.

Article 29

1. Everyone has duties to the community in which alone the free and full development of his personality is possible.
2. In the exercise of his rights and freedoms, everyone shall be subject only to such limitations as are determined by law solely for the purpose of securing due recognition and respect for the rights and freedoms of others and of meeting the just requirements of morality, public order

and the general welfare in a democratic society.

3. These rights and freedoms may in no case be exercised contrary to the purposes and principles of the United Nations.

Article 30

Nothing in this Declaration may be interpreted as implying for any State, group or person any right to engage in any activity or to perform any act aimed at the destruction of any of the rights and freedoms set forth herein.

6.
Wars the UN Failed to Prevent Involving 123 Countries, 1945-2009

(See p86)

Afghanistan
Civil War, 1979-2002
Al-Qaeda War, 2001-

Albania
Communist Regime, 1948-1989
Civil War, 1997

Algeria
War of Independence, 1954-1962
Fundamentalist Muslim uprising, 1992 *et seq.*

Angola
War of Independence, 1961-1975
Civil War, 1975-94

Argentina
Overthrow of Peron, 1955
Falklands War, 1982

Armenia
Nagorno-Karabakh, 1991 *et seq.*

Australia
Korean War, 1950-1953
Vietnam War, 1965-1972

Azerbaijan
1991 *et seq.*

Bangladesh
1971 massacres
Chittagong, 1975 *et seq.*

Belgium
Korean War, 1950-1953
Congo Crisis, 1960-1967

Bolivia
Civil War, 1952
Junta, 1971-1978

Bosnia and Herzegovina
1992-1995

Brazil
Indians, 1900-1985
Military regime, 1964-1985
Rightist terrorism, 1980
Death squads, 1985-1991
Yanomami Indians, 1987-1991

Bulgaria
Communist regime, 1948-1989

Burma
Rebellions, 1948 *et seq.*
Unrest, 1988

Burundi
1959-1995

Cambodia
Civil War, 1967-1975
Pol Pot, revolution, 1975-1978
Civil War, 1978-1991

Cameroon
1960s

Canada
Korean War, 1950-53

Central African Republic/Empire
Bokassa regime, 1965-1979
Kongo-Wara War, 1927-1931

Chad
Civil War, 1965 *et seq.*
Habré regime, 1982-1990

Chechnya
1994 *et seq.*

Chile
1973-1990

China
Wars with Tibet, 1950 *et seq.*
Korean War, 1950-1953
Sino-Indian War, 1962
Sino-Soviet War, 1963-1969
Sino-Vietnamese War, 1979
Tiananmen Square, 1989

Colombia
La Violencia, 1946-58
Korean War, 1951-53
Insurgencies, 1973-

North Congo (aka "French Congo", "Congo-Brazzaville", "People's Republic of the Congo.")
Coup, 1997

South Congo (aka "Belgian Congo", "Zaire", "Congo-Kinshasa", "Democratic Republic of the Congo.")
Congo Crisis, 1960-1964
Stanleyville revolt, 1964-1965
Mercenary uprising, 1967-1968
Uprisings and repression, 1970s
Conflicts, 1992-1994
Overthrow of Mobutu, 1997
Civil War, 1998-

Costa Rica
Civil War, 1948
War with Nicaragua, 1955

Croatia
1991-1992

Cuba
Batista regime & Civil War, 1952-1959
Angola, 1975-1995
Grenada, 1983

Cyprus
1955-1959
1963-1967
1974

Czechoslovakia

Post-WW2 expulsions of Germans, 1945-1947

1968 uprising

Dominican Republic

1965 *coup*

East Timor

1975 *et seq.*

Ecuador

War with Peru, 1995-1997

Egypt

Arab-Israeli Wars, 1947-1973

Yemen, 1962-1969

El Salvador

Football War, 1969

Civil War, 1979-1891

Equatorial Guinea

1969-1979

Eritrea

War of Independence, 1962-1992

War with Ethiopia, 1998-

Ethiopia

Korean War, 1951-1953

Civil Wars, 1962-1992

War with Eritrea, 1998-

France

Algeria, 1954-1962

Chad, 1982-

Indo-China War of Independence, 1945-1954

Korean War, 1951-1953
Lebanon 1983
Madagascar, 1947
Morocco 1953-1956
Tunisia 1952-1954, 1961

Gambia
1981

Georgia
1992-1993
War of 2008

Ghana
1981-1993

Greece
Civil War, 1946-1949
Korean War, 1951-1953

Grenada
1983

Guatemala
Civil War, 1960-1996

Guinea
Touré, 1969-1976
Civil War, 2000-

Guinea-Bissau
1962-1974

Haiti
Duvalier regime, 1957-1986
1991-1994

Honduras

War with Nicaragua, 1957

Football War, 1969

Death squads, 1980-1988

Hungary

1956 uprising

India

Partition violence, 1947

Hyderabad, 1948

Sino-Indian War, 1962

Indo-Pakistani War, 1965

Naxalites, 1968-

Bangladeshi War of Independence, 1971

Indo-Pakistani War, 1971

Assam, 1978-

Sikh uprising, 1984-1991

Indonesia

War of Independence, 1945-1950

Civil Wars, 1950s

War with Malaysia, 1962

Irian, 1962-

Coup and massacres, 1965-1967

East Timor, 1975-1999

Aceh, 1989

Jakarta, 1998

Moluccas, 1999-

Iran

Soviet occupation, 1945-1947

Pahlevi regime, 1953-1979

Overthrow of the Shah

Kurdistan

Iran-Iraq War, 1980-1988

Iraq

Kurds 1933, 1961-1970, 1980s

Coups, 1959-1966

Iran-Iraq War, 1980-1988

Gulf War, 1990-1991

Shia rebellion, 1991-1993

Bombing, 1998

US invasion, 2003

Insurgency, 2003-

Ireland

Northern Ireland, 1974-1998

Israel

British Palestine, 1945-1948

Arab-Israeli Wars, 1948-

Palestinians

Lebanon, 1982 *et seq.*

Gaza, 2008-2009

Jamaica

1980

Jordan

Arab-Israeli Wars, 1947-1973

Uprising, 1970-1971

Kashmir

Indo-Pakistani War, 1965

Civil War, 1989 *et seq.*

Kenya

Mau-Mau, 1952-1956

Border conflict, 1963

Ethnic clash, 1992

South Korea

Coup, 1948

Vietnam War, 1965-1973

Demonstrations, 1980

Korean War, 1950-1953

North Korea

1948 *et seq.*

Kosovo

1998-1999

Laos

French Indo-China, 1945-1954

Vietnam War, 1963-1973

Post-Vietnam War, 1975-1987

Lebanon

Civil War, 1958

Chaos, 1975-1992

Liberia

1989-1993

Libya

Egypt, 1977

Uganda, 1978-1979

Chad, 1982-

US attack, 1986

Madagascar

Revolt, 1947

Malawi

1964-1994

Malaysia
Emergency, 1948-1960
War with Indonesia, 1962

Mauritania
Western Sahara, 1975-1978

Moldova
1991-1997

Morocco
Independence, 1953-1956
Western Sahara, 1975-1978

Mozambique
Independence, 1961-1975
Civil War, 1975-1993

Nepal
1996-

Netherlands
Dutch East Indies, 1945-1946
Irian, 1962

New Guinea
Irian Jaya, 1962-

Nicaragua
War with Costa Rica, 1955
War with Honduras, 1957
Civil Wars, 1972-1991

Nigeria
Biafra, 1967-1970
Muslim uprising, 1980-1984
Internal conflicts, 1990s

Northern Ireland
1974-98

Pakistan
Partition violence, 1947
Indo-Pakistani War, 1965
Baluchi/Pathan separatists, 1973-1977
Bengali massacres, 1971
Sindh War, 1990s

Palestine
Israel, 1947-
Jordan, 1970-1971
Lebanon, 1975 *et seq.*

Panama
1989

Papua New Guinea
1989 *et seq.*

Paraguay
Civil War, 1947
Stroessner, 1954-1989
Ache Indians, 1968-1974
Coup, 1989

Peru
Uprising, 1965-1966
Shining Path, 1980-1993
War with Ecuador, 1995-1997

Philippines
Huk rebellion, 1946-1954
Korean War, 1950-1953
Vietnam War, 1965-1973
Rebellions, 1972-1992

Pol Pot, revolution, 1975-1978

Poland
Post-WW2 expulsions of Germans, 1945-1947

Portugal
Angola, 1961-1975
Mozambique, 1961-1975
Guinea-Bissau, 1962-1974

Rhodesia
1972-1979

Romania
Uprising, 1989

Russia
Chechnya, 1994 *et seq.*

Rwanda
1959-1995
1990

Saudi Arabia
Yemen, 1962-1969

Senegal
1982-

Sierra Leone
1991-

Somalia
Ogaden War, 1962-1992
Conflict with Kenya, 1963
Barre regime, 1971-1990
Chaos, 1992 *et seq.*

South Africa

Namibia, 1975-1990

Angola, 1975-1995

Spain

Basques, 1961 *et seq.*

Sri Lanka

1971 rebellion

1977-1995 War

Sudan

Civil War, 1955-1972

Civil War, 1983 *et seq.*

Syria

Arab-Israeli Wars, 1947-1973

Lebanon, 1976

Taiwan

1947

1954-1955

Tajikistan

1992-1996

Tanzania

Uganda, 1978-1979

Thailand

Korean War, 1950-1953

Vietnam War, 1965-1973

Tibet

Chinese occupation, 1950 *et seq.*

Timor, East
1975 *et seq.*

Tunisia
War of Independence 1952-1956
1961

Turkey
Kurdistan 1980s, 1990s
Korean War, 1950-1953
Cyprus, 1974

Uganda
Civil War, 1966
Civil War, 1979-1987
Civil War, 1987-

USSR
Occupation of Iran, 1945-1947
Hungarian uprising, 1956
Sino-Soviet War, 1963-1969
Afghanistan, 1979-1995

United Kingdom
Dutch East Indies, 1945-1946
Palestine, 1945-1948
Malaya, 1948-1960
Korean War, 1950-1953
Mau-Mau uprising, 1952-1956
Suez, 1956
Cyprus, 1955-1959
Malaysia, 1962
Aden, 1963-1967
Northern Ireland, 1969-
Falklands War, 1982

United States
Korean War, 1950-1953
Dominican Republic, 1965
Vietnam War, 1965-1973
Lebanon, 1983
Grenada, 1983
Panama, 1989
Gulf War, 1990-1991
Kosovo, 1998
Al-Qaeda War, 2001-

Vietnam
Indo-China War, 1946-1954
North Vietnam, 1954-1975
Vietnam War, 1965-1975
Post-Vietnam War, 1975-1987
Laos, 1975-1987
Cambodia Civil War, 1978-1991
Sino-Vietnamese War, 1979

Western Sahara
Morocco vs. Polisario Front, 1975-1978

North Yemen (aka "Kingdom of Yemen", "Yemen Arab Republic")
Civil War, 1948
Civil War, 1962-1969

South Yemen (aka "Aden", "Federation of South Arabia", "People's Republic of Southern Yemen")
British intervention, 1963-1967
Civil War, 1986

Zambia
1964

Zanzibar
1964

Zimbabwe
Rhodesian Civil War, 1972-1979
Chaos, 2007-

7.
37 Major Conflicts the UN Failed to Prevent after 1945: 689 UN Resolutions and 33,750,700 Deaths

(See p86)

Countries involved	War(s)	Deaths	UN Security Council Resolutions
Israel, Egypt, Syria, Iraq, Jordan, Lebanon, Palestinians, others	Arab-Israeli conflict (1948-present)	5,000,000	221
South Korea, North Korea, People's Republic of China, United Kingdom, United States, others	Korean War (1950-1953, ceasefire)	2,300,000	5
France, National Liberation Front, Front Algérie Française	Algerian War (1954-1962)	600,000	0
Sudan, Anyanya	First Sudanese Civil War (1955-1972)	500,000	0
United States, South Korea, South Vietnam, North Vietnam, Viet Cong	Vietnam War (1959-1975)	4,200,000	1
Congo, Zaire, South Kasai, United Nations	Congo Crisis (1960-1966)	100,000	6
Philippines, United States, New People's Army, Moro National Liberation Front, Moro Islamic Liberation Front, Abu Sayyaf, Rajah Solaiman Movement,	Insurgency in the Philippines (1960-present)	200,000	0

Jemaah Islamiyah			
Eritrean Liberation Front, Ethiopia, Cuba	Eritrean War of Independence	700,000	0
Portugal, African independence movements	Portuguese Colonial War (1961-1974)	140,700	1
Mutawakkilite Kingdom of Yemen, Saudi Arabia, South Kasai, Yemen Arab Republic, Egypt	North Yemen Civil War (1962-1970)	120,000	2
Khmer Rouge, Khmer Republic, United States, Democratic Republic of Vietnam	Cambodian Civil War (1967-1975)	1,000,000	1
Nigeria, Republic of Benin	Nigerian Civil War (1967-1971)	1,200,000	0
Pakistan, Mukti Bahini	Bangladesh Liberation War (March-December 1971)	2,800,000	2
Lebanon, Palestine Liberation Organization, Syria, South Lebanon Army, Israel, Lebanese National Movement	Lebanese Civil War (1975-1990)	250,000	43
MPLA, UNITA, National Liberation Front of Angola, United States, Soviet Union, South Africa, Cuba, Zaire	Angolan Civil War (1975-2002)	600,000	81
FRELIMO, RENAMO, United Nations Operation in Mozambique	Mozambican Civil War (1977-1992)	900,000	3

People's Democratic Party of Afghanistan, Soviet Union, Taliban, al-Qaeda, United States, United Kingdom, Mujahideen, Iran	Civil War in Afghanistan (1978-present)	1,700,000	28
China, Vietnam	Sino-Vietnamese War (February-March 1979)	200,000	0
Iran, Iraq	Iran-Iraq War (1980-1988)	1,000,000	8
Sudan, Lord's Resistance Army, Sudan People's Liberation Army/Movement, Eastern Front (Sudan), al-Qaeda, Egypt, Libya (1983-2005)	Second Sudanese Civil War	1,900,000	7
Sri Lanka, Liberation Tigers of Tamil Eelam	Sri Lankan Civil War (1983-2009)	140,000	0
Armed Forces of Liberia, National Patriotic Front of Liberia, Independent National Patriotic Front of Liberia, United Nations, United Liberation Movement of Liberia for Democracy	First Liberian Civil War (1989-1996)	200,000	18
India, al-Qaeda, Lashkar-e-Taiba, Harkat-ul-Mujahideen, Al-Badr (India), Hizbul Mujahideen, Pakistan	Islamic Insurgency in Jammu and Kashmir (1989-present)	100,000	0
Rwandan Patriotic Front, Rwandan Defence Forces, French Army, Uganda People's Defence Force, other	Rwandan Civil War (1990-1993)	800,000	4

Iraq, Kuwait, Coalition of the Gulf War	Gulf War (August 1990-February 1991)	80,000	19
Somalia, Al-Shabaab, Ethiopia, al-Qaeda, United States, United Nations	Somali Civil War (1991-present)	400,000	54
Sierra Leone, Liberia, West Side Boys, Armed Forces Revolutionary Council, United Kingdom, other	Sierra Leone Civil War (1991-2002)	100,000	24
Federal Republic of Yugoslavia, Croatia, Croatian Republic of Herzeg-Bosnia, Republika Srpska, NATO, other	Yugoslav wars (1991-2002)	130,000	67
Algeria, France, Islamic Salvation Front, Armed Islamic Group	Algerian Civil War (1991-1992)	170,000	0
Burundi, Union for National Progress, National Forces of Liberation	Burundi Civil War (1993-2005)	300,000	0
AFDL, Zaire, Ethiopia, Uganda, Rwanda, other	First Congo War (1996-1997)	200,000	0
Liberia, Liberians United for Reconciliation and Democracy, Movement for Democracy in Liberia, Economic Community of West African States Monitoring Group	Second Liberian Civil War (1999-2003)	150,000	8
Democratic Republic of the Congo, Movement for the Liberation of Congo, Namibia, Zimbabwe, Burundi, other	Second Congo War (1998-2003)	3,900,000	22

Russia, Chechnya, Chechen Republic of Ichkeria, Arag Mujahideen in Chechnya	Second Chechen War (1999-2009)	200,000	0
International Security Assistance Force, Afghanistan, United States, United Kingdom, Taliban, al-Qaeda, Lashkar-e-Taiba, other	War in Afghanistan (2001-present)	70,000	22
Multinational Force – Iraq, United States, United Kingdom, Iraq, Armed Islamic Group, Iraqi Insurgency	Iraq War (2003-present)	1,000,000	10
Sudan, Janjaweed, Justice and Equality Movement, Sudan Liberation Movement/Army, other	War in Darfur (2003-present)	400,000	32
	TOTAL	33,750,700	689

C. Freedom

1.
119 Electoral Democracies, 2009

(See pp5, 50)

Albania
Andorra
Antigua and Barbuda
Argentina
Australia
Austria
Bahamas
Bangladesh
Barbados
Belgium
Belize
Benin
Bolivia
Bosnia and Herzegovina
Botswana
Brazil
Bulgaria
Burundi
Canada
Cape Verde
Chile
Colombia
Comoros
Costa Rica
Croatia
Cyprus
Czech Republic
Denmark
Dominica
Dominican Republic
East Timor
Ecuador
El Salvador
Estonia
Finland
France
Germany
Ghana
Greece
Grenada
Guatemala
Guinea-Bissau
Guyana
Haiti
Honduras
Hungary
Iceland
India
Indonesia
Ireland
Israel
Italy
Jamaica
Japan
Kiribati
Latvia
Lesotho
Liberia
Liechtenstein
Lithuania
Luxembourg
Macedonia
Madagascar
Malawi
Mali
Malta
Marshall Islands
Mauritius
Mexico
Micronesia
Moldova
Monaco
Mongolia
Montenegro
Mozambique
Namibia
Nauru
Netherlands
New Zealand
Nicaragua
Niger
Norway
Palau
Panama
Papua New Guinea
Paraguay
Peru
Poland
Portugal
Romania
St. Kitts and Nevis
St. Lucia
St. Vincent and the

Grenadines
Samoa
San Marino
São Tomé and Principe
Senegal
Serbia
Seychelles
Sierra Leone
Slovakia
Slovenia
South Africa
South Korea
Spain
Sri Lanka
Suriname
Sweden
Switzerland
Taiwan
Trinidad and Tobago
Turkey
Tuvalu
Ukraine
United Kingdom
United States
Uruguay
Vanuatu
Zambia

2.
Freedom Ratings, 2009

(See pp5, 50, 155)

Of 192 UN countries and Taiwan, in 2009 89 were free, 62 partly free and 42 not free.

Countries are ranked according to political rights and civil liberties on a scale from 1.0 (most free) to 7.0 (least free).

The status designation of free, partly free or not free, which is determined by the combination of the political rights and civil liberties ratings, indicates the general state of freedom in a country.

A. Independent Countries

A. Independent Countries

Free

1.0

Andorra
Australia
Austria
Bahamas
Barbados
Belgium
Canada
Cape Verde
Chile
Costa Rica
Cyprus
Czech Republic
Denmark
Dominica
Estonia
Finland
France
Germany
Hungary
Iceland
Ireland
Kiribati
Liechtenstein
Lithuania

Luxembourg
Malta
Marshall Islands
Micronesia
Nauru
Netherlands
New Zealand
Norway
Palau
Poland
Portugal
St. Kitts and Nevis
St. Lucia
San Marino
Slovakia
Slovenia
Spain
Sweden
Switzerland
Tuvalu
United Kingdom
United States
Uruguay

1.5

Belize
Ghana
Greece
Grenada
Israel
Italy
Japan
Latvia
Monaco
Panama
St. Vincent and the Grenadines
South Korea
Taiwan

2.0

Antigua and Barbuda
Argentina
Benin
Botswana
Brazil
Bulgaria
Croatia
Dominican Republic
Mauritius
Mongolia
Namibia
Romania
Samoa
São Tomé and Principe
South Africa
Suriname
Trinidad and Tobago
Vanuatu

2.5

El Salvador
Guyana
India
Indonesia
Jamaica
Lesotho
Mali
Mexico
Peru
Serbia
Ukraine

Partly Free

3.0

Albania
Bolivia
Ecuador
Honduras
Macedonia
Montenegro
Mozambique
Paraguay
Senegal
Seychelles
Sierra Leone
Turkey
Zambia

3.5

Bosnia and Herzegovina
Colombia
Comoros
East Timor
Guatemala
Kenya
Liberia
Madagascar
Nicaragua
Niger
Papua New Guinea
Philippines
Solomon Islands
Tanzania

4.0

Bangladesh
Burkina Faso
Georgia
Guinea-Bissau
Kuwait
Malawi
Malaysia
Maldives
Moldova
Nepal
Sri Lanka
Tonga
Venezuela

4.5

Bhutan
Burundi
Gambia
Haiti
Kyrgyzstan
Lebanon
Morocco
Nigeria
Pakistan
Singapore
Thailand
Uganda

5.0

Armenia
Bahrain
Central African Republic
Djibouti
Ethiopia
Fiji
Gabon
Jordan
Togo
Yemen

Not Free

5.5

Afghanistan
Algeria
Angola
Azerbaijan
Brunei
Cambodia
Congo (Brazzaville)
Côte d'Ivoire
Egypt
Kazakhstan
Mauritania
Oman
Qatar
Russia
Rwanda
Tajikistan
United Arab Emirates

6.0

Cameroon	Iran	Tunisia
Congo (Kinshasa)	Iraq	Vietnam
Guinea	Swaziland	

6.5

Belarus	Cuba	Saudi Arabia
Chad	Eritrea	Syria
China	Laos	Zimbabwe

7.0

Burma	North Korea	Turkmenistan
Equatorial Guinea	Somalia	Uzbekistan
Libya	Sudan	

Of 16 related and disputed territories, in 2009 2 were free, 5 were partly free and 9 not free.
Related and disputed territories are also ranked from 1.0 (most free) to 7.0 (least free).

B. Related Territories

Free
1.0
Puerto Rico (United States)

Partly Free
3.5
Hong Kong (China)

C. Disputed Territories

Free
2.0
Cyprus (Northern [Turkish] Cyprus)

Partly Free

4.5

Kashmir (India)

Somaliland (Somalia)

5.0

Abkhazia (Georgia)

Nagomo-Karabakh (Armenia/Azerbaijan)

Not Free

5.5

Kashmir (Pakistan)

Kosovo (Serbia)

Palestinian-Authority-Administered Territories (Israel)

6.0

Israeli-Occupied Territories (Israel)

Transnistria (Moldova)

6.5

South Ossetia (Georgia)

Western Sahara (Morocco)

7.0

Chechnya (Russia)

Tibet (China)

3.
Freedom Ratings Table by Countries and Territories, 2009

(See pp5, 50, 155)

The table lists countries and territories in alphabetical order alongside ratings for political rights, civil liberties and freedom, and for recent trends:

- **PR** and **CL** stand for political rights and civil liberties, respectively; 1 represents the most free and 7 the least free rating. The ratings reflect an overall judgment based on survey results.

- ▲▼ up or down indicates a change in political rights, civil liberties, or status since the last survey.
- ↑↓ up or down indicate a trend of positive or negative changes that took place but were not sufficient to result in a change in political rights or civil liberties ratings of 1-7.
- * indicates a country's status as an electoral democracy.

A. Independent Countries

Trend Arrow	Country	PR	CL	Freedom Rating
	Afghanistan	5	6 ▼	Not Free
	Albania	3	3	Partly Free
	Algeria	6	5	Not Free
	Andorra*	1	1	Free
↑	Angola	6	5	Not Free
	Antigua and Barbuda*	2	2	Free
	Argentina*	2	2	Free
	Armenia	6 ▼	4	Partly Free
	Australia*	1	1	Free
	Austria*	1	1	Free
↓	Azerbaijan	6	5	Not Free
	Bahamas*	1	1	Free ↓
	Bahrain	5	5	Partly Free
	Bangladesh*	4 ▲	4	Partly Free
	Barbados*	1	1	Free
	Belarus	7	6	Not Free
	Belgium*	1	1	Free
	Belize*	1	2	Free
	Benin*	2	2	Free
	Bhutan	4 ▲	5	Partly Free ▲
	Bolivia*	3	3	Partly Free
	Bosnia and Herzegovina*	4	3	Partly Free
	Botswana*	2	2	Free
	Brazil*	2	2	Free

	Brunei	6	5	Not Free
	Bulgaria*	2 ▼	2	Free
	Burkina Faso	5	3	Partly Free
↓	Burma	7	7	Not Free
↓	Burundi*	4	5	Partly Free
	Cambodia	6	5	Not Free
↓	Cameroon	6	6	Not Free
	Canada*	1	1	Free
	Cape Verde*	1	1	Free
	Central African Republic	5	5	Partly Free
	Chad	7	6	Not Free
	Chile*	1	1	Free
	China	7	6	Not Free
	Colombia*	3	4 ▼	Partly Free
	Comoros*	3 ▲	4	Partly Free
	Congo (Brazzaville)	6	5	Not Free
	Congo (Kinshasa)	6	6	Not Free
	Costa Rica*	1	1	Free
	Côte d'Ivoire	6 ▲	5	Not Free
	Croatia*	2	2	Free
	Cuba	7	6 ▲	Not Free
	Cyprus*	1	1	Free
	Czech Republic*	1	1	Free
	Denmark*	1	1	Free
	Djibouti	5	5	Partly Free
	Dominica*	1	1	Free
	Dominican Republic*	2	2	Free
	East Timor*	3	4	Partly Free
	Ecuador*	3	3	Partly Free
	Egypt	6	5	Not Free
	El Salvador*	2	3	Free
	Equatorial Guinea	7	7 ▼	Not Free
	Eritrea	7	6	Not Free
	Estonia*	1	1	Free
	Ethiopia	5	5	Partly Free
↓	Fiji	6	4	Partly Free
	Finland*	1	1	Free

	France*	1	1	Free
↓	Gabon	6	4	Partly Free
↓	Gambia	5	4	Partly Free
↓	Georgia	4	4	Partly Free
	Germany*	1	1	Free
	Ghana*	1	2	Free
↓	Greece*	1	2	Free
	Grenada*	1	2	Free
	Guatemala*	3	4	Partly Free
	Guinea	7 ▼	5	Not Free
	Guinea-Bissau*	4	4	Partly Free
	Guyana*	2	3	Free
	Haiti*	4	5	Partly Free
	Honduras*	3	3	Partly Free
	Hungary*	1	1	Free
	Iceland*	1	1	Free
	India*	2	3	Free
	Indonesia*	2	3	Free
↓	Iran	6	6	Not Free
↑	Iraq	6	6	Not Free
	Ireland*	1	1	Free
	Israel*	1	2	Free
	Italy*	1	2 ▼	Free
	Jamaica*	2	3	Free
	Japan*	1	2	Free
	Jordan	5	5 ▼	Partly Free
	Kazakhstan	6	5	Not Free
	Kenya	4	3	Partly Free
	Kiribati*	1	1	Free
	Kuwait	4	4	Partly Free
↓	Kyrgyzstan	5	4	Partly Free
	Laos	7	6	Not Free
	Latvia*	2	1	Free
	Lebanon	5	4	Partly Free
	Lesotho*	2	3	Free
	Liberia*	3	4	Partly Free
	Libya	7	7	Not Free

	Liechtenstein*	1	1	Free
	Lithuania*	1	1	Free
	Luxembourg*	1	1	Free
↓	Macedonia*	3	3	Partly Free
	Madagascar*	4	3	Partly Free
	Malawi*	4	4	Partly Free
↑	Malaysia	4	4	Partly Free
	Maldives	4 ▲	4 ▲	Partly Free ▲
	Mali*	2	3	Free
	Malta*	1	1	Free
	Marshall Islands*	1	1	Free
	Mauritania	6 ▼	5 ▼	Not Free ▼
	Mauritius*	1	2	Free
↓	Mexico*	2	3	Free
	Micronesia*	1	1	Free
	Moldova*	4 ▼	4	Partly Free
	Monaco*	2	1	Free
	Mongolia*	2	2	Free
	Montenegro*	3	3	Partly Free
	Morocco	5	4	Partly Free
	Mozambique*	3	3	Partly Free
↓	Namibia*	2	2	Free
	Nauru*	1	1	Free
	Nepal	4 ▲	4	Partly Free
	Netherlands*	1	1	Free New
	New Zealand*	1	1	Free
	Nicaragua*	4 ▼	3	Partly Free
	Niger*	3	4	Partly Free
	Nigeria	5 ▼	4	Partly Free
	North Korea	7	7	Not Free
	Norway*	1	1	Free
	Oman	6	5	Not Free
	Pakistan	4 ▲	5	Partly Free ▲
	Palau*	1	1	Free
	Panama*	1	2	Free
	Papua New Guinea*	4 ▼	3	Partly Free
↑	Paraguay*	3	3	Partly Free

	Peru*	2	3	Free
	Philippines	4	3	Partly Free
	Poland*	1	1	Free
	Portugal*	1	1	Free
	Qatar	6	5	Not Free
	Romania*	2	2	Free
↓	Russia	6	5	Not Free
	Rwanda	6	5	Not Free
	St. Kitts and Nevis*	1	1	Free
	St. Lucia*	1	1	Free
	St. Vincent and the Grenadines*	2	1	Free
	Samoa*	2	2	Free
	San Marino*	1	1	Free
	São Tomé and Principe*	2	2	Free
	Saudi Arabia	7	6	Not Free
	Senegal*	3 ▼	3	Partly Free ▼
	Serbia*	3	2	Free
	Seychelles*	3	3	Partly Free
	Sierra Leone*	3	3	Partly Free
↓	Singapore	5	4	Partly Free
	Slovakia*	1	1	Free
	Slovenia*	1	1	Free
	Solomon Islands	4	3	Partly Free
	Somalia	7	7	Not Free
	South Africa*	2	2	Free
	South Korea*	1	2	Free
	Spain*	1	1	Free
	Sri Lanka*	4	4	Partly Free
	Sudan	7	7	Not Free
	Suriname*	2	2	Free
	Swaziland	7	5	Not Free
	Sweden*	1	1	Free
	Switzerland*	1	1	Free
	Syria	7	6	Not Free
	Taiwan*	2	1	Free
	Tajikistan	6	5	Not Free
	Tanzania	4	3	Partly Free

	Thailand	5 ▲	4	Partly Free
	Togo	5	5	Partly Free
	Tonga	5	3	Partly Free
	Trinidad and Tobago*	2	2	Free
	Tunisia	7	5	Not Free
	Turkey*	3	3	Partly Free
	Turkmenistan	7	7	Not Free
	Tuvalu*	1	1	Free
	Uganda	5	4	Partly Free
	Ukraine*	3	2	Free
	United Arab Emirates	6	5	Not Free
	United Kingdom*	1	1	Free
	United States*	1	1	Free
	Uruguay*	1	1	Free
	Uzbekistan	7	7	Not Free
	Vanuatu*	2	2	Free
↓	Venezuela	4	4	Partly Free
	Vietnam	7	5	Not Free
	Yemen	5	5	Partly Free
	Zambia*	3	3 ▲	Partly Free
↓	Zimbabwe	7	6	Not Free

B. Related Territories

Trend Arrow	**Country and Territory**	**PR**	**CL**	**Freedom Rating**
	China			
	Hong Kong	5	2	Partly Free
	United States			
	Puerto Rico	1	1	Free

C. Disputed Territories

Trend Arrow	Country and Territory	PR	CL	Freedom Rating
	Armenia/Azerbaijan			
	Nagomo-Karabakh	5	5	Partly Free
↓	*China*			
	Tibet	7	7	Not Free
	Cyprus			
	Northern [Turkish] Cyprus	2	2	Free
	Georgia			
	Abkhazia	5	5	Partly Free
	South Ossetia	7	6	Not Free
↑	*India*			
	Kashmir	5	4	Partly Free
	Israel			
↓	Israeli-Occupied Territories	6	6	Not Free
↓	Palestinian-Authority-Administered Territories	6	6	Not Free
	Moldova			
	Transnistria	6	6	Not Free
	Morocco			
	Western Sahara	7	6	Not Free
	Pakistan			
	Kashmir	6 ▲	5	Not Free
	Russia			
	Chechnya	7	7	Not Free
	Serbia			
	Kosovo	6	5	Not Free
	Somalia			
	Somaliland	5 ▼	4	Partly Free

4.
The World's 20 Worst Dictators, 2009

(See pp50-51)

A "dictator" is a head of state who exercises arbitrary authority over the lives of his citizens and who cannot be removed from power by legal means. The worst dictators commit terrible human-rights abuses. This list draws in part on reports by global human-rights organizations.

Dictator	Nation-State
1. Robert Mugabe	Zimbabwe
2. Omar Al-Bashir	Sudan
3. Kim Jong-Il	North Korea
4. Than Shwe	Myanmar (Burma)
5. King Abdullah	Saudi Arabia
6. Hu Jintao	China
7. Sayyid Ali Khamenei	Iran
8. Isayas Afewerki	Eritrea
9. G. Berdymuhammedov	Turkmenistan
10. Muammar al-Gaddafi	Libya
11. Islam Karimov	Uzbekistan
12. Bashar al-Assad	Syria
13. Raul Castro	Cuba
14. Teodoro Obiang Nguema	Equatorial Guinea
15. Aleksandr Lukashenka	Belarus
16. Meles Zenawi	Ethiopia
17. Idriss Déby	Chad
18. King Mswati III	Swaziland
19. Paul Biya	Cameroon
20. Hosni Mubarak	Egypt

D. Regions and Nation-States

1.
Regional Populations as Percentages of World Population, 2008
(See p144)

Region	Per cent of Global Population*
Asia	56.6%
Europe	12%
North America	5.1%
Latin America/Caribbean	8.6%
Africa	14.3%
Middle East	3%
Oceania/Australia	0.5%

(* Approximate, rounded up to one decimal point.)

2.
Historical and Predicted Regional Populations as Percentages of World Population
(See p144)

World historical and predicted populations (in millions)

Region	1750	1800	1850	1900	1950	1999	2008	2050	2150
World	791	978	1,262	1,650	2,521	5,978	6,707	8,909	9,746
Africa	106	107	111	133	221	767	973	1,766	2,308
Asia	502	635	809	947	1,402	3,634	4,054	5,268	5,561
Europe	163	203	276	408	547	729	732	628	517
Latin America and the Caribbean	16	24	38	74	167	511	577	809	912
Northern America	2	7	26	82	172	307	337	392	398
Oceania	2	2	2	6	13	30	34	46	51

World historical and predicted populations by percentage distribution

Region	1750	1800	1850	1900	1950	1999	2008	2050	2150
World	100	100	100	100	100	100	100	100	100
Africa	13.4	10.9	8.8	8.1	8.8	12.8	14.5	19.8	23.7
Asia	63.5	64.9	64.1	57.4	55.6	60.8	60.4	59.1	57.1
Europe	20.6	20.8	21.9	24.7	21.7	12.2	10.9	7.0	5.3
Latin America and the Caribbean	2.0	2.5	3.0	4.5	6.6	8.5	8.6	9.1	9.4
Northern America	0.3	0.7	2.1	5.0	6.8	5.1	5.0	4.4	4.1
Oceania	0.3	0.2	0.2	0.4	0.5	0.5	0.5	0.5	0.5

3.
Nation-States' Populations as Percentages of World Population

(See pp133, 137, 144)

Based on the July 1, 2009 estimate by the United Nations Department of Economic and Social Affairs – Population Division.

Letter on pp129-132	Rank	Country/ Territory	Population	Date Last Updated	Approx % of World Population	Source
		World	6,788,400,000		100%	US Census – International Programs Department
A	1	China	1,333,910,000	Nov 3, 2009	19.63%	Chinese population clock
A	2.	India	1,172,090,000	Nov 3, 2009	17.25%	Indian population clock
A	3	United States	307,855,000	Nov 3, 2009	4.53%	Official USA population clock
C	4	Indonesia	229,965,000		3.38%	UN estimate

C	5	Brazil	191,982,000	Nov 3, 2009	2.83%	Official Brazilian population clock
C	6	Pakistan	167,854,500	Nov 3, 2009	2.47%	Official Pakistani population clock
C	7	Bangladesh	162,221,000		2.39%	UN estimate
C	8	Nigeria	154,729,000		2.28%	UN estimate
B	9	Russia	141,881,000	Nov 3, 2009	2.09%	Russian State Statistics Service
C	10	Japan	127,560,000	Oct 1, 2009	1.88%	Official Japan Statistics Bureau estimate
C	11	Mexico	107,550,697		1.58%	INEGI estimate National Population Statistics of Mexico
C	12	Philippines	92,226,600	Mid-2009	1.36%	National Statistics Office medium projection
C	13	Vietnam	85,789573	Apr 1, 2009	1.26%	Official preliminary results of the 2009 census
A	14	Germany	82,002,000	Dec 31, 2008	1.21%	Federal Statistical Office
C	15	Ethiopia	79,221,000	Jul 2008	1.17%	Ethiopia Central Statistics Agency
D	16	Egypt	77,279,837	Nov 3, 2009	1.14%	Official Egyptian population clock
D	17	Iran	74,196,000		1.09%	UN estimate
D	18	Turkey	71,517,100	Dec 31, 2008	1.05%	Turkish

						Statistical Institute estimate
D	19	Democratic Republic of Congo	66,020,000		0.97%	UN estimate
B	20	France	65,073,482	Jan 1, 2009	0.96%	Official INSEE estimate. The figure for France without the overseas collectivities is 64,303,482
D	21	Thailand	63,389,730	Dec 31, 2008	0.93%	Official Thai Statistics estimate
B	22	United Kingdom	61,634,599	Jan 1, 2009	0.91%	Eurostat estimate
A	23	Italy	60,157,214	Apr 2009	0.88%	Official ISTAT estimate
D	24	Myanmar (Burma)	50,020,000		0.74%	UN estimate
D	25	South Africa	49,320,500	Jul 1, 2009	0.73%	Statistics South Africa
D	26	South Korea	48,333,000		0.71%	UN estimate
D	27	Ukraine	46,029,281	Jul 1, 2009	0.68%	Official UKRSTAT estimate
A	28	Spain	45,967,632	Oct 1, 2009	0.68%	Official INE estimate
D	29	Colombia	45,161,000	Nov 3, 2009	0.66%	Official Colombian population clock
D	30	Tanzania	43,739,000		0.64%	UN estimate
D	31	Argentina	40,134,425	Jun 30, 2009	0.59%	Official INDEC estimate

D	32	Kenya	39,802,000		0.59%	UN estimate
D	33	Sudan	39,154,490	Apr 22, 2008	0.58%	2008 Sudanese census
A	34	Poland	38,100,700		0.56%	Official Central Statistics Office of Poland
D	35	Algeria	34,895,000		0.51%	UN estimate
E	36	Canada	33,831,000	Nov 3, 2009	0.5%	Official Canadian population clock
E	37	Uganda	32,710,000		0.48%	UN estimate
E	38	Morocco	31,629,000	Nov 3, 2009	0.47%	Official Moroccan population clock
E	39	Iraq	30,747,000		0.45%	UN estimate
E	40	Nepal	29,331,000		0.43%	UN estimate
E	41	Peru	29,132,013	Jun 30, 2009	0.43%	Official INEI estimate
E	42	Venezuela	28,536,000	Nov 3, 2009	0.42%	Official Venezuelan population clock
E	43	Malaysia	28,310,000	Jul 31, 2009	0.41%	Statistics Department of Malaysia
E	44	Afghanistan	28,150,000		0.4%	UN estimate
E	45	Uzbekistan	27,488,000		0.4%	UN estimate
E	46	Saudi Arabia	25,721,000		0.38%	UN estimate
E	47	North Korea	24,051,706	Oct 2008	0.35%	UNFPA
E	48	Ghana	23,837,000		0.35%	UN estimate
E	49	Yemen	23,580,000		0.35%	UN estimate
E	50	Taiwan	23,069,345	Jun 30, 2009	0.34%	Official National Statistics Taiwan estimate
E	51	Mozambique	22,894,000		0.34%	UN estimate
E	52	Australia	22,040,000	Nov 3, 2009	0.32%	Official Australian population clock

E	53	Syria	21,906,000		0.32%	UN estimate
A	54	Romania	21,498,616	Jan 1, 2009	0.32%	Eurostat estimate
E	55	Côte d'Ivoire	21,075,000		0.31%	UN estimate
E	56	Sri Lanka	20,238,000		0.3%	UN estimate
F	57	Madagascar	19,625,000		0.29%	UN estimate
F	58	Cameroon	19,522,000		0.29%	UN estimate
F	59	Angola	18,498,000		0.27%	UN estimate
F	60	Chile	16,986,000	Nov 3, 2009	0.25%	Official INE projection
A	61	Netherlands	16,571,400	Nov 3, 2009	0.24%	Official Netherlands population clock
F	62	Kazakhstan	15,776,492	Jul 1, 2009	0.23%	National Statistics Agency estimate
F	63	Burkina Faso	15,757,000		0.23%	UN estimate
F	64	Niger	15,290,000		0.23%	UN estimate
F	65	Malawi	15,263,000		0.22%	UN estimate
F	66	Cambodia	14,805,000		0.22%	UN estimate
F	67	Ecuador	14,073,000	Nov 3, 2009	0.21%	Official Ecuadorian population clock
F	68	Guatemala	14,027.000		0.21%	UN estimate
F	69	Mali	13,010,000		0.19%	UN estimate
F	70	Zambia	12,935,000		0.19%	UN estimate
F	71	Senegal	12,534,000		0.18%	UN estimate
F	72	Zimbabwe	12,523,000		0.18%	UN estimate
F	73	Chad	11,274,106	Jun 2009	0.17%	Chadian 2009 census
A	74	Greece	11,257,285	Jan 1, 2009	0.17%	Eurostat estimate
F	75	Cuba	11,204,000		0.16%	UN estimate
A	76	Belgium	10,754,528	Jan 1, 2009	0.16%	Eurstat estimate
A	77	Portugal	10,627,250	Jan 1, 2009	0.16%	Eurostat estimate
A	78	Czech Republic	10,476,543	Mar 31, 2009	0.15%	Czech Statistical Office
F	79	Tunisia	10,327,800	Jul 1, 2008	0.15%	National Statistics Institute of Tunisia

F	80	Dominican Republic	10,090,000		0.15%	UN estimate
F	81	Guinea	10,069,000		0.15%	UN estimate
F	82	Haiti	10,033,000		0.15%	UN estimate
A	83	Hungary	10,031,208	Jan 1, 2009	0.15%	Eurostat estimate
F	84	Rwanda	9,998,000		0.15%	UN estimate
F	85	Bolivia	9,879,000		0.15%	UN estimate
F	86	Serbia	9,850,000		0.14%	UN estimate
F	87	Belarus	9,671,900	Jan 1, 2009	0.14%	Official Statistics of Belarus
A	88	Sweden	9,316,256	Aug 31, 2009	0.14%	Statistics Sweden
F	89	Somalia	9.133,000		0.13%	UN estimate
F	90	Benin	8,935,000		0.13%	UN estimate
F	91	Azerbaijan	8,896,900	Apr 1, 2009	0.13%	State Statistical Committee of Azerbaijan
A	92	Austria	8,355,260	Jan 1, 2009	0.12%	Eurostat estimate
F	93	Burundi	8,303,000		0.12%	UN estimate
F	94	Switzerland	7,753,600	Aug 31, 2009	0.11%	Official Switzerland Statistics estimate
A	95	Bulgaria	7,606,551	Jan 1, 2009	0.11%	Eurostat estimate
G	96	Honduras	7,466,000		0.11%	UN estimate
G	97	Israel	7,459,900	Aug 31, 2009	0.11%	Israeli Central Bureau of Statistics
A	98	Hong Kong	7,008,900	Dec 31, 2008	0.103%	Hong Kong Census and Statistics Department
G	99	Tajikistan	6,952,000		0.102%	UN estimate
G	100	Papua New Guinea	6,732,000		0.099%	UN estimate
G	101	Togo	6,619,000		0.097%	UN estimate
G	102	Libya	6,420,000		0.094%	UN estimate
G	103	Paraguay	6,349,000		0.093%	UN estimate
G	104	Laos	6,320,000		0.093%	UN estimate

G	105	Jordan	6,316,000		0.093%	UN estimate
G	106	El Salvador	6,163,000		0.091%	UN estimate
G	107	Nicaragua	5,743,000		0.085%	UN estimate
G	108	Sierra Leone	5,696,000		0.084%	UN estimate
A	109	Denmark	5,519,441	Jun 30, 2009	0.081%	Statistics Denmark
G	110	Kyrgyzstan	5,482,000		0.081%	UN estimate
A	111	Slovakia	5,413,548	Mar 31, 2009	0.08%	Statistics Slovakia
A	112	Finland	5,349,200	Nov 4, 2009	0.079%	Official Finnish Population clock
G	113	Turkmenistan	5,110,000		0.075%	UN estimate
G	114	Eritrea	5,073,000		0.075%	UN estimate
G	115	Singapore	4,987,600	Mid-2009	0.073%	Statistics Singapore
G	116	Norway	4,843,700	Nov 4, 2009	0.071%	Official Norwegian population clock
G	117	United Arab Emirates	4,599,000		0.068%	UN estimate
G	118	Costa Rica	4,579,000		0.067%	UN estimate
A	119	Ireland	4,459,300	Apr 1, 2009	0.065%	Irish Central Statistics Office estimate
G	120	Croatia	4,435,056	Jan 1, 2009	0.065%	Eurostat estimate
G	121	Central African Republic	4,422,000		0.065%	UN estimate
G	122	Georgia	4,385,400	Jan 1, 2009	0.065%	Statistics Georgia
G	123	New Zealand	4,336,100	Nov 4, 2009	0.064%	Official New Zealand population clock
G	124	Lebanon	4,224,000		0.062%	UN estimate
I	125	Puerto Rico	3,982,000		0.059%	UN estimate
G	126	Bosnia and Herzegovina	3,767,000		0.055%	UN estimate

I	127	Palestine	3,761,646	Dec 1, 2007	0.055%	2007 Palestinian Bureau Census
G	128	Republic of the Congo	3,683,000		0.054%	UN estimate
G	129	Moldova	3,567,500	Jan 1, 2009	0.053%	National Bureau of Statistics of Moldova
G	130	Liberia	3,476,608	Mar 21, 2008	0.051%	2008 Population and Housing Census
G	131	Panama	3,454,000		0.051%	UN estimate
G	132	Uruguay	3,361,000		0.049%	UN estimate
G	133	Lithuania	3,349,872	Jan 1, 2009	0.049%	Eurostat estimate
G	134	Mauritania	3,291,000		0.048%	UN estimate
G	135	Armenia	3,230,100	Jan 1, 2008	0.048%	
G	136	Albania	3,170,000	Jan 1, 2008	0.047%	
G	137	Kuwait	2,985,000		0.44%	UN estimate
G	138	Oman	2,845,000		0.042%	UN estimate
G	139	Jamaica	2,719,000		0.04%	UN estimate
G	140	Mongolia	2,671,000		0.039%	UN estimate
A	141	Latvia	2,254,000	Sep 2009	0.033%	Official Statistics of Latvia
G	142	Namibia	2,171,000		0.032%	UN estimate
G	143	Lesotho	2,067,000		0.03%	UN estimate
H	144	Republic of Macedonia	2,048,620	Jan 1, 2009	0.03%	Official Slovenian population clock
A	145	Slovenia	2,048,480	Nov 4, 2009	0.03%	Official Slovenian population clock
H	146	Botswana	1,950,000		0.029%	UN estimate
H	147	Gambia	1,705,000		0.025%	UN estimate
H	148	Guinea-Bissau	1,611,000		0.024%	UN estimate
H	149	Gabon	1,475,000		0.022%	UN estimate
H	150	Qatar	1,409,000		0.021%	UN estimate
A	151	Estonia	1,340,415	Jan 1, 2009	0.02%	
H	152	Trinidad and Tobago	1,339,000		0.02%	UN estimate
H	153	Mauritius	1,288,000		0.019%	UN estimate

H	154	Swaziland	1,185,000		0.017%	UN estimate
H	155	East Timor	1,134,000		0.017%	UN estimate
H	156	Djibouti	864,000		0.013%	UN estimate
H	157	Fiji	849,000		0.012%	UN estimate
A	158	Cyprus	793,963	Jan 1, 2009	0.012%	Eurostat estimate
H	159	Bahrain	791,000		0.012%	UN estimate
H	160	Guyana	762,000		0.011%	UN estimate
H	161	Bhutan	697,000		0.01%	UN estimate
H	162	Comoros	676,000		0.01%	UN estimate
H	163	Equatorial Guinea	676,000		0.01%	UN estimate
H	164	Montenegro	624,000		0.009%	UN estimate
J	165	Macau	546,200	Mar 31, 2009	0.008%	Macau Statistics and Census Service
H	166	Solomon Islands	523,000		0.008%	UN estimate
H	167	Suriname	520,000		0.008%	UN estimate
J	168	Western Sahara	513,000		0.008%	UN estimate
H	169	Cape Verde	506,000		0.007%	UN estimate
A	170	Luxembourg	493,500	Jan 1, 2009	0.007%	Eurostat estimate
A	171	Malta	413,627	Jan 1, 2009	0.006%	Eurostat estimate
H	172	Brunei	400,000		0.006%	UN estimate
H	173	Bahamas	342,000		0.005%	UN estimate
H	174	Belize	322,100	Jun 30, 2008	0.005%	Statistical Institute of Belize
H	175	Iceland	319,246	Jul 1, 2009	0.005%	Statistics Iceland
H	176	Maldives	309,000		0.005%	UN estimate
H	177	Barbados	256,000		0.004%	UN estimate
H	178	Vanuatu	240,000		0.004%	UN estimate
J	179	Netherlands Antilles	198,000		0.003%	UN estimate
H	180	Samoa	179,000		0.003%	UN estimate
J	181	Guam	178,000		0.003%	UN estimate
H	182	St. Lucia	172,000		0.003%	UN estimate
H	183	São Tomé	163,000		0.002%	UN estimate

		and Principe				
H	184	Federated States of Micronesia	111,000		0.002%	UN estimate
J	185	US Virgin Islands	110,000		0.002%	UN estimate
H	186	St. Vincent and the Grenadines	109,000		0.002%	UN estimate
J	187	Aruba	107,000		0.002%	UN estimate
H	188	Grenada	104,000		0.002%	UN estimate
H	189	Tonga	104,000		0.002%	UN estimate
H	190	Kiribati	98,000		0.001%	UN estimate
J	191	Jersey	89,300	Dec 31, 2006	0.001%	States of Jersey Statistics Unit
H	192	Antigua and Barbuda	88,000		0.001%	UN estimate
J	193	Northern Mariana Islands	87,000		0.001%	UN estimate
H	194	Andorra	86,000		0.001%	UN estimate
H	195	Seychelles	84,000		0.001%	UN estimate
J	196	Isle of Man	80,000		0.001%	UN estimate
H	197	Dominica	67,000		0.001%	UN estimate
J	198	American Samoa	67,000		0.001%	UN estimate
J	199	Bermuda	65,000		0.001%	UN estimate
H	200	Marshall Islands	62,000		0.001%	UN estimate
J	201	Guernsey	61,811	Mar 1, 2007	0.001%	UN estimate: Series A, Table 2
J	202	Greenland	57,000		0.001%	UN estimate
J	203	Cayman Islands	56,000		0.001%	UN estimate
H	204	St. Kitts and Nevis	52,000		0.001%	UN estimate

J	205	Faroe Islands	49,006	Aug 1, 2009	0.001%	Official statistics of the Faroe Islands
H	206	Liechtenstein	35,593	Jan 1, 2009	0.0005%	
H	207	Monaco	33,000		0.0005%	UN estimate
J	208	Turks and Caicos Islands	33,000		0.0005%	UN estimate
J	209	Gibraltar	31,000		0.0005%	UN estimate
H	210	San Marino	30,800	Jan 1, 2008	0.0005%	
J	211	British Virgin Islands	23,000		0.0003%	UN estimate
J	212	Cook Islands	20,000		0.0003%	UN estimate
H	213	Palau	20,000		0.0003%	UN estimate
J	214	Anguilla	15,000		0.0002%	UN estimate
H	215	Tuvalu	10,000		0.0001%	UN estimate
H	216	Nauru	10,000		0.0001%	UN estimate
J	217	Montserrat	5,900		0.0001%	UN estimate
J	218	St. Helena	4,500		0.0001%	UN estimate
J	219	Falkland Islands	3,000		0.00005%	UN estimate
J	220	Niue	1,500		0.00003%	UN estimate
J	221	Tokelau	1,200		0.00003%	UN estimate
H	222	Vatican City	800		0.00002%	UN estimate
J	223	Pitcairn Islands	50		0.000001%	UN estimate
K	224-231	See * below				

*K. 8 disputed territories not on this UN-based list: Kashmir, Abkhazia, Nagomo-Karabakh, Kosovo, Transnistria, South Ossetia, Chechnya, Tibet

4.
8 Regions and 195 Nation-States

(See pp78, 145, 147)

(Kosovo, Taiwan and Vatican City were not in the UN in 2009)

Asia (27 nation-states)

Bangladesh
Bhutan
Brunei
Cambodia
China
India
Indonesia
Japan
Kazakhstan
North Korea
South Korea
Kyrgyzstan
Laos
Malaysia
Maldives
Mongolia
Myanmar
Nepal
Philippines
Singapore
Sri Lanka
Taiwan
Tajikistan
Thailand
Turkmenistan
Uzbekistan
Vietnam

Middle East and North Africa (23 nation-states)

Afghanistan
Algeria
Azerbaijan
Bahrain
Egypt
Iran
Iraq
Israel
Jordan
Kuwait
Lebanon
Libya
Morocco
Oman
Pakistan
Qatar
Saudi Arabia
Somalia
Syria
Tunisia
Turkey
United Arab Emirates
Yemen

Europe (48 nation-states)

Albania
Andorra
Armenia
Austria
Belarus
Belgium
Bosnia and Herzegovina
Bulgaria
Croatia
Cyprus
Czech Republic
Denmark
Estonia
Finland
France
Georgia
Germany
Greece
Hungary
Iceland
Ireland
Italy
Kosovo
Latvia
Liechtenstein
Lithuania
Luxembourg
Macedonia
Malta
Moldova

Monaco
Montenegro
Netherlands
Norway
Poland
Portugal
Romania
Russia
San Marino
Serbia
Slovakia
Slovenia
Spain
Sweden
Switzerland
Ukraine
United Kingdom
Vatican City

North America (3 nation-states)

Canada
Mexico
United States of America

Central America and the Caribbean (20 nation-states)

Antigua and Barbuda
Bahamas
Barbados
Belize
Costa Rica
Cuba
Dominica
Dominican Republic
El Salvador
Grenada
Guatemala
Haiti
Honduras
Jamaica
Nicaragua
Panama
St. Kitts and Nevis
St. Lucia
St. Vincent and the Grenadines
Trinidad and Tobago

South America (12 nation-states)

Argentina
Bolivia
Brazil
Chile
Colombia
Ecuador
Guyana
Paraguay
Peru
Suriname
Uruguay
Venezuela

Africa (47 nation-states)

Angola
Benin
Botswana
Burkina Faso
Burundi
Cameroon
Cape Verde
Central African Republic
Chad
Comoros
Congo, Democratic Republic of the
Côte d'Ivoire
Djibouti
Equatorial Guinea
Eritrea
Ethiopia
Gabon
Gambia
Ghana
Guinea
Guinea-Bissau
Kenya
Lesotho
Liberia
Madagascar
Malawi
Mali
Mauritania
Mauritius
Mozambique
Namibia

Niger
Nigeria
Rwanda
São Tomé and Principe
Senegal
Seychelles
Sierra Leone
South Africa
Sudan
Swaziland
Tanzania
Togo
Uganda
Zambia
Zimbabwe

Australia and Oceania (15 nation-states)

Australia
East Timor
Fiji
Kiribati
Marshall Islands
Micronesia, Federated States of
Nauru
New Zealand
Palau
Papua New Guinea
Samoa
Solomon Islands
Tonga
Tuvalu
Vanuatu

5.
18 Mini-Regions and 209 Nation-States

(See pp145-146, 147)

(The 209 nation-states comprise 192 UN nation-states; 16 related and disputed territories; and Taiwan, which was not in the UN in 2009)

AFRICA

Northern Africa

Algeria
Egypt
Libya
Morocco
Sudan
Tunisia
Western Sahara

Western Africa

Benin
Burkina Faso
Cape Verde
Côte d'Ivoire
Gambia
Ghana
Guinea
Guinea-Bissau
Liberia
Mali
Mauritania
Niger
Nigeria
Senegal
Sierra Leone
Togo

Eastern Africa

Burundi
Comoros
Djibouti
Eritrea
Ethiopia
Kenya
Madagascar
Malawi
Mauritius
Mayotte
Mozambique
Réunion
Rwanda
Seychelles
Somalia
Tanzania
Uganda
Zambia
Zimbabwe

Middle Africa

Angola
Cameroon
Central African Republic
Chad
Congo
Congo, Democratic Republic of the
Equatorial Guinea
Gabon
São Tomé and Principe

Southern Africa

Botswana
Lesotho
Namibia
South Africa
Swaziland

AMERICAS

Northern America

Canada
United States

Central America

Belize
Costa Rica
El Salvador
Guatemala
Honduras
Mexico
Nicaragua
Panama

Caribbean

Antigua and Barbuda
Bahamas
Barbados
Cuba
Dominica
Dominican Republic
Grenada
Guadeloupe
Haiti
Jamaica
Martinique
Netherlands Antilles
Puerto Rico
St. Kitts and Nevis
St. Lucia
St. Vincent and the Grenadines
Trinidad and Tobago

South America

Argentina
Bolivia
Brazil
Chile
Colombia
Ecuador
French Guiana
Guyana
Paraguay
Peru
Suriname
Uruguay
Venezuela

ASIA

Western Asia

Armenia
Azerbaijan
Bahrain
Cyprus
Georgia
Iraq
Israel
Jordan
Kuwait
Lebanon
Oman
Palestinian Territory
Qatar
Saudi Arabia
Syria
Turkey
United Arab Emirates
Yemen

South Central Asia

Afghanistan
Bangladesh
Bhutan
India
Iran
Kazakhstan
Kyrgyzstan
Maldives
Nepal
Pakistan
Sri Lanka
Tajikistan
Turkmenistan
Uzbekistan

Southeast Asia

Brunei
Cambodia
Indonesia
Laos
Malaysia
Myanmar
Philippines
Singapore
Thailand
Timor-Leste
Vietnam

East Asia

China
China, Hong Kong
China, Macao
Japan
Korea, North
Korea, South
Mongolia
Taiwan

EUROPE

Northern Europe

Channel Islands
Denmark
Estonia
Finland
Iceland
Ireland
Latvia
Lithuania
Norway
Sweden
United Kingdom

Western Europe

Austria
Belgium
France
Germany
Liechtenstein
Luxembourg
Monaco
Netherlands
Switzerland

Eastern Europe

Belarus
Bulgaria
Czech Republic
Hungary
Moldova
Poland
Romania
Russia
Slovakia
Ukraine

Southern Europe

Albania
Andorra
Bosnia and Herzegovina
Croatia
Greece
Italy
Kosovo
Macedonia
Malta
Montenegro
Portugal
San Marino
Serbia
Slovenia
Spain

OCEANIA

Australia
Federated States of Micronesia
Fiji
French Polynesia
Guam
Kiribati
Marshall Islands
Nauru
New Caledonia
New Zealand
Palau
Papua New Guinea
Samoa
Solomon Islands
Tonga
Tuvalu
Vanuatu

6.
Club of Rome's 10 Zones

(See p144)

A revised plan for a world government was outlined in 1973 by the "Rockefellerite" Club of Rome, which split the world into 10 political/economic regions or zones that would unite the entire world under one government. These were originally called "Kingdoms" to reflect the 10 kingdoms within Atlantis in Plato's account in *Critias*. The word "Kingdoms" was omitted when the plan was published in a book, *Mankind at the Turning Point*, which argued that the world's problems could only be solved "in a global context". These zones are:

1. North America
2. Western Europe
3. Japan
4. The rest of the developed market economies (Israel, Australia, Tasmania, New Zealand, Oceania, South Africa)
5. Eastern Europe include the free Soviet Union
6. Latin America
7. North Africa and the Middle East
8. Main Africa
9. South and South Eastern Asia including India
10. "Centrally-planned Asia", meaning Communist Asia (Mongolia, North Korea, North Vietnam, and China)

7.
The IMF's 190 Countries, 2009
(See p78)

A

Afghanistan, Islamic Republic of
Albania
Algeria
Angola
Antigua and Barbuda
Argentina
Armenia, Republic of Aruba,
Kingdom of the Netherlands
Australia
Austria
Azerbaijan, Republic of

B

Bahamas, The
Bahrain, Kingdom of
Bangladesh
Barbados
Belarus, Republic of
Belgium
Belize
Benin
Bhutan
Bolivia
Bosnia and Herzegovina
Botswana
Brazil
Brunei Darussalam
Bulgaria
Burkina Faso
Burundi

C

Cambodia
Cameroon
Canada
Cape Verde
Central African Republic
Chad
Chile
China, People's Republic of
Colombia
Comoros
Congo, Democratic Republic of the
Congo, Republic of the
Costa Rica
Côte d'Ivoire
Croatia, Republic of
Cyprus
Czech Republic

D

Denmark
Djibouti
Dominica
Dominican Republic

E

Ecuador
Egypt, Arab Republic of
El Salvador
Equatorial Guinea
Eritrea
Estonia, Republic of
Ethiopia

F

Fiji
Finland
France

G

Gabon
Gambia
Georgia
Germany
Ghana
Greece
Grenada
Guatemala
Guinea
Guinea-Bissau
Guyana

H

Haiti
Honduras
Hong Kong Special Administrative Region of the People's Republic of China
Hungary

I

Iceland
India
Indonesia
Iran, Islamic Republic of
Iraq
Ireland
Israel
Italy

J

Jamaica
Japan
Jordan

K

Kazakhstan, Republic of
Kenya
Kiribati
Korea, Republic of
Kosovo
Kuwait
Kyrgyz Republic

L

Lao People's Democratic Republic
Latvia, Republic of
Lebanon
Lesotho
Liberia
Libyan Arab Jamahiriya, Socialist People's
Lithuania, Republic of
Luxembourg

M

Macao Special Administrative Region of the People's Republic of China
Macedonia, former Yugoslav Republic of
Madagascar
Malawi
Malaysia
Maldives
Mali
Malta
Marshall Islands, Republic of the
Mauritania
Mauritius
Mexico
Micronesia, Federated States of
Moldova, Republic of
Mongolia
Montenegro, Republic of
Morocco
Mozambique, Republic of
Myanmar

N

Namibia
Nepal
Netherlands, Kingdom of the
Netherlands Antilles, Kingdom of the
New Zealand
Nicaragua
Niger
Nigeria
Norway

O

Oman

P

Pakistan
Palau, Republic of
Panama
Papua New Guinea
Paraguay
Peru
Philippines
Poland, Republic of
Portugal

Q

Qatar

R

Romania
Russian Federation
Rwanda

S

Samoa
San Marino
São Tomé and Principe
Saudi Arabia
Senegal
Serbia, Republic of
Seychelles
Sierra Leone
Singapore
Slovak Republic
Slovenia, Republic of
Solomon Islands
Somalia
South Africa
Spain
Sri Lanka
St. Kitts and Nevis
St. Lucia
St. Vincent and the Grenadines
Sudan
Suriname
Swaziland, Kingdom of
Sweden
Switzerland
Syrian Arab Republic

T

Tajikistan, Republic of
Tanzania
Thailand
Timor-Leste, Democratic Republic of
Togo
Tonga
Trinidad and Tobago
Tunisia
Turkey
Turkmenistan

U

Uganda
Ukraine
United Arab Emirates
United Kingdom
United States
Uruguay
Uzbekistan, Republic of

V

Vanuatu
Venezuela, Republica Bolivariana de
Vietnam

Y

Yemen, Republic of

Z

Zambia
Zimbabwe

8.
Overview of the EU's Institutions

(See pp76-77)

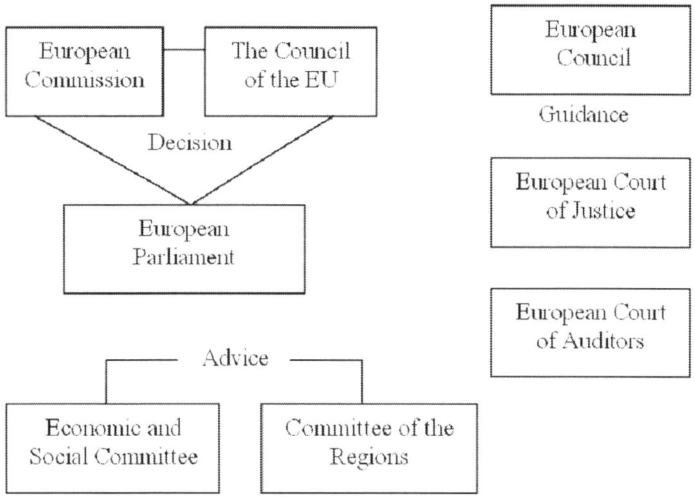

List of Websites Supporting Data

(Material has often been updated and adapted)

Page No.	**Website**
182-186	Declaration of Independence No website, taken from Hagger, *The Secret Founding of America*
186-190	The North Atlantic Treaty http://www.nato.int/cps/en/natolive/official_texts_17120.htm
190-192	Project for the New American Century http://www.newamericancentury.org/statementofprinciples.htm
193	Overview of the UN Structure http://mpsinfo.files.wordpress.com/2008/12/400px-un_institu-tionssvg.png
194	Structure of UN Agencies http://www.stanford.edu/group/Jonsson/appendb.gif
195-200	UN Organizations http://en.wikipedia.org/wiki/United_Nations_System
200-203	The UN's 192 Member States http://www.encyclopedia.com/doc/1E1-UNmmbrTABLE.html
203-210	The UN Universal Declaration of Human Rights 1948 http://www.un.org/en/documents/udhr/
210-255	Wars the UN Failed to Prevent Involving 123 Countries, 1945-2009 http://answers.google.com/answers/threadview?id=55124

225-229 37 Major Conflicts the UN Failed to Prevent after 1945: 689 UN Resolutions and 33,750,700 Deaths
http://en.wikipedia.org/wiki/Criticism_of_the_United_Nations#Comparison_of_UNSC_resolutions_on_various_conflicts

230-231 119 Electoral Democracies, 2009
http://www.freedomhouse.org/template.cfm?page=477&year=2009

231-235 Freedom Ratings, 2009
http://www.freedomhouse.org/template.cfm?page=475&year=2009
and
http://www.freedomhouse.org/template.cfm?page=476&year=2009

235-242 Freedom Ratings Table by Countries and Territories, 2009
http://www.freedomhouse.org/template.cfm?page=478&year=2009
and
http://www.freedomhouse.org/template.cfm?page=474&year=2009

243 The World's 20 Worst Dictators, 2009
http://www.parade.com/dictators/2009/

244 Regional Populations as Percentages of World Population, 2008
http://www.data360.org/dsg.aspx?Data_Set_Group_Id=644&transpose=row

244-245 Historical and Predicted Regional Populations as Percentages of World Population
http://en.wikipedia.org/wiki/World_population

245-255 Nation-States' Populations as Percentages of World Population
http://en.wikipedia.org/wiki/List_of_countries_by_population

256-258 8 Regions and 195 Nation-States
http://geography.about.com/od/lists/a/officiallist.htm

258-261 18 Mini-Regions and 209 Nation-States
http://www.docstoc.com/docs/10157039/2009-World-Population-Data-Sheet

262 Club of Rome's 10 Zones
No website, taken from Hagger, *The Syndicate*

263-267 The IMF's 190 Countries, 2009
http://www.imf.org/external/country/index.htm

267 Overview of the EU's Institutions
http://www.dadalos-europe.org/int/grundkurs4/eu-struktur_1.htm

NOTES AND REFERENCES

Prologue: World Government and Peace

1. Nicholas Hagger, *The New Philosophy of Universalism*, pp355-357.
2. Hagger, *The Syndicate*, pp283-284 and 291-293.
3. Survey conducted by Freedom House, an organization opposed to tyranny that supports the expansion of freedom in the world, between 1972 and 2005. In this survey, updated to 2009, "free" nations up to a certain ranking were considered to be liberal democracies. See http://www.freedomhouse.org/template.cfm?page=477&year=20
4. Freedom House Survey of 2009. See http://www.freedomhouse.org/template.cfm?page=475&year=20 and 20http://www.freedomhouse.org/template.cfm?page=476&year=20
5. John Milton, *The Ready and Easy Way to Establish a Free Commonwealth*, ed. by Evert Mordecai Clark. See http://all.libertyfund.org/?option=com_staticxt&staticfile=show.php%3Ftitle=272&chapter=41706&layout=html&Itemid=27
6. Sir Charles Firth, *Oliver Cromwell and the Rule of Puritans in England*, p382.

PART ONE
THE WORLD GOVERNMENT DREAM

1. History's Inexorable Flow towards World Government

1. See http://geography.about.com/od/lists/a/officiallist.htm?p=1. See also http://en.wikipedia.org/wiki/Future_enlargement_of_the_European_Union.
2. Alexander Wendt, 'Why a World State is Inevitable', European Journal of International Relations, 2003, 9, 4: pp491-542.
3. Wendt, *op. cit.*, p491.
4. Daniel Deudney, 'Nuclear Weapons and the Waning of the *Real*-State', *Daedalus*, 124, 2 (1995), pp209-31; *see also* 'Geopolitics and Change' in *New Thinking in International Relations Theory*, M. Doyle and G.J. Ikenberry (eds.), Boulder, Colorado: Westview Press.
5. Wendt, *op. cit.*, pp505-506.

2. The Long Yearning for a World State

1. For a full examination of *rta*, see Jeanine Miller, *The Vision of Cosmic Order in the Vedas*, e.g. p283.
2. Fung Yu-Lan, *The Spirit of Chinese Philosophy*, p27.
3. *Encyclopedia Britannica*, 15th edition, 'Chinese Philosophy', 4.416.
4. See http://en.wikiquote.org/wiki/Socrates#Plutarch, Socrates' words seem to contradict his view in *Crito*.
5. Dante, *Convivio*, in *Readings in Medieval Political Theory 1100-1400*, C.J. Nederman and K.L. Forhan (eds.).
6. Richard Kay, *Dante's Monarchia*, ppxxiii-xxv, quoted in Barbara Reynolds, *Dante, The Poet, the Political Thinker, the Man*, pp328-329.
7. Dante, *Monarchia*, pp13, 15, 21-2, 43-4, xvii and 19, xxxiii for the citings of *Monarchia* in this paragraph.
8. See John J. Reilly, *The Perfection of the West* and his related essay 'Dante's World Government: *De Monarchia* in the 21st Century', www.johnreilly.info/dwg.htm.
9. For this and the previous extracts, see the translation of *De Monarchia*, Dante, *On World-Government*, trans. Herbert W. Schneider. See also another translation, Dante, *Monarchy*, trans. and ed. Prue Shaw, who translates the extract from 1:11 as: "Justice is at its strongest only under a monarch; therefore for the best ordering of the world there must be a monarchy or empire."
10. For this extract see Marsilius of Padua, *The Defender of Peace*, trans. by Alan Gewirth.
11. For this extract see, Francesco Petrarch, *Canzoni 128*, trans. Morris Bishop in *Petrarch and His World*, p234.
12. Thomas Hobbes, *Leviathan*, p286.
13. Abbé de Saint-Pierre, *Extrait du projet de paix perpétuelle*, trans. H.H. Bellot. See also another translation, *A Lasting Peace through the Federation of* Europe, trans. C.E. Vaughn. See also Jean-Jacques Rousseau, *A Lasting Peace through the Federation of Europe and The State of War* (1756), pp61-64.
14. Rousseau, *op. cit.*, pp91, 93, 112.
15. To find this on the Internet, see the version with a slightly different end to the title (explained on p39) Immanuel Kant, *Idea for a Universal History from a Cosmopolitan Point of View* (1784), trans. by Lewis White Beck, in Immanuel Kant, *On History*,

http://www.marxists.org/reference/subject/ethics/kant/universal-history.htm. The quotations that follow are taken from the version referred to in note 16.

16. Immanuel Kant, *Idea for a Universal History with a Cosmopolitan Purpose* (1784) and *Perpetual Peace: A Philosophical Sketch* (1795), in *Political Writings*, trans. by H.B. Nisbet, ed. by Hans Reiss, pp41, 47, 48 and 105.
17. Kant, *op. cit.*, pp41-53 and 93-130, here citing pp100, 102, 104, 106, 113 and 114.
18. J. Christopher Harold, *The Age of Napoleon*, p123.
19. Kant, *op. cit.*, p100.
20. John Rawls, *A Theory of Justice*, pp11-16.
21. P. Kleingeld and E. Brown, 'Cosmopolitanism', *Stanford Encyclopedia of Philosophy* (Fall 2006 Ed.)
22. See http://www.globalpolitician.com/22960-world-government
23. Joseph E. Schwartzberg, 'Reform of the General Assembly', in *Revitalizing the United Nations: Reform Through Weighted Voting*, Institute for Global Policy, World Federalist Movement, p3.
24. H.G. Wells, *The Outline of History*, p1153.
25. Albert Einstein, 'Towards a World Government' (1946), in *Out Of My Later Years: The Scientist, Philosopher and Man Portrait Through His Own Words*, New York: Wings Books, 1956.
26. Gandhi, speech, March 1947. In Gandhi, *All Men are Brothers, Autobiographical Reflections*, p112.
27. Bertrand Russell, 'The Atomic Bomb and Prevention of War' in the *Bulletin of the Atomic Scientists*, 1 October 1946.
28. In Dennis Laurence Cuddy, *Secret Records Revealed: The Men, the Money & The Methods Behind the New World Order*, p89.
29. The Russell-Einstein Manifesto (1955), issued in London on 9 July 1955 by Bertrand Russell.
30. Wendell L. Willkie, *One World*, p165.
31. Emery Reves, *The Anatomy of Peace*, p247.
32. Einstein, 'Economic war or Peace' in Albert Einstein, *Ideas and Opinions*, p122.
33. See http://magazine.uchicago.edu/9512/9512Salvation.html
34. See http://www.worldservice.org/gov.html
35. For copies of visas, see http://www.worldgovernment.org/visas.html?s=1

36. Joseph P. Baratta, *The Politics of World Federation*, p470.
37. E. Adamson Hoebel, *The Law of Primitive Man*, pp331-333.
38. E. Goodman, 'The Soviet Union and World Government', in *The Journal of Politics* 15, 2, 1953, pp231-253.

3. History's Progress to an End-Point: The Collapse of the Old Order

1. Kant, *Idea for a Universal History from a Cosmopolitan Point of View* (1784), trans. by Lewis White Beck, in Immanuel Kant, *On History*. See http://www.marxists.org/reference/subject/ethics/kant/universal-history.htm. All the quotations regarding the nine theses are taken from this translation.
2. *An Idea for a Universal History from a Cosmopolitan Point of View*, in Immanuel Kant, *On History*, p16.
3. Francis Fukuyama, *The End of History and the Last Man*, p66.
4. Jacques Derrida, *Specters of Marx*.
5. Hagger, *The Fire and the Stones*; *The Light of Civilization* and *The Rise and Fall of Civilizations*.
6. For further details, see Hagger, *The Fire and the Stones*, *The Light of Civilization* and *The Rise and Fall of Civilizations*.
7. See Freedom House Survey of 2009. See http://www.freedomhouse.org/template.cfm?page=475&year=20 and 20http://www.freedomhouse.org/template.cfm?page=476&year=20
8. See Hagger, *The Libyan Revolution*.
9 *The New Oxford American Dictionary*, 2nd edn., ed. by Erin McKean.
10. For Europe removing 80 per cent of laws from European nation-states, see www.norwich1.com/europe.htm. Also see Note 13. For the German figure of 84 per cent, see http://www.openeurope.org.uk/analysis/herzog .pdf, Roman Herzog and Lüder Gerken: "The German Ministry of Justice has compared the legal acts adopted by the Federal Republic of Germany between 1998 and 2004 with those adopted by the European Union in the same period. Results: 84 per cent came from Brussels, with only 16 per cent coming originally from Berlin." For a figure of 85 per cent see http://openeuropeblog.blogspot.com/2009/04/how-many-of-our-laws-are-made-in.html. For Pöttering's comment see http://bnp.org.uk/2009/06/eu-president-after-lisbon-treaty-%e2%80%9cn: "The president of the European Union Parliament, Hans Gert Pöttering, has stated unequivo-

cally that once the Lisbon Treaty is fully implemented, the EU will be responsible for 'nearly 100 per cent' of all laws made in Europe."

11. For *FREE* see the Appendix of Hagger, *The Revolution That Didn't Happen*.
12. Hobbes, *Leviathan*, p188.
13. For Europe making 80 per cent of British laws, see Peter Lilley, House of Commons, *Daily Hansard*, 3 June 2008: "The European Union has supremacy over British Law. 80 per cent of Britain's laws are now made in Brussels and Parliament has no power to reject or amend them." See also note 10.
14. See http://en.wikipedia.org/wiki/Collective_security.
15. See Hagger, *Armageddon*, pp582-595.
16. Thomas Paine, *The Age of Reason*, p22.
17. Hagger, *The Fire and the Stones*, pp3-344. Updated as *The Light of Civilization*.

PART TWO
THE WORLD GOVERNMENT AS A REALITY IN OUR TIME

4. Models of a Supranational Authority: the *Status Quo*

1. *Catholic Encyclopedia* (1913), Henry IV.
2. *The Law of War and Peace*, trans. by Francis Kelsey, prol. sect. 28. (The book title does not reflect the Latin *De*, "on" or "concerning".)
3. See http://www.guardian.co.uk/news/datablog/2009/sep/06/nuclear-weapons-world-us-north-korea-russia-iran
4. See http://www.thesun.co.uk/sol/homepage/news/article1076910.ece Also http://www.telegraph.co.uk/news/1527886/New-EU-map-makes-Kent-part-of-same-nation-as-France.html
5. For a much fuller account of the American Constitutional Convention, see Hagger, *The Secret Founding of America*, pp152-158.
6. Writ of Certiorari, Supreme Court, http://www.watchblog.com/thirdparty/archives/004636.html
7. Anthony and Andrew Cowgill, *The European Constitution in Perspective*, 'The Treaty establishing a Constitution for Europe', p5.

5. Models of a Supranational Authority: Reforming the UN

1. Arthur M. Schlesinger, Jr, *A Thousand Days: John F. Kennedy in the*

White House, p484.

6. Models of a Supranational Authority: Global Governance

1. Derek Wilson, *Rothschild: A Story of Wealth and Power*, pp9-33; Frederic Morton, *The Rothschilds, A Family Portrait*, pp17-36; Count Egon Caesar Corti, *The Rise of the House of Rothschild*, pp1-26; George Armstrong, *The Rothschild Money Trust*, pp21-22.
2. Armstrong, *op. cit.*, p21; Wilson, *op. cit.*, p32.
3. Corti, *op. cit.*, p402; Morton, *op. cit.*, p17.
4. Armstrong, *op. cit.*, p24.
5. Niall Ferguson, *The World's Banker, The History of the House of Rothschild*, pp1034-1035.
6. Ferguson, *op. cit.*, pp78-79.
7. Armstrong, *op. cit.*, p35.
8. Morton, *op. cit.*, pp150-152.
9. Hagger, *The Syndicate*, pp10-13.
10. Emanuel M. Josephson, *The "Federal" Reserve Conspiracy and Rockefeller*, p75.
11. Emanuel M. Josephson, *The Truth about Rockefeller, Public Enemy No. 1*, pp2, 54.
12. David Allen Rivera, *Final Warning, A History of the New World Order*, p44.
13. Rivera, *op. cit.*, p65.
14. Ron Chernow, *Titan, The Life of John D. Rockefeller Sr.*, p557.
15. Josephson, *The "Federal" Reserve Conspiracy and Rockefeller*, pp74-75.
16. Emanuel M. Josephson, *Rockefeller "Internationalist", The Man Who Misrules the World*, pp204-231, particularly p212; Josephson, *The Truth about Rockefeller, Public Enemy No. 1*, *op.cit.*, pp44, 133.
17. John Loftus and Mark Aarons, *The Secret War against the Jews*, p168.
18. Josephson, *Rockefeller "Internationalist", The Man who Misrules the World*, *op.cit.*, p24.
19. Armstrong, *op. cit.*, p36.
20. For Rumsfeld and Iraq, see Jim Tucker, *Bilderberg Diary*, p9. For the Bilderberg Group, see Daniel Estulin, *The True Story of The Bilderberg Group*, *passim*; also Hagger, *The Syndicate*, pp34-36.
21. Estulin, *op. cit.*, pp149-165; also Hagger, *The Syndicate*, pp37-38.
22. *Global 2000 Report to the President*, vol.1, pp1, 41-42 and *Global Future*,

p50. See also Hagger, *The Syndicate*, pp267-272.

23. The Kissinger Report, *National Security Study, Memorandum 200*, April 1974, on the need for massive population reduction, implying that war, famine and disease can reduce the world's population of "useless eaters" to an acceptable (i.e. cost-effective) level.
24. Eisenhower, farewell address on radio and TV, 17 January 1961, Public Papers of the Presidents of the United States at http://www.presidency.ucsb.edu/ws/
25. Charles Griffin, 'New Light on Eisenhower's Farewell Address', *Presidential Studies Quarterly*, 22 (1992), pp469-479.
26. See http://www.guardian.co.uk/news/datablog/2009/sep/06/nuclear-weapons-world-us-north-korea-russia-iran
    The US high for possession of nuclear warheads was in 1965 (32,040), which had come down by 1985 (to 24,401), and the USSR high was in 1985 (45,000). In early May 2010 the US Secretary of State Hillary Clinton declassified the size of the US nuclear arsenal to galvanize efforts to rid the world of nuclear weapons. According to a report in the *Times* of 4 May she revealed that the Pentagon's figures show that the US stockpile consisted of 5,113 nuclear warheads and "several thousand" more retired warheads awaiting dismantling. The 5,113 and "several thousand" can be expected to amount to 9,552. The UK figure of 225 nuclear weapons was announced by Foreign Secretary William Hague on 26 May 2010.
27. Woodrow Wilson, address to Congress, 8 January 1918, in *Papers Relating to the Foreign Relations of the United States, 1918: Supplement I, The World War* (2 vols., Washington, DC, US Government Printing Office, 1933), I, pp15-16. See http://www.historyplace.com/speeches/wilson-points.htm
28. Hagger, *The Syndicate*, p41; also Hagger, *The Secret Founding of America*, p139.
29. A. Ralph Epperson, *The New World Order*, pxiv; quoting Jean-Michel Angebert, *The Occult and the Third Reich*, p192.
30. Hermann Rauschning, *Hitler* Speaks, p87; alternatively translated in Epperson, *op. cit.*, pxiv, quoting Jean-Michel Angebert, *op. cit.*, p192.
31. Hagger, *The Syndicate*, pp120-121, 132.
32. All these quotations about the New World Order are sourced in Hagger, *The Syndicate*, pp121-122.
33. Hagger, *The Syndicate*, p23.

34. George Soros, *The Bubble of American Supremacy*, pvii. For Senator Jay Rockefeller see Hagger, *The Syndicate*, p185 and *The Secret American Dream*, ch 8.
35. Hagger, *The Secret Founding of America.*
36. See video by Representative Paul Kanjorski, http://www.youtube.com/watch?v=pD8viQ_DhS4, accessed on 9.3.2010
37. See http://bushstole04.com/monetarysystem/rothschild_bank.htm
38. James P. Tucker, 'Bilderberg Surreptitiously Pushes Global Treasury Department', *American Free Press*, 22 March 2010.
39. See http://www.webpal.org/a_reconstruction/nwo/charter99.htm

PART THREE
THE STATECRAFT OF WORLD GOVERNMENT: A BLUEPRINT FOR A WORLD STATE

7. The Ideal Form of World State

1. Lenin, *Collected Works*, Progress Publishers, 1974, Moscow, vol.21, pp339-343, *Sotsial-Demokrat*, No. 44, August 23, 1915, trans. by Charles Farrell, see http://www.marxists.org/archive/lenin/works/1915/aug/23.htm.
2. Hagger, *The Fire and the Stones*; *The Rise and Fall of Civilizations.*
3. Bank for International Settlements, Triennial Central Bank Survey, December 2007, http://www.bis.org/publ/rpfxf07t.pdf

8. The Structure of the New World State

1. See list http://en.wikipedia.org/wiki/List_of_countries_by_population#cite_note-unpop-3.
2. See Hagger, *The Syndicate*, pp257-260.
3. Hagger, *The Syndicate*, pp110-111, citing *Spotlight*, 22.April 1996, pp4-5: "Sources have told the *Spotlight* Chernomyrdin and David Rockefeller are secret partners in Russian energy combines."
4. See http://www.flickr.com/photos/redxdress/365219901/

9. Peering into the Future: A Glimpse of the World State

1. Hagger, *The Fire and the Stones*; revised in two volumes as *The Light of Civilization* and *The Rise and Fall of Civilizations.*

2. For full details, see Hagger, *Armageddon*, pp582-595; and *The Secret American Dream*, Appendix.
3. Hagger, *Armageddon*, "Useful Sources", ppx-xiii.
4. Report in *American Free Press*, 2 November 2009, p14.
5. UN Population Estimates and Projections, August 2009. See http://esa.un.org/unpp/.
6. UN Report based on 2004 data. See http://www.un.org/esa/population/publications/sixbillion/sixbilpart1.pdf.
7. See http://www.hubbertpeak.com/campbell/Campbell_02-3.pdf.
8. See http://www.ukerc.ac.uk/support/tiki-index.php?page=Global+Oil+Depletion.
9. See http://www.need.org/needpdf/infobook_activities/SecInfo/NGasS.pdf
10. For details of these predictions, see Hagger, *The Rise and Fall of Civilizations*, pp282-293, and pp532-546.
11. http://oai.dtic.mil/oai/oai?verb=getRecord&metadataPrefix=html&identifier=ADA482785
12. See http://www.homelandsecurityresearch.com/2008/05/cost-of-war-on-terror/
13. Joseph Stiglitz and Linda Bilmes, *The Three Trillion Dollar War*.
14. See http://www.cbsnews.com/blogs/2009/03/17/politics/politicalhot-sheet/entry4872310.shtml.
15. Office for National Statistics, see http://www.economicshelp.org/blog/uk-economy/uk-national-debt/.
16. See http://en.wikipedia.org/wiki/Military_of_the_European_Union
17. For alternative totals of global military spending in 2008, see http://daga.dhs.org/icp/faithpeace/2009/90220a.htm for $1.4727 trillion; see http://en.wikipedia.org/wiki/List_of_countries_by_military_expenditures for $1.47 trillion; see http://www.globalissues.org/article/75/world-military-spending#WorldMilitarySpending for $1.464 trillion (quoting the Stockholm International Peace Research Yearbook, 2009); and see http://news.therecord.com/article/550332 for $1.46 trillion.
18. Hagger, *Collected Poems 1958-2005*, pp93-94.
19. Carl Haub, "How Many People Have Ever Lived on Earth?", *Population Today* (Population Reference Bureau). November/December 2002. See http://www.prb.org/pdf/PT_novdec02.pdf.
20. Hagger, *The Rise and Fall of Civilizations*, p536, no.12.

21. My study shows that the previous stage, stage 16, sees the surfacing of epic poetry set in the time of early growth, which reflects the God of growth, the Universalist Light. Homer's *Iliad* was about the early growth of the Aegean-Greek civilization, Virgil's *Aeneid* about the early growth of the Roman civilization. Epic poetry can be expected about the early growth of the North-American civilization. It so happens that the two poetic epics I have written are about American leaders, Eisenhower in the Second World War and George W. Bush in the War on Terror, and both therefore qualify as American epics.
22. Quoted in Edith Starr Miller, *Occult Theocrasy*, vol.1, p.221; also quoted in John Daniel, *Scarlet and the Beast*, vol.1, pp.393-394. Pike's letter was read on 14 July 1889 at the annual Congress of 23 Grand Lodge Supreme Councils in Paris. The reading was noted in a letter in an English Masonic periodical *The Freemason* on 19 January 1935. See also Hagger, *The Syndicate*, pp285-290, 312-314.

Epilogue: Making a Golden Age Happen

1. Fyodor Dostoevsky, *The Brothers Karamazov*, trans. by David Magarshack, vol. 1, p302

BIBLIOGRAPHY

Abbé de Saint-Pierre, *A Lasting Peace through the Federation of Europe*, trans. by C.E. Vaughn, London: Constable and Co., 1917.

Abbé de Saint-Pierre, *Extrait du projet de paix perpétuelle*, trans. by H.H. Bellot, London, 1927; republished by Kessinger Publishing, 2009.

Angebert, Jean-Michel, *The Occult and the Third Reich*, MacMillan Publishing Company, 1974.

Armstrong, George, *The Rothschild Money Trust*, Omni Publications, California, 1940.

Baratta, Joseph P., *The Politics of World Federation, United Nations, UN Reform, Atomic Control*, 2 vols., Westport, Connecticut: Praeger, 2004.

Bishop, Morris, *Petrarch and His World*, Indiana University Press, 2002.

Chernow, Ron, *Titan, The Life of John D. Rockefeller Sr.*, Little, Brown, 1998.

Clark, Grenville, and Sohn, Louis, *Introduction to World Peace Through World Law*, World Without War Publications, 1973.

Clark, Grenville, and Sohn, Louis, *World Peace Through World Law*, two alternative plans, 3rd edition enlarged, Harvard University Press, 1966.

Corti, Count Egon Caesar, *The Rise of the House of Rothschild*, Western Islands, USA, 1928, 1972.

Cowgill, Anthony and Andrew, *The European Constitution in Perspective*, British Management Data Foundation, 2004.

Cuddy, Dennis Laurence, *Secret Records Revealed: The Men, the Money & The Methods Behind the New World Order*, Hearthstone Publishing Ltd., 1999.

Daniel, John, *Scarlet and the Beast*, vol. I, JKI Publishing, 1995.

Dante, *Convivio* (*The Banquet, c.*1304), in *Readings in Medieval Political Theory 1100-1400*, ed. by C.J. Nederman and K.L. Forhan, Indianapolis: Hackett, 1993.

Dante, *Monarchy*, trans. and ed. by Prue Shaw, Cambridge, Cambridge University Press, 1996.

Dante, *On World-Government*, trans. by Herbert W. Schneider, 2nd rev. ed., New York: Liberal Arts, 1957.

Derrida, Jacques, *Specters of Marx*, Routledge, 1st edition, 1994.

Dostoevsky, Fyodor, *The Brothers Karamazov*, trans. by David Magarshack, Penguin, 1958.

Einstein, Albert, *Ideas and Opinions*, New York: Bonanza Books, Crown Publishers, 1954.

Epperson, A. Ralph, *The New World Order*, Publius Press, 1990.

Estulin, Daniel, *The True Story of The Bilderberg Group*, TrineDay LLC, 2009.

Ferguson, Niall, *The World's Banker, The History of the House of Rothschild*, Weidenfeld & Nicolson, London, 1998.

Firth, Sir Charles, *Oliver Cromwell and the Rule of Puritans in England*, Oxford University Press, 1900, reprinted in 1961.

Fukuyama, Francis, *The End of History and the Last Man*, Hamish Hamilton, 1992.

Gandhi, Mahatma, *All Men are Brothers, Autobiographical Reflections*, ed. Krishna Kripalani, New York: Continuum, 1982.

Global Future, Time to Act, Council on Environmental Quality, 1981/ University of Michigan Library, reprint.

Global Report to the President - Entering the Twenty-First Century, Council on Environmental Quality, 1981/ Penguin, 1982.

Grotius, Hugo, *The Law of War and Peace*, trans. by Francis Kelsey, Carnegie edition, 1925.

Hagger, Nicholas, *Armageddon*, O Books, 2010.

Hagger, Nicholas, *Collected Poems 1958-2005*, O Books, 2006.

Hagger, Nicholas, *The Fire and the Stones*, Element, 1991.

Hagger, Nicholas, *The Libyan Revolution*, O Books, 2009.

Hagger, Nicholas, *The Light of Civilization*, O Books, 2006.

Hagger, Nicholas, *The New Philosophy of Universalism*, O Books, 2009.

Hagger, Nicholas, *The Revolution That Didn't Happen*, awaiting publication.

Hagger, Nicholas, *The Rise and Fall of Civilizations*, O Books, 2008.

Hagger, Nicholas, *The Secret American Dream*, Watkins Publishing, 2011.

Hagger, Nicholas, *The Secret Founding of America*, Watkins Publishing, 2007.

Hagger, Nicholas, *The Syndicate*, O Books, 2004.

Harold, J. Christopher, *The Age of Napoleon*, The American Heritage Library, 1963.

Hobbes, Thomas, *Leviathan*, Penguin, 1986.

Hoebel, E. Adamson, *The Law of Primitive Man*, Harvard University Press, 1954.

Huntington, Samuel, *The Clash of Civilizations*, Simon and Schuster, 1996.

Josephson, Emanuel M., *Rockefeller "Internationalist", The Man who Misrules the World*, Chedney Press, New York, 1952.

Josephson, Emanuel M., *The "Federal" Reserve Conspiracy and Rockefeller*, Chedney Press, New York, 1968.

Josephson, Emanuel M., *The Truth about Rockefeller, Public Enemy No. 1*, Chedney Press, New York, 1964.

Kagan, Robert, *The Return of History and the End of Dreams*, Atlantic Books, 2008.

Kant, Immanuel, *Idea for a Universal History from a Cosmopolitan Point of View* (1784), in Immanuel Kant, *On History*, The Bobbs-Merrill Co., 1963.

Kant, Immanuel, *Idea for a Universal History with a Cosmopolitan Purpose* (1784) and *Perpetual Peace: A Philosophical Sketch* (1795), in *Political Writings*, trans. by H.B. Nisbet, ed. by Hans Reiss, 2nd ed., New York: Cambridge University Press, 1991.

Kant, Immanuel, *On History*, Indianapolis: Bobbs-Merrill, 1963.

Kay, Richard, *Dante's Monarchia*, PIMS, 1998.

Loftus, John and Aarons, Mark, *The Secret War against the Jews*, St. Martin's Press, New York, 1994.

Marsilius of Padua, *The Defender of Peace*, trans. by Alan Gewirth, Harper & Row, 1957.

Miller, Edith Starr, *Occult Theocrasy*, vol.1, 1933; Christian Book Club of America, Hawthorne, CA, 1980.

Miller, Jenine, *The Vision of Cosmic Order in the Vedas*, Routledge & Kegan Paul, 1985.

Milton, John, *The Ready and Easy Way to Establish a Free Commonwealth*, ed. by Evert Mordecai Clark, Yale University Press, 1915.

Morton, Frederic, *The Rothschilds, A Family Portrait*, Atheneum, New York, 1962.

Paine, Thomas, *The Age of Reason*, Dover Publications Inc., 2004.

Rauschning, Hermann, *Hitler Speaks*, London: Thornton Butterworth, 1939.

Rawls, John, *The Law of Peoples*, Cambridge, Mass.: Harvard University Press, 1999.

Reilly, John J., *The Perfection of the West*, Xlibris Corporation 2003.

Reves, Emery, *The Anatomy of Peace*, Penguin, 1947 (first published in USA in 1945).

Reynolds, Barbara, *Dante, The Poet, the Political Thinker, the Man*, I.B. Tauris, 2007.

Rivera, David Allen, *Final Warning, A History of the New World Order*, Rivera Enterprises, 1984-1994.

Rousseau, Jean-Jacques, *A Lasting Peace through the Federation of Europe and the State of War* (1756), trans. by C.E. Vaughan, London: Constable and Co., 1917.

Schlesinger, Arthur M., Jr, *A Thousand Days: John F. Kennedy in the White House*, Andre Deutsch, 1965.

Schwartzberg, Joseph E., *Revitalizing the United Nations: Reform through Weighted Voting*, Institute for Global World Federalists, 2004.

Stiglitz, Joseph and Bilmes, Linda, *The Three Trillion Dollar War*, Allen Lane, 2008.

The New Oxford American Dictionary, 2nd edn., ed. by Erin McKean, 2051 pages, Oxford University Press, 2005.

Tucker, Jim, *Bilderberg Diary*, American Free Press, 2005.

Wells, H.G., *The Outline of History*, Cassell & Co., 8th revision, 1927.

Willkie, Wendell L., *One World*, Cassell, 1943.

Wilson, Derek, *Rothschild: A Story of Wealth and Power*, Mandarin, London 1988.

Yu-Lan, Fung, *The Spirit of Chinese Philosophy*, Routledge & Kegan Paul, 1962.